Why Trust Matters

Why Trust Matters

DECLINING POLITICAL TRUST AND THE

DEMISE OF AMERICAN LIBERALISM

Marc J. Hetherington

PRINCETON UNIVERSITY PRESS

PRINCETON AND OXFORD

Library of Congress Cataloging-in-Publication Data

Hetherington, Marc J., 1968–
Why trust matters : declining political trust and the demise of
American liberalism / Marc J. Hetherington.
p.   cm.
Includes bibliographical references and index.
ISBN 0-691-11776-4 (cl : alk. paper)
1. Political participation—United States. 2. Political alienation—United States.
3. Public opinion—United States. 4. Voting—United States. 5. Progressivism
(United States politics). 6. United States—Politics and government. I. Title.
JK1764.H48 2005
320.973—dc22   2004044513

British Library Cataloging-in-Publication Data is available

This book has been composed in Galliard

Printed on acid-free paper. ∞

pup.princeton.edu

Printed in the United States of America

10 9 8 7 6 5 4 3 2 1

For Suzanne, my love

Contents

List of Figures   ix

List of Tables   xi

Acknowledgments   xiii

CHAPTER ONE
Why Political Trust Matters   1

CHAPTER TWO
Political Trust and Its Evolution   8

CHAPTER THREE
Political Distrust, *Not* Conservatism   36

CHAPTER FOUR
The Dynamic Importance of Political Trust   62

CHAPTER FIVE
Political Trust and Public Support for Government Spending   75

CHAPTER SIX
Political Trust and the Racial Policy Preferences of Whites   99

CHAPTER SEVEN
Political Trust and the Demise of Health Care Reform   120

CHAPTER EIGHT
Political Trust and the Future of American Politics   138

Notes   155

References   163

Index   171

Figures

2.1. Changes in Political Trust, 1964–2000   18
2.2. Political Trust among Whites, South versus Non-South,
     1964–80   21
2.3. Changes in Trust in Government, 2000–2003   31
3.1. Policy Liberalism, 1953–2001   37
3.2. Public Support for More Federal Services and Spending,
     1982–2000   42
3.3. Percentage Supporting Federal Spending Cuts on Various
     Programs, 1984–2002   44
3.4. Changes in Various Measures of Conservatism, 1964–2000   46
3.5. Political Trust and Policy Liberalism, 1964–2001   54
3.6. The Causes of Policy Liberalism   58
4.1. The Causal Dynamics of Political Trust in Temporal
     Sequence   68
4.2. Cross-Lagged Models: Political Trust and Racial Policy
     Preferences, 1972–76, White Respondents, OLS
     and Ordered Probit Estimates   71
4.3. Cross-Lagged Models: Political Trust and Racial Policy
     Preferences, 1990–94, White Respondents, OLS and
     Ordered Probit Estimates   73
5.1. Support for Welfare Spending Cuts and Lagged Political
     Trust, 1970–2002   77
5.2. Spending Preferences as a Function of Political Trust,
     Symbolic Attitudes, Risk, and Sacrifice   83
5.3. Spending Preferences as a Function of Political Trust,
     Symbolic Attitudes, Risk, and Sacrifice, and Appropriate
     Interactions   84
5.4. The Effect of Political Trust on Support for Spending on
     Financial Aid, Parents vs. Nonparents   91
5.5. The Effect of Political Trust on Support for Racialized
     Spending Programs, Conditional on Racial Attitudes   94
5.6. The Effect of Political Trust on Support for Spending to
     Assist Blacks, Conditional on Sacrifice and Risk   96
6.1. Support for a Federal Role in School Integration and
     Lagged Political Trust, 1964–2000   104
6.2. Racial Policy Preferences as a Function of Political Trust,
     Other Symbolic Attitudes, and Social Characteristics   109

6.3. The Effect of Political Trust on Support for Higher-
Education Quotas Conditional on Having a Child   116
6.4. The Effect of Political Trust on Support for Various
Race-Based Programs Conditional on Antiblack Stereotypes   118
7.1. Perceptions of Bill Clinton on Health Insurance as a Function of Political Distrust, Other Symbolic Attitudes, Ability
to Afford Health Insurance, and Social Characteristics   129
7.2. The Effect of Political Trust on Distance People Perceive
Clinton from Center on Government-Sponsored Health
Insurance, 1994   134

Tables

2.1. Differences in Political Trust by Social Characteristics, 1992   17

2.2. Feelings about the Federal Government as a Function of
Feelings about a Range of People, Institutions, and
Groups, 1996   28

3.1. Measures of Policy Liberalism as a Function of Political
Trust, Policy Mood, and the Partisan Composition of
Government, 1953–2001   55

5.1. Percentage Supporting Cuts in Federal Spending on
Various Programs by Levels of Political Trust   81

5.2. How Political Trust Should Affect Support for Different
Spending Programs   85

5.3. Benefits Distributed Universally, No Sacrifice   88

5.4. Benefits Distributed Widely, Sacrifice Asked of a Small
Group of People   89

5.5. Benefits Distributed Widely, Sacrifice Asked of a Small
Group of People, with Interactions   90

5.6. Benefits Distributed Narrowly, Sacrifice Asked of a Large
Group of People   92

5.7. Benefits Distributed Narrowly, Sacrifice Asked of a Large
Group of People, with Interactions   93

5.8. Benefits Distributed Narrowly, Sacrifice Asked of a Large
Group of People, with Interactions, by Beneficiary Group   95

5.9. Benefits Distributed outside the United States, Sacrifice
Is Universal   97

6.1. Percentage Supporting Various Racial Policies by Levels of
Political Trust, 1992   110

6.2. Whites' Support for Race-Conscious Agenda, 1990–94   111

6.3. Whites' Support for Social Welfare Agenda, 1990,
1992, 1994   112

6.4. Whites' Support for Equal Treatment Agenda, 1990–94   113

6.5. Testing the Sacrifice Hypothesis, Education Quotas, 1992   115

6.6. Testing the Risk Hypothesis, White Respondents, 1992   117

7.1. Perceived Position of the Democratic Party, Democratic
Presidents, Democratic Presidential Candidates, and
People's Self-Placement on NES Health Insurance
Scale, 1970–96   125

7.2. Difference in Mean Perception of Democratic Standard-
Bearer's Position on Government-Sponsored Health Care
by Political Trust, 1988, 1994, 1996   130
7.3. Perceptions of Clinton's Position on Government-
Sponsored Health Care as a Function of Political Trust
and Other Variables, 1988, 1994, 1996   131
7.4. Perceptions of Clinton's Position on Government-
Sponsored Health Care with an Interaction between
Political Trust and Sacrifice, 1994   133
7.5. The Effect of Political Trust on Congressional Voting,
1992 versus 1994   135

Acknowledgments

I AM NOT altogether certain why I began to focus my attention on trust in government toward the end of my graduate career at the University of Texas at Austin. I can think of a few potential reasons. First, my father was the press secretary for Senator Hugh Scott (R-Pa.) when he was Senate minority leader during Watergate. His experiences with this crisis in public trust were among my first political experiences. Maybe something from 25 years ago lodged in my brain. Second, the 1994 Republican revolution occurred during this time, confirming that the center of American politics was shifting to the right. Yet the key explanatory variables in the public opinion/political behavior literature, such as party identification and ideology, had all remained basically constant. Perhaps the fact that political trust had deteriorated significantly since the 1960s caught my attention. Third, I am a great fan of underdogs, counting the Washington Capitals, Boston Red Sox, and New Orleans Saints among my favorite sports teams. If there has ever been an underdog among variables in the National Election Study surveys, it is the trust in government battery. No other measure has been singled out for more abuse and derision. Like my choking dog sports teams, maybe I figured that it couldn't be that bad.

Whatever the explanation, my dissertation included a little something about trust in government, although the media remained the center of my research agenda until I headed to the University of Virginia for my first job. While there, I published a couple papers on the effect of political trust on feelings about the president and Congress and also on presidential vote choice. But neither had anything to do with policy preferences or the drift to the right in American politics. Toward the end of my time at Virginia and the start of my time at Bowdoin, I began to put the thesis in this book together. The public's desire for less government was more pragmatic than ideological. They wanted more of the things they benefited from and less of the things that they paid the costs for. Since political trust plausibly would affect support for the latter but not the former, it likely provided the solution to the puzzle. My earliest work in this area appeared in an edited volume called *Communication in U.S. Elections: New Agendas,* published by Rowman and Littlefield. I wish to thank Rowman and Littlefield for their permission to reprint a little of my chapter from that book, which appears in the theory section of chapter 3.

The juxtaposition of Lyndon Johnson and Bill Clinton, which provides an organizing frame for much of the analysis that follows, comes from my experiences in Austin and my many trips to the Johnson presidential library and the Johnson ranch in Johnson City, Texas, during the time that Bill Clinton was president. These trips reminded me of the optimism that Johnson had about the role of government in solving social problems. I have no doubt that Johnson was legitimately moved by the plight of the less fortunate. His reflex was to use the federal government to improve people's lives. In the context of the 1990s, that optimism seemed old-fashioned. The impulse to use government to solve problems was missing from Bill Clinton's approach to politics. Moreover, Clinton's different approach did not come from a different political tradition or from early life experiences that were fundamentally different from Johnson's. In fact, the more I learned about the two of them, the more similar I found them. Given their personal similarities, their differing approaches to governing must have resulted from a change in the political environment. And nothing about the political environment was more different than the loss of public trust in government that occurred between the 1960s and 1990s.

I could not have presented these observations as I do in the pages that follow without a legion of helpers. Bob Luskin stands out as one of the two most valuable. No one did more to turn a person who was interested in politics into a political scientist than Bob did. As I went through my graduate training, I sometimes felt that it might be better to have a mentor with lower standards. Just getting done seemed to me, at times, more important than doing well. I even felt cursed to have Bob prodding me about things as seemingly arcane as conceptualization, measurement, and recursivity. It is too painful to recount what he used to do to my writing. Now nearly seven years later, I realize that no advisor could have provided a student gifts greater than learning how to approach problems rigorously and write clearly.

Of course, other people at Texas helped me out a great deal, too. Brian Roberts was a great friend and mentor, as were Daron Shaw, Tse-min Lin, and Phil Paolino. Phil, in particular, has continued to provide me an endless supply of helpful feedback on my work. Rod Hart and Walter Dean Burnham taught me new ways to think about problems. In some ways, it was Burnham's belief that certain periods in American political history are organized by identifiable characteristics that got me thinking about how political trust might play such a role in explaining the most recent 40 years in American politics. Since much of my work relies on survey data, I would be remiss if I failed to recognize Joe TenBarge. No one taught me more about data analysis and management, not to mention how to set a solid screen on the basketball court, than Joe. Jay Mason, Joe Smith, John Nugent, and Mark Warren spent countless hours listening to me talk about my work. John provided me with an exhaustive reading of the book along with plenty of useful feedback. Jasmine Farrier, another wonderful friend, also provided many helpful comments

When I moved to Virginia, I was most fortunate to meet Steve Finkel. He had serious doubts about my use of simultaneous equation models. His skepticism drove me to find more evidence, statistical and otherwise, to support my theories. It was awfully gratifying to receive an email from Steve, after he had read a draft of this book, indicating that he finally believed me. I also met a great friend and colleague at Virginia in the person of Bruce Larson. In addition to being one of the most supportive people in the world, Bruce gave me great feedback on a draft of this book as well. Dave Klein and Paul Freedman also provided me lots of help, enthusiasm, and friendship at Virginia.

My time at Bowdoin College has also brought me together with some great colleagues who have been generous enough to listen to me ramble on and on about trust in government. Consistent with the culture at a liberal arts college, these are people from a variety of backgrounds. Included among them are a computer scientist, Eric Chown, a historian, Matt Lassiter, a couple of political theorists, Joe Lane and Paul Franco, a surprisingly rigorous English professor, Pete Coviello, and a sociologist, Joe Bandy. All their perspectives have helped to round out my work, with Matt doing yeoman work with the manuscript itself during Pete's wedding weekend. No one at Bowdoin was more generous with his time than Jonathan Weiler. Without Jonathan, this book would be substantially less interesting. He is uniquely able to see the connection between seemingly disparate events, and he has a way of making you feel that you found these connections on your own. Members of my own department have also been very supportive. Indeed, had Marcia Weigle not figured a way to hire me back in 1998, I was looking at a forced career change. Henry Laurence, Janet Martin, Dick Morgan, Chris Potholm, Allen Springer, and Jean Yarbrough have all made me feel very welcome.

Several talented undergraduates also helped me with the preparation of the manuscript. Mehran Ahmed carried out media content analysis work that appears in chapter 2. Melanie Keane and David Butler took care of myriad details, both big and small, that made the process much more manageable. More generally, the members of my Controversies in Voting Behavior seminar, which met in the fall of 2002, critiqued my work and explained to me why certain parts might not be accessible to a general audience. They also helped me make these parts more so.

Most of this book was written during the 2001–2 academic year after Larry Bartels gave me the opportunity of a lifetime in the form of a fellowship at the Center for the Study of Democratic Politics at Princeton University. While there, I was surrounded by extraordinary people like Larry, Chris Achen, Keith Krehbiel, Fred Greenstein, Doug Arnold,

Nolan McCarty, Howard Rosenthal, Eric Oliver, Tali Mendelberg, Adam Berinsky, and Josh Tucker, all of whom took the time to help me with my work. The junior fellows that year at the CSDP, Dave Campbell, Amber Seligson, and Rose Razaghian, were also great colleagues. There is no way to measure how much I benefited from the frequent talks and conferences put on by the Center. During my research talk early on in the year, Keith Krehbiel showed me that my argument would be much more compelling if I could find an aggregate-level dependent variable that told the story that I was trying to tell with individual level data. Some months later, Bob Erikson came to the Center to give a talk in which he introduced me to the policy liberalism variables that I use in chapter 3. Had Keith not raised his point, I would likely have not made the connection with Bob's work. I should also thank Keith for helping me to become a more consistent bowler.

Two people at Princeton deserve particular mention. It will come as no surprise to those who know him that Larry Bartels is a remarkable person. Not only did he take a chance on a guy from a small liberal arts college in Maine, he did everything he could to make my experience exceptional. He organized a conference on trust in government; he always dropped everything to talk about my research; and, perhaps most important to me, he found an office for my wife, so she could finish her dissertation that year. In addition to Larry, Fred Greenstein requires special notice. If not for Fred, this book never would have reached the finish line. He read numerous drafts and painstakingly explained to me what distinguished a book from a series of articles. A note to any future fellows at the Center: listen to Fred. No one will help you more in explaining the architecture of a book. To the extent that I have come up short, it is entirely my fault, not Fred's.

John Hibbing has given me a lot of support throughout this process. In addition, he brought me together with some great people. John and Elizabeth Theiss-Morse hosted a conference in 1999 on political trust and related issues at the University of Nebraska. While there, I had the opportunity to meet a number of people who have given me a hand here and there throughout the process, including Bill Bianco, Jack Citrin, Virginia Chanley, and Ric Uslaner. In addition, Wendy Rahn, Bob Erikson, and Bryan Jones have also provided me considerable encouragement with my work.

These professional colleagues have been great, but the contributions made by my family have been still more fundamental. My parents got me started thinking about politics when I was about five years old, maybe even earlier. I distinctly remember being very frustrated with myself as a seven-year-old because during a parent-as-teacher day at school I had misidentified the former Pennsylvania senator, Richard Schweiker (R-Pa.), as Milton Shapp (D-Pa.), the governor at the time. My goodness, they were of opposite parties. However, my parents provided me something even more important than an exhaustive political education: support in everything that I have ever done. Nothing gives a child more confidence than knowing that his parents are proud of him. In addition, I would like to thank my in-laws, Elaine and Jerry Globetti, for all the support they have provided me over the years. They have done everything imaginable to allow me to focus on this book.

Finally, the person who has been most important in this whole process is my wife, Suzanne Globetti. There is not a page in this book that she has not edited at least twice. She and I have coauthored so much together that it is impossible to distinguish where my thinking stops and hers picks up. In fact, chapter 6 is a version of an article that Suzanne and I published in the *American Journal of Political Science* in 2002. (I would like to thank Blackwell Publishing for their permission to reprint some of this material.) Suzanne is more than a great help, though. Since we met a decade ago, she has been everything to me. She has made my life incredibly happy, rewarding, and fun. Whenever I get discouraged, she has a unique ability to make things better. Everything has gone so well since she came into my life. She is my good luck charm. And, now that we share our lives with a wonderful little boy named Ben, I feel even more fortunate still.

Why Trust Matters

CHAPTER ONE

Why Political Trust Matters

> Government cannot solve our problems, it cannot set our goals, it cannot define our vision. Government cannot eliminate poverty or provide a bountiful economy or reduce inflation or save our cities or cure illiteracy or provide energy. And government cannot mandate goodness.
> —Jimmy Carter, State of the Union Address, 1978

> Government is not the solution to our problem; government *is* the problem.   —Ronald Reagan, Inaugural Address, 1981

> The era of big government is over.
> —Bill Clinton, State of the Union Address, 1995

SINCE THE LATE 1960s and especially since Watergate, not even those who head the federal government have had much good to say about it. Democrats like Jimmy Carter and Bill Clinton expressed very little confidence in government, while Republicans like Ronald Reagan expressed outright contempt. Without doubt, their rhetoric reflects the public's antipathy toward government, but it also guarantees that such antipathy will continue. While scholars and commentators have focused considerable attention on declining political trust, they have focused much less on if, why, and in what concrete ways the decline matters. In fact, declining political trust has had such profound effects on American politics that, in many ways, it has defined American political landscape over the last several decades.

Political candidates have capitalized on this distrust, even catapulting themselves into the White House with it. In September 2000, George W. Bush's campaign was in terrible shape. Al Gore emerged from the Democratic convention like a house afire. His vice presidential selection of Senator Joseph Lieberman, a pro-business Democrat and the first Jewish candidate for national office, won high praise. The party successfully reengaged key elements of the Democratic coalition, namely women, union members, and racial minorities. And, perhaps most importantly, Gore finally seemed to find his voice during his well-received acceptance speech. Whereas Gore had consistently trailed Bush by up to 15 points in public opinion polls in the days before the Democratic convention, he roared out of it leading by 10.

While Gore was catching fire, Bush was losing it. The perception that Bush was intellectually lazy at best and not smart enough to be president at worst started to take its toll. Each campaign stop seemingly brought another gaffe, whether it was confusing billions with trillions in explaining how he would spend the budget surplus, or getting caught by a live microphone using vulgar language to describe *New York Times* reporter Adam Clymer.

Bush's campaign operatives were not doing much better. During the second week in September, the press hammered the campaign for allegedly inserting a subliminal message into a television advertisement. In what would become known as the "Rats" ad, the word "bureaucrats" tumbled from the top of the screen to the bottom, and, for less than a half second, the word "Rats" was frozen in the bottom corner. Democratic political operatives had a field day charging the Bush team with unethical conduct. Worse yet, at a press event in Milwaukee where Bush attempted to put the "Rats" flap behind him, he repeatedly mispronounced *subliminal* as "subliminable," casting further doubt on his intelligence.

By early October, however, Bush had righted the ship. By doing better than expected in the first presidential debate on October 3, Bush convinced many Americans that he belonged on the same stage as Gore. Indeed, according to data collected by political scientist James Stimson, Bush led Gore in the polls every day but one from October 5 through Election Day.[1]

In addition to marking a decisive turn in the polls, October 5 is significant for another reason. It was the day that the Bush campaign debuted a very effective political advertisement. In this 60-second spot, Bush in effect made the claim that huge philosophical differences distinguished him from Gore. Bush's tagline summed up the contrast: "He [Al Gore] trusts government. I trust you." The campaign hierarchy judged the ad so effective that they ran it in each of the battleground states for the duration of the campaign and inserted the charge in numerous other ads that ran in the campaign's final month. In addition, Bush used this turn of phrase in all three presidential debates, and he made it a regular feature of his stump speech as well.[2]

Bush's tagging of Gore with the government was effective because so few people trust it. In 2000, 60 percent of Americans trusted the government to do what was right only "some of the time" or "never"; 60 percent thought it wasted "a lot" of money. Nearly twice as many thought it was run for a few big interests looking out for themselves as thought it was run for the benefit of all Americans.[3] In short, people viewed the government as unethical, inefficient, wasteful, and unrepresentative. In this environment, Bush could increase his support by framing people's choice for president as one between someone who trusts the people and someone who trusts the government.

Recent history supports running a presidential campaign against Washington. Since 1968, being identified with Washington has become political poison. The incumbent party has won only four of the last nine presidential elections, the worst showing for the ins since the days of Andrew Jackson. The only successful nonincumbent presidential candidate with recent Washington ties was George H. W. Bush, and he benefited handsomely from his opponent, Michael Dukakis, running perhaps the worst campaign of the last half-century.[4] Vice presidents and former vice presidents such as Hubert Humphrey, Walter Mondale, and Al Gore have been consistent losers, and senators like George McGovern and Bob Dole have fared no better. Indeed, prior to Bush in 1988, the last federal officeholder to win the White House was Senator John F. Kennedy in 1960.[5] In contrast to much of American political history, it helps to be a former governor these days, as were Jimmy Carter, Ronald Reagan, Bill Clinton, and George W. Bush. When it comes to choosing a president, Americans' lack of trust in the federal government in a post-Vietnam, post-Watergate political culture matters profoundly.

POLITICAL TRUST AND PUBLIC POLICY

Even more importantly, declining political trust has played the central role in the demise of progressive public policy in the United States over the last several decades. My claim defies the conventional wisdom. In explaining why public policy has grown more conservative since the 1960s, pundits and political scientists alike tend to identify a conservative turn in public opinion as the cause. However, little evidence exists to support this explanation. There remains constant and widespread support for big government in areas where most Americans benefit. For example, almost everyone wants to maintain or increase investment in the vast majority of federal programs, such as Medicare, Social Security, education, highways, environmental protection, and the like. Had public opinion truly grown more conservative, support for these initiatives would have decreased because conservatives have a philosophical aversion to government.

Contemporary political rhetoric fuels this misunderstanding. By railing against "big government" in general, conservative and moderate politicians imply that people want less government across the board. However, public opposition to government is focused entirely on programs that require political majorities to make sacrifices for political minorities, such as antipoverty and race-targeted initiatives. In short, Americans continue to support big government when they benefit from it, but they want limited government when they are asked to make sacrifices.

The massive deterioration in political trust that has occurred since the 1960s explains this disjuncture. Declining trust should not affect support for all things that government does. Indeed, people do not need to trust the government much when they benefit from it. Instead, people need to trust the government when they pay the costs but do not receive the benefits, which is exactly what antipoverty and race-targeted programs require of most Americans. When government programs require people to make sacrifices, they need to trust that the result will be a better future for everyone. Absent that trust, people will deem such sacrifices as unfair, even punitive, and, thus, will not support the programs that require them.

Judging by their anti-Washington media campaigns, politicians understand the power of political distrust. They have learned that among the surest ways to rally public opposition to a proposed government-sponsored initiative is to remind ordinary Americans that the federal government will be involved. This tactic proved effective during the health care reform debate of the early 1990s. When Bill Clinton ran for president in 1992, he promised to provide health insurance to all Americans, including the more than 30 million uninsured. With so many already lacking insurance and tens of millions of others struggling to afford it, the issue seemed electorally promising. Indeed, the top of Clinton's campaign hierarchy, James Carville and Paul Begala, knew its potential first hand. They had run Harris Wofford's (D-Pa.) successful U.S. Senate bid to fill John Heinz's seat after his untimely death in 1991. Although no one gave the politically obscure Wofford, the Pennsylvania labor secretary and former Bryn Mawr College president, much of a chance, he erased a 55-point deficit in the polls to defeat former two term Pennsylvania governor and sitting U.S. attorney general, Dick Thornburgh. Most observers believe Wofford won largely on the strength of his health care reform promise. In 1992, a relatively obscure Arkansas governor, Bill Clinton, enjoyed similar success.

Things changed markedly for Clinton over the next two years as he attempted to move health care reform from campaign promise to law. Although the secret meetings of the Health Care Task Force, the complexity of the final proposal, and the negative feelings that most Americans had about Hillary Clinton, the Task Force's leader, damaged the reform effort (see Johnson and Broder 1996; Skocpol 1996), the biggest problem was Americans' negative feelings toward government. At the time, only about 20 percent of Americans thought they could trust the government in Washington to do what was right "just about always" or even "most of the time," the lowest reading since polling organizations started asking the question in the 1950s. Moreover, 75 percent thought the government was run for a few big interests looking out for themselves. Such an opinion environment makes it extraordinarily difficult for leaders to marshal support for a large federally administered program that might require many people to make sacrifices for others. Most Americans simply do not think government is capable of doing the job well enough or fairly enough to help the less well off at the same time it protects the interests of the better off.[6]

Things used to be much different. When political trust was high in the 1960s, John F. Kennedy promised Americans a New Frontier, and Lyndon Johnson promised a Great Society. Both trumpeted programs designed to aid historically discriminated-against groups and those at the bottom of the socioeconomic ladder. With political trust today in much lower reserve, only the most resolute liberals even talk much about race and poverty, much less enact new policies to confront these problems.[7] Instead, most left-of-center politicians search for a "third way" by splitting the difference between conservative and liberal ideas. They try to avoid using racial terms or making references to racialized programs, such as welfare and food stamps (Gilens 1999).

Centrists like Clinton and Gore have replaced liberals like Kennedy and Johnson because most Americans, whether conservative or liberal, do not trust the delivery system for most progressive public policy. Even if people support progressive policy goals, they do not support the policies themselves because they do not believe that the government is capable of bringing about desired outcomes. While almost all Americans would like to eradicate poverty and racial discrimination, most simply do not think the federal government is up to the task. As evidence, a 1995 poll by the *Washington Post*, Harvard University, and the Kaiser Family Foundation found that among those who were not willing to have "the federal government spend more to help low-income minorities," fully 59 percent said their opposition was based on the belief that "the federal government [could] not do the job right." In contrast, only 25 percent voiced a principled objection to spending in this policy area.[8] Given such a dim view of the government's ability to solve problems, it should be no surprise that Republicans have dominated the last 35 years in American politics, which has been mostly characterized by low levels of public trust in government.

STRUCTURE OF THE BOOK

This book is about the importance of political trust, a concept that has caused a great deal of scholarly debate about both its definition and its measurement. In chapter 2, I define political trust and detail scholarly concerns about its measurement. I review the scholarly and political explanations for fluctuations in political trust over time, and augment this understanding of why trust changes using a priming-based theory based on post–September 11 data. Next, I track the pattern of trust's decay since the 1960s, and discuss the theoretical and normative importance of a lack of political trust in a democratic society.

I argue that declining political trust explains why the center in American politics has shifted to the right in recent decades. Although increasing conservatism is an alternative explanation, I demonstrate in chapter 3 that conservatism, by any number of measures, has remained constant. It, therefore, cannot explain why the policy agenda has become so much more conservative over this same period. Only increasing political distrust can. In this chapter, I detail an individual-level theory about the importance of political trust in generating support for programs that require either perceived sacrifice or entail some perceived risk, exactly the types of programs that have seen a deterioration in public support over time. In addition, I show that, in the aggregate, the pattern of policy liberalism implemented by the federal government follows the pattern of political trust over time. When the public is more trustful, the government responds with more liberal public policy, and when the public is more distrustful, the government responds with more conservative public policy. I also demonstrate that political trust is a more compelling aggregate-level explanation for variation in policy liberalism than other competing factors, most notably policy mood.

Chapter 4 details the changing causal dynamic between political trust at the individual level and support for specific public policies. My work challenges the scholarly conventional wisdom about the causal importance of trust. Most scholars have treated political trust as a dependent variable (e.g. Citrin 1974; Miller 1974a, 1974b), attempting to explain why it changes. While I demonstrate that this approach was appropriate in the 1970s, the contemporary information environment has transformed political trust into a potent causal force.

The next three chapters provide individual-level evidence that declining political trust undermines support for a range of progressive public policies. In chapter 5, I demonstrate that political trust helps bridge the divide in public opinion between distributive and redistributive issues. Americans have always been more supportive of spending for programs that benefit them directly, such as spending on highways, than programs for which most make sacrifices, such as spending on welfare or food stamps (Free and Cantril 1967). In fact, this gap has grown larger over the last 30 years. The reason is the decline in political trust. While support for distributive spending has remained constant, support for redistributive spending has ebbed and flowed with increases and decreases in political trust. My theory suggests that trust should be influential only when a program requires sacrifice or risk, which are both characteristics of redistributive spending.

Chapter 6 extends the theory to include racial policy. For whites, race-targeted policies require at least perceived sacrifices for a somewhat intangible outcome, greater racial equality. Hence whites should need to trust the government to support race-targeted programs. In fact, I demonstrate that this is the case. The results in this chapter have strong normative implications as well. Why do white Americans support racial equality in principle but not the programs designed to make equality a reality? The main reason is that they do not trust the government to administer race-targeted programs either well or fairly.

In chapter 7, I demonstrate political trust's importance in understanding the failure of the Clinton health care reform plan and the administration's subsequent turn to the right. While opponents attacked the plan in several different ways, I show that antigovernment appeals were decisive in explaining its defeat. Although trust in government had no bearing on support either before or after 1994, opponents made it a critically important component in 1994 by framing the debate in terms of sacrifice and clumsy government bureaucracy. Since trust reached its survey era low during 1994, the politicization of trust defeated Clinton's last major effort to add to the nation's social safety net. In addition, I show that political trust played a major role in congressional voting decisions in 1994, but not in other years, helping to usher in a different kind of politics that has further marginalized progressive public policy.

Chapter 8 discusses the implications of the findings. That Americans are more distrustful today rather than more conservative has important implications for the behavior of political elites. For example, the post-1994 Clinton administration governed consistently to the right on most issues, apparently believing that a fundamental reordering of ideological preferences had occurred. But, ideology had not changed, and, indeed, the public's preference for government intervention actually increased toward the end of his presidency. If Clinton had realized that increasing political distrust was the source of his problem in 1994, he might have charted a much more progressive route through the rest of his administration.[9]

In addition, the concluding chapter discusses larger normative issues. Since political trust is necessary to generate support for redistributive and race-targeted policies, low levels of political trust have a particularly negative effect on those who rely most on government programs, specifically the economically disadvantaged and racial minorities. For government to provide them adequate representation, political trust cannot be in short supply. Otherwise, the haves will be unwilling to make the sacrifices necessary to aid the have-nots.

CHAPTER TWO

Political Trust and Its Evolution

THAT AMERICANS HAVE lost faith in the federal government to implement and administer public policy is the key change in American public opinion over the last 40 years. While many have suggested that the ideological center has shifted to the right, this is not exactly correct. People do not want less federal intervention across the board, only in areas that demand sacrifices from most Americans. These are the areas where people will need to trust the government to support government policy. Thus, anti-Washington attitudes advantage conservatives, but they should not be confused with conservatism.

To the extent that Americans appear more conservative, it is because programs offered by progressives generally use the government to deliver services or ensure rights. If people do not trust the delivery system and, therefore, do not want it involved in providing policy solutions, it automatically limits the range of possibilities available to them. While the early to middle 1960s were perhaps anomalous in their high levels of public trust, they allowed policymakers great leeway in proposing and implementing federal solutions to America's problems. That leeway is now gone. As political trust has deteriorated, those tasks have become infinitely harder for advocates of an activist federal government.

This chapter provides the foundation for my argument. I discuss what political trust is and explore the role that it plays in normative democratic theory. I then turn to a discussion of how scholars have measured trust, and the controversies that issues of measurement have raised. Next I track changes in political trust over time to highlight the causes of political trust and to provide evidence that the often noted measurement issues are overblown. Finally, using data taken from the months before and after the September 11 terrorist attacks, I test a theory that suggests that what people are thinking about when they evaluate the government affects their trust in it. Specifically, it explains why political trust has been relatively high since September 11, and, more importantly, it also explains why people evaluate government more negatively today than they did 40 years ago. After the Great Society, people started to think about government in terms of unpopular redistributive programs instead of more universal programs, which caused them to express less trust in the federal government.

WHAT IS POLITICAL TRUST?

Political trust, in general, is a concept that people think they understand until they are asked to define it. Thus, it is not surprising that definitions are numerous in the scholarly literature. Some consider political trust a commodity that helps political actors achieve their goals (Luhmann 1979), while others conceptualize it as people's willingness to follow the political leadership of others (Warren 1999). Definitions like these are too instrumental to suit my purposes. They do little to explain the conditions under which individuals are more or less willing to follow political leadership, and hence, more or less willing to support public policy alternatives.

Still others define political trust more broadly as a sense of shared moral community, both political and social, with an agreement on what values a society ought to pursue (Fukuyama 1995). This suggests that political trust originates outside the political sphere and is in large measure determined by how much people trust each other. Those living in more trusting societies tend to trust their government more than those living in less trusting societies. While attractive on one level, this definition conflates two separate concepts, political trust and social trust. In American life, one can easily identify people who trust other people but do not trust government, and, with a little more difficulty, one can also identify the reverse. Indeed, as an empirical matter, measures of political and social trust are positively but only weakly correlated, further suggesting vast conceptual differences (see Mishler and Rose 2001). In addition, social and political trust are related to different things. Robert Putnam (2000) and others have demonstrated that social trust affects whether individuals vote or participate more actively in politics, while political trust does not (see Citrin 1974).[1]

A definition of political trust should incorporate both instrumental and normative aspects. I define political trust as the degree to which people perceive that government is producing outcomes consistent with their expectations (see Stokes 1962; Coleman 1990). One might think about it as a pragmatic running tally of how people think the government is doing at a given point in time. Morris Fiorina (1981) conceptualized party identification in much the same way. Economic evaluations were central to Fiorina's treatment, but they are only part of what people have in mind when they evaluate the government as a whole. Hence trust in government is necessarily broader in a conceptual sense. To ideologues, this running tally will be conditioned by who is running the government at a given point in time; conservatives will be more positive than liberals when conservatives run Washington and vice versa (Citrin 1974; see also Anderson and LoTempio 2002). But, for most Americans, policy ends are more important than policy means (Brody 1991), so political trust will be a reflection of how positively citizens perceive government performance relative to their expectations.

A key term in my definition is *perceptions*. People's view of government is far different than its actual performance would predict. Haynes Johnson and David Broder (1996) point out this contradiction.

> In those years of growing negativism [toward government], government actions brought about the greatest expansions of basic civil rights in the nation's history; a measurably cleaner, safer environment; a significant improvement in the health and well-being of senior citizens; and countless breakthroughs in science and technology that helped fuel the growth of an economy that was the envy of the world. That same government also trained and equipped the most powerful military forces in the world and led an international alliance that thwarted expansionary international communism, won the Cold War, and ushered in the peaceful liberation of the Soviet Union and Eastern Europe. With such a record of success, America was the model for all other societies to emulate.

Derek Bok (1997) provides further evidence that, while there are areas where it could improve, the federal government has done a reasonably good job in the administration and provision of services since the 1960s. Al Gore's Reinventing Government Commission actually turned up much less waste in the federal bureaucracy than most would expect, perhaps no more than 3 cents on the dollar.

Yet most people think that the majority of politicians pursue their own selfish interests rather than those of the country (Hibbing and Theiss-Morse 2002), and many believe that urban neighborhoods are full of Cadillac-driving "welfare queens" because government bureaucrats are too inept to stop them. Instead of the 3 cents turned up by the Gore commission, the average American perceives that the government wastes nearly 50 cents on the dollar (Langer 2002).[2] Such misperceptions are likely the result of, or at least reinforced by, a relentlessly negative news media (Patterson 1993; Orren 1997). Regardless, as is often the case in politics, the perception of government performance is more important than the reality.

It is also imperative to understand that my research focuses on Americans' trust in the *federal* government, not state or local governments. At least today, Americans generally trust their state and local governments significantly more than they trust the federal government because they view them as more responsive and more efficient (Blendon et al. 1997). As evidence, the 1996 National Election Study asked respondents which level of government would do the best job handling environmental, welfare, and anticrime programs. In all three cases, a plurality of respondents chose state government. When asked which level of government they had the most "faith" in, a plurality again chose state government (37 percent), with local government finishing second (33 percent) and the federal government last (30 percent).[3] And, when asked which level of government they had the least faith in, the federal government (48 percent) was the clear winner, with local (34 percent) and state government (19 percent) lagging well behind. Although I sometimes write about government generically, I am referring to the federal government unless otherwise noted.

In understanding what political trust is, it is also useful to note what it is not. Political trust should not be confused with trust in a specific political figure. Political trust is a general evaluation of the entire government, while trust in a given figure is but one dimension of a more complete evaluation of that figure.[4] This distinction is important. People can trust the government while, at the same time, distrusting the president and vice versa. Indeed, during the last six years of the Clinton presidency, Americans took an increasingly dim view of his personal trustworthiness while, at the same time, political trust increased markedly. Similarly, people might have trusted Jimmy Carter personally because he made his personal ethics an important part of his presidential persona, but most did not trust the government much during his term in office because it performed so poorly. More often than not, those who are trustful of the political figure tend to be trustful of the government, but the correlation is far from perfect.

POLITICAL TRUST AND AMERICAN DEMOCRACY

With very few exceptions, classical political theorists have taken a normatively positive view of political trust, describing it as "essential to a democratic community's well being" (Mara 2001, 820). To the extent that democratic theorists disagree over trust, they differ over why, not whether, it is positive. In *On Liberty*, John Stuart Mill (1982) notes the importance of deliberation in helping a society decide on a policy direction that will allow it to achieve the greatest good. Indeed, the number of conceptions of the "greatest good" covaries closely with the number of political parties in a political system. Since parties tend not to agree, they need political trust to provide the context to discuss, and ultimately arrive at, what is best for society (Mara 2001).

In democracies made up of political majorities and minorities, political trust is also a necessary ingredient to ensure the proper representation of all interests. When the interests of majorities and minorities conflict, the representation of minority interests requires that majorities be willing to make some sacrifices for the greater good. Race provides an example. Many whites might benefit materially from racial discrimination in hiring. If a white person has to compete only against other white applicants, it increases the probability that he or she will get the job because the talent pool will be shallower. Government can act to ban such discrimination.

For a white person to support the government's action, however, he or she must trust that the government is working in the nation's best interest, even if it is not in his or her personal self-interest (Gamson 1968). Absent that trust, minority interests are unlikely to be adequately represented.

In addition, since most democracies are representative in nature, their functioning depends heavily on public trust. Representation demands that people trust their individual representatives and the institutions they occupy. If people come to think that institutions are not working in either their or the nation's best interest, it is not clear why they would continue to follow the laws set by these institutions. In fact, there is ample evidence to suggest that those who do not trust government are significantly less likely to obey its laws. For example, distrusters are significantly less likely to pay their taxes than trusters (Scholz and Lubell 1998).

The founding of the United States provides a useful example of the desirability of public trust in government. The alternative to a representative form of democracy is one that emphasizes direct citizen control over policy decisions. Certainly, the Framers had little confidence that the unwashed masses had the wherewithal to manage the affairs of the day, fearing that mob rule would almost certainly result from direct mass participation. Mob rule would, in turn, produce politics driven by passion rather than reason. If people lost trust in representative institutions, it would likely lead to direct democracy, exactly what the Framers hoped to avoid. With this in mind, it is interesting to note that in contemporary America, the initiative revolution grew particularly strong during the 1970s, the period when political trust was in its steepest decline.[5] Indeed, Jeffrey Karp (1995) demonstrates that low political trust was the root cause of the mass drive for more direct democracy in the 1970s and 1980s.

There are also less obvious, but still important, reflections of political trust's importance to the Founders. People commonly note that the Constitution suggests the understandable distrust that Americans had of government, given their experiences as colonists. The Framers, however, were more distrustful of power than of government itself. As a result, they created a system that fragmented power throughout the government such that it would be difficult for one person or one faction to capture its reins.

Was the Framers' concern about power born of concerns about the nature of human beings or the nature of government? People were clearly the stronger concern. The model of political abuse was the English monarchy. Hence the Framers wanted to avoid putting too much power in the hands of too few people. Madison believed that it was human nature to abuse power. In *Federalist* No. 10, he notes, "Enlightened statesmen will not always be at the helm," and, in *Federalist* No. 51, he argues that government would not be necessary if men were angels. Madison, therefore, proposed institutions disparate enough to curb the worst human instincts while still sufficiently powerful to administer the affairs of the nation. While the Founders would have wanted people to be skeptical of government, because men would run it, government itself was not the target of their distrust.

Indeed, since the Founders wanted to frustrate the natural human impulse to aggregate power, it follows that they would have *wanted* ordinary people to trust the institutions designed to check the worst human ambitions. Government with strong public trust would do a better job than government without it. From the Founders' perspective, the public has more to fear from too much trust in the people running the government than from too much trust in the machinery of government. Hence they would likely be dismayed by the personalization of politics that has occurred during the television age (Hart 1994). Only as officeholders, such as Lyndon Johnson, came to see and present themselves as the government did too much trust in government become a problem, as it no doubt was in the mid-1960s. For example, as Johnson was preparing to board the wrong helicopter during one of his visits to Vietnam, a helpful young aide attempted to point Johnson in the right direction by saying "This is your helicopter, Mr. President." "Son, they're all my helicopters," Johnson replied.[6] The concern might be extended to Rep. Tom DeLay (R-Tex.), the House Majority Leader, in 2003. When an employee attempted to dissuade DeLay from smoking a cigar on government property, the majority leader responded by shouting, "I am the federal government."[7]

This discussion is not to suggest that the represented ought to blindly trust those who represent them. Citizens must hold leaders and their institutions accountable for their mistakes if democracy is to function properly. Indeed, over the last 40 years government has made mistakes ample enough to justify a distrustful response from the electorate. The Gulf of Tonkin incident, continued official misinformation about the prosecution of the Vietnam War, failed economic policy in the 1970s, Watergate, the Iran-Contra affair, and Bill Clinton's serial problems with the truth all provide good examples (see Hardin 2002 for a discussion about legitimate distrust).

A problem develops, however, when people begin to reflexively respond to politics with distrust even when it is not justified, and that is what has happened in contemporary American politics. In this book, I demonstrate that the gap between perceptions of government performance and its actual performance matters profoundly, particularly for racial minorities and the poor. These groups lose the most from the hardened distrust that has developed about the federal government.[8] That certain identifiable groups are disproportionately affected suggests that low levels of political trust have important implications for the representativeness of American democracy.

Measuring Political Trust

Measuring political trust has also proved elusive to scholars. In the late 1950s and early 1960s, researchers at the University of Michigan took a stab at the problem in their National Election Study (NES), and they developed the following set of measures, which I use throughout this book.

> *Trust.* How much of the time do you think you can trust the government in Washington to do what is right—just about always, most of the time, or only some of the time?
>
> *Waste.* Do you think that people in government waste a lot of the money we pay in taxes, waste some of it, or don't waste very much of it?
>
> *Interest.* Would you say the government is pretty much run by a few big interests looking out for themselves or that it is run for the benefit of all the people?
>
> *Crooked.* Do you think that quite a few of the people running the government are crooked, not very many are, or do you think hardly any of them are crooked?

These survey questions have come under a great deal of criticism, much of it justified. In fact, research on political trust essentially disappeared from the mid-1980s to the late 1990s due, in large part, to concerns over measurement. I readily admit that there are problems. First, some of the terms are losing meaning, particularly the word "crooked" in the last of the items. In the 1960s and 1970s, Richard Nixon might have seemed crooked, but in the 1990s, people would have been more likely to describe Bill Clinton as sleazy.

In addition, the two or three fixed options provided by the questions limit variation in responses. Surely, most ordinary Americans do not see the political world in the stark categories available to them. Indeed, since 1972, the most common response to each of these items has been the least trustful one. What do we make of this? Timothy McVeigh, the Oklahoma City bomber, distrusted government, but surely a plurality of Americans does not share his attitudes. Responding that you trust the government only some of the time means different things to different people (Lodge and Tursky 1979).

Third, the NES measures do not measure institutional legitimacy, as many critics have argued. Typically, Easton's (1965, chaps. 11–13, 17–21; 1975) work on political support has framed these scholarly exchanges. Most relevant to these debates, Easton distinguishes between specific and diffuse support. Specific support refers to satisfaction with government outputs and the performance of political authorities, while diffuse support refers to the public's attitude toward regime-level political objects regardless of their performance.

Some suggest the trust measure correlates only with specific support, so they believe that the decline of trust is of somewhat limited consequence (Citrin 1974; Citrin and Green 1986; Lipset and Schneider 1983). According to this view, an improvement in incumbent job performance should remedy low levels of political trust, although it has not done so thus far. In contrast, others suggest a connection between political trust and some measures of diffuse support (Miller 1974a, 1974b; Miller, Goldenberg, and Erbring 1979; Miller and Listhaug 1990), implying that sustained low trust ultimately challenges regime legitimacy.

The distinction between specific and diffuse support is useful, but it obscures more important issues. As previous research has consistently suggested, the NES's trust measure contains elements of both types of support (e.g. Hetherington 1998). Indeed, because the government is largely composed of institutions operated by incumbents, the objects of support are difficult, if not impossible, to separate. Lost in this debate, however, is whether declining trust has had meaningful effects on variables of normative import.

Viewed in this way, declining trust can have long-term consequence even if it is not a measure of institutional legitimacy. For example, lower levels of political trust cause people to approve of the president less (Hetherington 1998). Since distrust causes disapproval and disapproval makes it more difficult for leaders to marshal resources to solve problems (Neustadt 1990; Rivers and Rose 1985), government will, on average, solve fewer problems when political trust is low. This, in turn, will cause more distrust and more disapproval, which, absent some exogenous change, will continue the cycle.

In fact, because it is not a measure of institutional support, the NES measure is actually more useful than one that is. Support for the basic structure of the American constitutional system has remained virtually unchanged during the survey era even as people have become increasingly dissatisfied with the people running the institutions (Hibbing and Theiss-Morse 1995; Hibbing and Theiss-Morse 2002). Things that have not changed over time, such as institutional support, cannot explain things that have. If we want to understand what has changed about American politics, we should be interested in a measure that taps feelings that have varied over time, exactly what the NES measure of political trust does.

That said, researchers must use care in interpreting responses to the NES. If 75 percent of Americans say they trust the government only some of the time, we need not fear that government overthrow is imminent. But their response does mean that the president and Congress will be less popular (Hetherington 1998), a third-party presidential candidate may find fertile ground (Hetherington 1999), people will be more supportive of antigovernment devices like initiative and referendum and term limits (Karp 1995), and, as I demonstrate in this book, government will produce less progressive public policy.

This slippage between the concept of political trust and the survey items used to measure it, which is called measurement error, is very common with survey data. The biggest problem with measurement error is that it reduces the correspondence between the concept to be measured and other attitudes and behaviors that might be correlated with it. For example, if I think political trust might cause people to be less supportive of government spending on welfare programs and I know that my measure of political trust contains some measurement error, then the correlation between my measure of political trust and my measures of support for spending on welfare programs is reduced. Hence, if I find any significant relationship, it is all the more impressive. It means that, were a better measure of political trust available, its relationship with support for welfare programs would be still stronger.

Explaining Variation in Political Trust

To understand how political trust has changed American politics, it is first important to understand what makes trust increase and decrease. In general, scholars have found that political trust depends on a number of factors, including policy satisfaction (Miller 1974a; King 1997), economic evaluations (Citrin and Green 1986; Weatherford 1984), media negativity (Patterson 1993; Cappella and Jamieson 1997), major political scandals (Weatherford 1984), war (Parker 1995), the president's personal characteristics (Citrin and Green 1986), and the size and scope of government (Mansbridge 1997). The direction of these effects is rather obvious. In general, when people are satisfied with the policy direction that the country is taking, when the economy is growing, when the president has attractive personal characteristics, when the country is threatened, and when media criticism is relatively low, political trust increases. Major scandals and unpopular wars decrease political trust.

It is also important to note what political trust does not depend on. While one might expect disadvantaged groups to be more distrustful than advantaged ones, generally they are not (but see Abramson 1983). Table 2.1 compares levels of trust by different social characteristics. To measure political trust, scholars generally combine the four items outlined above to make an index. Although there are several ways to do this, I begin by arraying the responses such that the most trustful is always at the top of the scale. Next, the most trustful response to each of the items is assigned

TABLE 2.1
Differences in Political Trust by Social Characteristics, 1992

Social Characteristic	Mean	N
Gender		
Male	0.211	1,040
Female	0.220	1,204
|Difference|	0.009	
Race		
Black	0.226	287
Nonblack	0.214	1,957
|Difference|	0.012	
Age		
Below median	0.226	1,117
Above median	0.206	1,127
|Difference|	0.020	
Education		
Below median	0.227	1,151
Above median	0.203	1,037
|Difference|	0.024	
Income		
Below median	0.227	1,047
Above median	0.210	967
|Difference|	0.017	

Source: American National Election Study, 1992.

a 1 and the least trustful response a 0. If the question has three response options, as is the case for all the items except Interest, the middle option receives a score of 0.5. Finally, each person's score for the four items is totaled and the mean taken. Individuals can score anywhere from 0 (completely distrustful) to 1 (completely trustful). I employ this measure throughout the book.

Since the political trust scale is on a (0, 1) interval, the differences can be interpreted as the percentage difference between groups. All are substantively insignificant, with differences between 1 and 2 percentage points. Men and women share about the same levels of political trust, as do whites and blacks, the better and less well educated, those with higher and lower incomes, and older and younger people. While the data presented come from 1992 only, these insignificant differences have generally been the rule.[9]

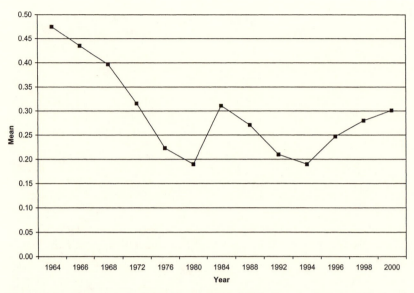

Figure 2.1. Changes in Political Trust, 1964–2000. Source: American National Election Study, Cumulative File, 1948–2000.

Political Trust from Johnson through Clinton

Tracing changes in political trust since the four-item index debuted in 1964 provides evidence for what affects it. Figure 2.1 illustrates Americans' average score on the political trust index for all presidential years and a couple key off years between 1964 and 2000. The trend line shows that political trust has deteriorated greatly since the 1960s, but there have been increases during the period as well. That trust follows such a pattern over time bolsters the validity of the measure. It drops when one would expect, as with the deepening morass in Vietnam after 1968 and the Watergate scandal in 1974, and it rises when one would expect, as with the major economic expansions of the early 1980s and late 1990s.

Its high point is 1964, the first year the NES asked this particular battery of questions.[10] The mid-1960s were a good time for the government. Although U.S. involvement in Vietnam was on the rise, public opinion was still solidly behind the war. In addition, economic prosperity had returned after a relatively deep recession in the late Eisenhower and early Kennedy years. The political leadership of the era was important as well. John F. Kennedy provided tremendous optimism about what government might accomplish. Certainly the country has not seen a more forceful spokesperson for progressive, government-sponsored programs since his assassination in November 1963, except perhaps his successor, Lyndon Johnson. Unlike politicians today, Kennedy and Johnson unabashedly articulated their belief that government could solve social problems.

Rhetorical support of "big government" has important implications for public opinion. When people receive information from elites on both sides of an issue, they can choose the side that they find most persuasive. John Zaller (1992) refers to this as a two-sided information flow. Usually, ordinary Americans attempt to match their opinions with those of elites with whom they identify. While conservatives like Barry Goldwater in the 1960s criticized government intervention in antipoverty policy and race as beyond its purview, Kennedy and Johnson argued that federal involvement would produce a better America. It follows that public trust was high in this period, since the most popular leaders of the day supported big government.

The information environment has changed radically since. It is rare to find a prominent elected leader who advocates government solutions to social problems. Although most of the 2004 Democratic presidential hopefuls promised big government programs like universal health insurance, they assiduously avoid mentioning what role government might play in accomplishing this goal. Indeed, even though many experts believe the most cost-efficient system would be one run by the government, most candidates propose plans that will ultimately cost more money but provide government a smaller role in the administration of service because they know how unpopular government is in the public's eye. In 1992, Bill Clinton took the same tack on this issue. Since a progovernment position is not well represented in the political discourse, while critics of government are both numerous and voluble, ordinary Americans will naturally tend toward the more prominently articulated view that government is incapable, incompetent, and thus unworthy of their trust. Thus, it is no surprise that people began to trust the government less as government friendly voices exited the political stage.

Over the 16 years following Johnson's election in 1964, political trust experienced a freefall. While most observers point to dramatic events like Vietnam and Watergate as causes, the decline began before opinion turned against the war, with the first hints of trouble occurring in 1966. Indeed, declining trust in government in the United States was part of a larger trend also affecting much of Western Europe during the middle to late 1960s (Lipset and Schneider 1987).

Although empirical evidence is thin, the most plausible explanations for the pre-1968 decline are public dissatisfaction with an expanding welfare state coupled with social problems that persisted (Mansbridge 1997). When politicians promised that they could solve problems that had previously been beyond the government's reach, it naturally raised the public's expectations about what government might accomplish. No longer was it sufficient for the federal government to provide peace and prosperity to maintain the public's trust; now it had to end poverty, solve racial discord, and protect the American family. While politicians promised solutions, these problems did not abate overnight. Indeed, the race riots of the late 1960s suggested that government policy was causing more, not less, racial discord.

It is also of consequence that this increase in the government's involvement occurred in an area in which most people could not directly evaluate performance. Most Americans neither benefited directly from the government's antipoverty efforts nor knew people who did. All they knew was that they were paying taxes to help the poor, a group that many felt just needed to work harder (see Kinder and Sanders 1996). While great strides were, in fact, made during the 1960s, it would be difficult for most Americans to receive tangible evidence of progress. Without evidence of success, it would be reasonable to conclude that government was wasting money. This interpretation of the American case is consistent with the simultaneous declines in political trust occurring in western Europe, which also coincided with sizable increases in the size and scope of their welfare states (Lipset and Schneider 1987).

Federal efforts to include the non-South in implementation of racial policy almost certainly contributed to the decline. A major cause of the seeming public consensus regarding New Deal, New Frontier, and Great Society issues was the ability of political leaders to submerge race, which was evident in Franklin Roosevelt's approach to Social Security, John F. Kennedy's reluctance to take an active stand on civil rights, and Lyndon Johnson's using West Virginia, not a major city, as the backdrop for his declarations on the War on Poverty (Wilson 1987). The North was no bastion of racial liberalism. In the 1940s and 1950s, normally solid Democrats in cities like Detroit voted for conservative Republicans when blacks started to move into white neighborhoods and competed for their jobs (Sugrue 1996). Nonsoutherners could embrace the Civil Rights Act of 1964 and Voting Rights Act of 1965 because until the 1970s they pertained only to the South, allowing northerners to dismiss race as a regional problem. As the 1960s came to a close, however, events caused that consensus in the non-South to erode.

It was during this period that urban race riots rocked nonsouthern cities like Detroit and Los Angeles, the media replaced the rural white face of poverty and antipoverty programs with a less popular urban black one (see Gilens 1999), and Lyndon Johnson signed the Fair Housing Act of 1968, which applied to the entire nation, not just the South. During the Nixon presidency, the National Association for the Advancement of Colored People (NAACP) brought a series of school segregation lawsuits against non-

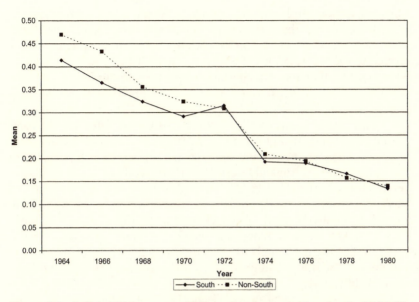

Figure 2.2. Political Trust among Whites, South versus Non-South, 1964–80.
Source: American National Election Study, Cumulative File, 1948–2000.

southern school districts, which led, starting in 1971, to forced busing plans in cities such as Denver, Detroit, Boston, and Los Angeles. That the nationalization of implicitly and explicitly racial policies was a root cause for the drop in political trust in the late 1960s is evident from the data in figure 2.2. It traces change in political trust between 1964 and 1980, comparing southern whites with whites from outside the South. From 1964 to 1970, when the reach of civil rights legislation was largely confined to the South, southerners were less trustful of the federal government than nonsoutherners, although the gap had begun to close by 1968.[11] By 1972, with progressives no longer able to submerge the race issue outside the South, trust levels among southerners and nonsoutherners became indistinguishable. When race policy confronted Jim Crow laws and voting discrimination *in the South*, northerners and westerners felt they could trust the government. When the federal courts, in particular, made race policy a national issue, nonsoutherners began to trust the government less.

Although the rate of decay in political trust was greater for nonsoutherners than for southerners from the late 1960s through the mid-1970s, these data demonstrate that trust was dropping rapidly for both. The more universal explanations for the decline in political trust during this period are easy to identify. It had become increasingly clear that the United States was not on the verge of winning the war in Vietnam and that government officials had been misleading the public for years. In early 1968, the Tet offensive exploded the myth of imminent American victory for Walter Cronkite, and thus the nation as a whole. Soon after, Americans were treated to the assassinations of Martin Luther King and Robert Kennedy, Soviet tanks rolling into Czechoslovakia, the tumultuous Democratic National Convention in Chicago, and the racist presidential candidacy of George Wallace. In succeeding years, "America's Century" appeared at a premature end. The prosperity of the 1960s turned into chronic bouts with inflation and unemployment in the 1970s. Since people's evaluations of the economy are paramount in understanding how much people trust the government (Citrin and Green 1986), this economic downturn was a severe blow (Weatherford 1984). Through the early 1970s, the situation in Vietnam continued to deteriorate no matter the number of troops committed or bombs dropped, ultimately leading to the embarrassing withdrawal of U.S. troops. Americans seeing the poignant images of servicemen clinging desperately to helicopters leaving Saigon could not help but notice that things had changed significantly since the United States won World War II, and not for the better.

The Watergate scandal provided another blow. Not only did Nixon knowingly mislead the public for nearly two years about his involvement in the cover-up of the break-in at the Democratic National Committee in 1972, other unsavory details about his use of executive power against his personal and political enemies came to light.

Things only got worse during Jimmy Carter's presidency, as trust reached its lowest point yet. During Carter's successful run for the White House in 1976, he raised expectations about government ethics by assuring voters that he would clean up Washington, promising that he would never lie. But his administration was quickly wracked by scandal, with the forced resignation of his budget director, Bert Lance, for past misdeeds and, ultimately, lying to the public.

Beyond the ethics problems, most Americans viewed the country's performance during the Carter years as quite poor, including Carter himself. His "Malaise Speech," which identified a crisis of national confidence as a root problem in American life, confirmed that the nation's faith in political institutions had eroded under his watch. In stark contrast to Kennedy's optimism, Carter failed to make people believe that government could play a valuable role. Indeed, his securing the presidency by running against government all but precluded a restoration of such belief. In addition, economic success eluded the Carter administration, as the United States experienced both high unemployment and high inflation, with prime lending rates exceeding 20 percent.

Things were even worse abroad, with events in Iran providing the clearest glimpse of national weakness. In November 1979, students loyal to the Ayatollah Khomeni seized 52 hostages at the U.S. embassy in Iran. With Carter unable to secure their return by either diplomatic or military means, Americans were forced to acknowledge that the country had been brought to its knees by a group of students.

As figure 2.1 shows, Ronald Reagan returned trust to levels not seen since the late 1960s. Jack Citrin and Donald Green (1986) suggest that this happened for two reasons. First, economic performance improved. After 1982, at least, unemployment and, particularly, inflation dropped markedly and change in gross domestic product (GDP), a leading measure of economic growth, skyrocketed. Second, Reagan exuded confidence and optimism about America, often using patriotic symbols to his advantage. The public often rewards optimistic presidents, like Kennedy, Reagan, and Clinton, with increasing levels of political trust (Nelson 2001). Moreover, Reagan accomplished quite a lot. He kept his early agenda very simple: tax cuts, defense spending increases, and a balanced budget. In going two for three, his batting average was significantly higher than his predecessor's.

The increase in trust did not last long, however. It began to decline during Reagan's second term, coinciding with Senate hearings into the Iran-Contra scandal. In addition, Arthur Miller and Stephen Borelli (1991) demonstrate that people became concerned about the country's ideological direction. The gap between where people saw themselves on the issues and where they saw the government started to grow, which is not surprising given Reagan's unabashed conservatism and the public's consistent desire for moderation. This disparity caused political trust to drop as well.

Trust continued to deteriorate through the George H. W. Bush years. Despite victory in the Cold War and Gulf War, Americans' evaluations of government did not improve. This was likely the result of the persistent recession that stretched from late 1990 into 1992. Without doubt, economic difficulties trumped foreign policy successes during the Bush years, as his defeat in the election of 1992 shows.

During Clinton's rocky first two years in office, trust reached its survey-era nadir. This likely owed, in part, to scandals like Whitewater, the misuse of FBI files, and the firing of the White House travel office. The public also came to see Clinton as ideologically extreme. During his first two years in office, he became linked to the far Left on cultural issues like gays in the military and abortion policy. As David King (1997) shows, the pattern of policy dissatisfaction in the 1960s had been inverted by the 1990s. Whereas Arthur Miller (1974a) suggested that centrist politics were to blame for low trust in the 1960s, polarized politics are to blame today. In other words, those in the political center—the majority of Americans—are now less likely to trust the government because they see the parties as too far from ordinary people and too close to the ideological poles (see also Jacobs and Shapiro 2000).

After the Republicans swept to power in Congress in 1994 and the economy continued its rapid expansion, political trust increased for the rest of the decade. Improved perceptions of government effectiveness and improved evaluations of Congress' job performance fueled the increase between 1994 and 1996 (Hetherington 1998) and probably beyond. In addition, the election of the first Republican Congress in 40 years provided the public with an increased sense that the political system could respond to citizen discontent. Once in office, the minor but well-publicized institutional changes that Congress adopted in early 1995 contributed to the improvement as well. That these changes were institutional in nature is noteworthy, given the continued unpopularity of congressional leaders like Newt Gingrich and some congressional decisions like the government shutdown (see Hibbing and Theiss-Morse 1995).

That the increase in political trust continued throughout the 1990s even with the constant scandals experienced by Bill Clinton and others in his administration is testament to the importance of economic performance. Indeed, had it not been for Kenneth Starr's prosecution of the Lewinsky matter, there is every reason to believe that political trust would have been quite a lot higher. According to the NES's cumulative data file, Americans' perceptions of the nation's economic performance in the past year, which is the most politically relevant measure of economic performance (Kinder and Kiewiet 1979, 1981), were more favorable in 1998 than at any time since the NES debuted these questions in the 1970s.[12] The increase in trust in the late 1990s despite the constant media focus on scandal allows us to generalize Stephen Weatherford's (1984) claim that poor economic performance during the mid-1970s affected political trust during that period more than did the Watergate affair. Both scandal and economic performance matter, but it is increasingly clear that the economy matters more.

What Are People Thinking About?

A small amount of scholarly literature on political trust has also explored what precisely people are thinking about when they answer the NES's standard battery of questions (Lodge and Tursky 1979). This deserves more attention. The federal government is a large amorphous entity, and certain parts of it and certain things it does are more popular than others. Hence understanding the criteria that people use to evaluate government at any given point should also help explain its relative popularity.

Information-processing theories tell us that the criteria most accessible in memory when someone is asked a survey question will carry the most weight in the answer given (Krosnick 1988). By determining what will be accessible, the mass media has a disproportionately large influence in making certain things seem more important. Since people tend to think that what they have heard most recently is most important (McCombs and Shaw 1972), recent information becomes the criterion that people use to evaluate leaders and institutions (Iyengar and Kinder 1987). This is called *priming*.

Importantly, the various potential criteria for evaluating government differ in popularity. Hence what people happen to be considering at different points in time can influence their overall evaluation of government. Regarding the three branches of government, specifically, John Hibbing and Elizabeth Theiss-Morse (1995) demonstrate that people feel more warmly toward the Supreme Court and the president than they do toward Congress. Not surprisingly, given the unpopularity the federal government has registered over the last 30 years, scholars have demonstrated that political trust is more closely associated with feelings about Congress than the other branches (Chanley, Rudolph, and Rahn 2000; Feldman 1983; Hetherington 1998; Williams 1985), although there is also strong evidence that people consider the president as well (Citrin 1974). As one might expect, political trust among Democrats tends to increase to some degree when a Democrat occupies the White House, and vice versa (Citrin 1974).

Many Americans also likely have in mind "typical politicians" when they evaluate the federal government. John Hibbing and Elizabeth Theiss-Morse (2002) cite the fact that Americans tend to believe that politicians care more about their personal ambitions than the greater good as the key reason for people's distaste for Congress. More generally, they argue that Americans hate government because they overwhelmingly believe that congresspeople are playing them for suckers, lining their own nest with big salaries, taxpayer-funded trips, and other perquisites while ignoring the needs of ordinary people. Consistent with this view, when the Kaiser Family Foundation asked Americans why people do not trust government, the most commonly cited reason was that leaders say what they think will get them elected, not what they really believe.[13]

Of course, the federal government is more than just the president, Congress, and Supreme Court. It also includes myriad executive branch departments and agencies, not to mention the institutions linked to them. Some of these entities and the programs they administer are more popular than others. For example, people do not seem to have much problem with parts of the government that might provide them direct benefits. You do not hear much complaint about federal spending on the interstate highway system, except maybe from Hawaiians. While some states with well-placed members of Congress surely get more, everyone gets some. Similarly, the 2000 presidential campaign reminds us that all Americans want to see Social Security and Medicare well funded because they will more than likely benefit from these programs in the future. In fact, the major party presidential candidates featured traditional New Deal programs in a higher percentage of their ads than in any election in the television era (Geer 2003). When the information environment focuses on these programs and the agencies that administer them, trust, other things being equal, will be higher.

Executive branch offices responsible for redistributive programs are another story. Before the 1960s, most government programs distributed benefits more widely, making it hard to argue that a relatively small number of people were taking advantage of the system and that government was doing a poor job stopping them. The burgeoning number and reach of antipoverty programs designed during the Great Society years changed that. An overwhelming percentage of Americans did not benefit directly from these programs; the problems these programs were intended to solve did not go away quickly; and the people receiving the benefits were not held in very high esteem.

As a result, redistributive programs and the agencies administering them became targets for attack from media sources and officeholders alike. Americans growing up in the television era have been fed a steady diet of stories about the urban poor buying liquor with food stamps, Cadillac-driving "welfare queens," and teenage mothers intentionally having more children to increase the size of their welfare checks, all while inept bureaucrats did nothing. Ronald Reagan, in particular, was fond of telling these, most often apocryphal, stories to public audiences. This publicity places such programs on tops of people's heads when they are asked to evaluate the government's trustworthiness. Indeed, the tendency to think about government in terms of redistributive policies is so ingrained in the public mind that, when people hear references made to government spending in general, they think about redistributive spending specifically (Jacoby 1994). Since this type of spending is less popular than spending on programs that distribute benefits widely, the trend toward increasing government distrust after the proliferation of redistributive federal programs makes perfect sense.

Perhaps the main reason that Americans think about government in terms of redistributive programs is that they wildly overestimate how much government spends on them relative to the more universal ones. In the 2002 fiscal year budget, nearly a quarter of federal spending was directed toward Social Security (the largest federal outlay), one-sixth went to national defense, and Medicare received just over a tenth of federal spending. These percentages of the federal budget are typical. In contrast, redistributive programs like Aid to Families with Dependent Children (AFDC), when it still existed, and food stamps programs combined to receive about 5 percent of the budget. Foreign aid received between 1 and 2 percent.

The public perceives a markedly different picture. In a January 1995 poll taken by the *Los Angeles Times*, more than 40 percent of respondents identified either foreign aid (22 percent) or welfare/aid to families with dependent children (21 percent) as the programs or areas receiving the most federal spending. Only 6 percent correctly identified Social Security.[14] Instead of the 5 or so percent of the budget that was spent on AFDC and food stamps at the time, a CBS News–*New York Times* poll taken in April 1995 showed that three-quarters of Americans mistakenly believed that welfare programs accounted for more than 10 percent of the federal budget, and nearly half pegged the amount above 20 percent.[15] The largest misperceptions involve foreign aid. Whereas these outlays make up between 1 and 2 percent of the budget, an April 2002 poll sponsored by the Pew Charitable Trusts found that 63 percent of Americans thought that the federal government spent more money on foreign aid than on Social Security even though Social Security receives ten times the funding. Only 14 percent correctly identified Social Security as the costlier program.[16] If people so wildly overestimate federal involvement in these areas, it follows that they will weight these considerations more heavily than is warranted in their overall evaluations of government.

And, in fact, the evidence suggests that people make just this mistake. Table 2.2 presents the results from a regression analysis that estimates the effect that feelings about a range of different people, institutions, and groups have on feelings about the federal government. Regression is a tool that allows researchers to estimate the independent effect of a range of explanatory variables at the same time, while holding constant all the others. For example, whether someone votes for a Democrat or Republican will depend on both a person's party identification and ideology. Even though these two explanations are correlated (that is, Republicans will tend to be conservatives and Democrats liberals), regression allows us to sort out what independent influence each has on vote choice, controlling for the other.

In this analysis, I use a number of the NES feeling thermometer questions, on which people rate things from a cold 0 degrees to a hot 100 degrees. Respondents are instructed to provide higher scores to groups that they feel positively about and lower scores to groups they feel negatively about. If people have neutral feelings about a group, they are instructed to give it a score of exactly 50 degrees. In a handful of recent presidential election years, the NES has asked people to rate their feelings

Table 2.2
Feelings about the Federal Government as a Function of Feelings about a Range of People, Institutions, and Groups, 1996

Variable	Parameter Estimate (SE)
Constant	−10.068***
	(2.355)
Congress thermometer	0.434***
	(0.026)
Supreme Court thermometer	0.160***
	(0.026)
Clinton thermometer	0.198***
	(0.018)
People on welfare thermometer	0.094***
	(0.022)
Older Americans thermometer	0.004
	(0.030)
Military thermometer	0.050*
	(0.023)
Blacks thermometer	−0.008
	(0.026)
Whites thermometer	−0.034
	(0.027)
Conservatives thermometer	−0.000
	(0.025)
Liberals thermometer	0.060**
	(0.025)
Labor unions thermometer	0.092***
	(0.020)
Big business thermometer	0.097***
	(0.024)
Poor people thermometer	−0.028
	(0.028)
Adj. R^2	.54
N	1,297

* $p < .05$.   ** $p < .01$.   *** $p < .001$. One-tailed test.
Source: American National Election Study, 1996.

toward "the federal government." I am interested in what people are thinking about when they are asked to evaluate it. If feelings about institutions, people, and groups are significant predictors of feelings about the federal government, it must be the case that they are on people's minds when they evaluate the federal government. I present the results from 1996 NES data, although the results from the other years prior to September 11, 2001, in which the federal government thermometer appears (1988, 1992, and 2000) are substantively the same.

Since all the variables are on a 0–100 scale, the estimated effects can be compared to get a sense of which variables are most and least influential. If a variable has an estimated effect of .10, it means that, moving from the coldest to the warmest evaluation of that object would increase feelings about the federal government by 10 degrees, or, 10 percent of the dependent variable's range. My analysis confirms that Congress is the main element that people have on their minds when they are asked about the federal government. Its effect is more than twice as large as any other variable. Feelings about the Supreme Court and about Bill Clinton, the sitting president, are also very influential. In addition, feelings about "Big Business," "Labor Unions," "Liberals," and "the Military" are on people's minds when they are asked to rate the federal government.

Most important for my purposes, however, is the fact that feelings about "People on Welfare" inform people's view of the federal government while feelings about "Older People" do not. Specifically, the estimated effect for "People on Welfare" is positively signed and statistically significant, meaning that the more warmly they feel about people on welfare, the more warmly they feel about the federal government and vice versa. However, their feelings about older people have no bearing on their feelings about the federal government. This is true despite the fact that programs that directly benefit older Americans, such as Social Security and Medicare, make up more than 35 percent of the federal budget, whereas traditional welfare programs make up less than 10 percent. Of course, people think welfare programs make up more of the budget than they do, which places these less popular programs and their recipients on the tops of people's heads when they think about the federal government.[17]

Taken together, this evidence paints a problematic picture. Americans express much less trust in the federal government today than decades ago in part because they are now evaluating the government based on their feelings about redistributive and foreign aid programs rather than more universal programs like Social Security, defense, and Medicare. They do this because they mistakenly believe that redistribution and foreign aid make up a much larger part of the federal budget than they really do. In fact, most Americans think these programs make up more of the budget than the true budget elephants. Hence, as was the case for misperceptions of government wastefulness, it seems that at least some of the decline in political trust between the Johnson and Clinton years is based on misperception of what government really does.

Evidence for the Priming Theory: Political Trust after September 11, 2001

Of course, news reporting and, therefore, the criteria that people use to evaluate political leaders and institutions changed fundamentally after Al Qaeda's September 11, 2001, attack on New York City and Washington, D.C. Consistent with the rally-round-the-flag literature (e.g. Mueller 1973), the public rallied behind George W. Bush. Bush's approval numbers jumped from 51 percent, as measured by Gallup in the days just prior to the attack, to 90 percent on September 22, the highest rating ever achieved by a president in the survey era. Bush, moreover, maintained his higher approval ratings longer than other rally beneficiaries because the public remained focused on foreign affairs and domestic security for an extended period of time (Hetherington and Nelson 2003).

Less widely noticed, support for American political institutions also shot up after September 11, with the percentage of people providing trusting responses to the standard political trust question increasing from 30 percent in the last survey taken before the attacks to 64 percent in the first survey taken after. This enormous spike encouraged polling organizations to ask the standard trust-in-government question more often than usual, which allows a test of the priming theory explicated above. Figure 2.3 tracks the percentage of people answering either "just about always" or "most of the time" (as opposed to "only some of the time" or "never") to this question (Trust) between November 2000 and July 2003.[18]

It is remarkable how closely the pattern of trustful responses mirrors changes in the information environment. As the criteria on which we might expect people to evaluate the government change, the level of public trust in government changes. A big dip in political trust occurred between the NES's 2000 postelection study and January 2001. Two major events took place during this period that likely account for the drop. First, the court proceedings following the election fiasco in Florida, which culminated in the Supreme Court's ending any further recounts, took center stage in the news media. Most Americans were unhappy with all the legal wrangling. Since Americans do not like to see contentious political processes played out in public (Hibbing and Theiss-Morse 1995, 2002), it follows that people's evaluations of government suffered.[19]

Second, economic news turned sour in the weeks leading up to and immediately following George W. Bush's inauguration, which suggests the enduring importance of performance evaluations in understanding trust in government. The following headlines about the economy provide

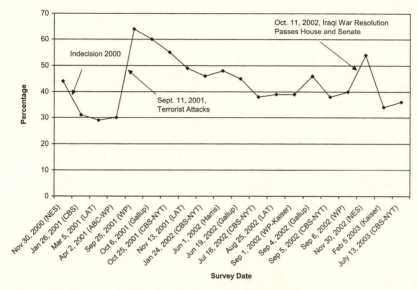

Figure 2.3. Changes in Trust in Government, 2000–2003.

a sample of front section *New York Times* reporting: "Consumer Confidence Plunges to Two-Year Low" (December 29), "Roots of a Slowdown" (January 13), and "Many Sense Good Times Slipping Away" (January 18). In early January, the Federal Reserve cut the discount rate half a percentage point in an effort to help what was consistently described in the press as a lagging economy drifting into recession. Given the importance that scholars have attributed to economic performance in explaining trust in government (e.g. Citrin and Green 1986), it is likely that the focus on a deteriorating economy contributed to the 15-percentage-point drop in trust between November 2000 and April 2001.

Data on trust in government are scarce for the first nine months of 2001. The last survey with a trust question before September was in early April 2001, and only 30 percent of Americans provided trusting responses. By early September, it is likely that trust had slipped even further. In a Gallup poll taken on April 6, Bush's approval rating was 59 percent, but it had dropped to 51 percent just before September 11. Since trust and presidential approval often move in tandem (Citrin 1974; Hetherington and Globetti 2003), the September 11 surge depicted in figure 2.3 is probably understated. Either way, in the weeks after the attacks, trust in government numbers rebounded to highs resembling the mid-1960s.

Although trust levels remained high relative to the last 20 years, they started to erode quickly, even during the successful military campaign in

Afghanistan in October and November 2001. These data are a reminder that rallies do not last forever. Moreover, the reason rallies do not last forever is noteworthy. People had started to think about things different from the event(s) that caused the rally. An ABC News poll taken on January 9, 2002, provides some evidence. Rather than just asking the general trust-in-government question, this poll prefaced it with two different phrases. In one, people were asked, "When it comes to handling social issues like the economy, health care, Social Security, and education, how much of the time do you trust the government . . ." In the other, people were asked, "When it comes to handling national security and the war on terrorism, how much of the time do you trust the government . . ." When primed to evaluate government on social policy, only 38 percent of Americans provided trusting responses, not that much higher than the 29 percent recorded in March 2001. When primed to evaluate the government based on the war on terrorism, however, 69 percent provided trusting responses, almost identical to the 65 percent in the *Washington Post* poll taken right after the attacks. As the shock of the attacks began to ebb, people started to think more about the usual things.[20]

In June 2002, with the September 11 attacks nine months in the past, trust in government dropped to the same level recorded in the 2000 NES. In the spring and early summer of 2002, the news media turned its attention away from foreign entanglements and domestic security to stories of corporate malfeasance, the resultant negative effect it had on investor confidence, and the persistent weakness in the broader economy. In mid-June, the media covered the guilty verdict handed down by a federal jury against the accounting firm Arthur Andersen for obstruction of justice in helping Enron in its illegal accounting schemes. In July, reporting turned to Congress's efforts to pass legislation aimed at restoring public confidence in financial markets. Much of this reporting focused heavily on the chummy relationship that many of the corporate wrongdoers had with President Bush, members of his administration, and both Republicans and Democrats in Congress.

It should come as no surprise, then, that a CBS News–*New York Times* poll taken on July 16, 2002, showed only 38 percent of Americans providing trustful responses to the standard political trust question. Hence, between the September 25, 2001, *Washington Post* poll that showed a return to 1960s trust levels and this July 2002 CBS News–*New York Times* poll, trust in government had dropped by fully 26 percentage points. Between July and early September 2002 trust held steady. Without a major change in the information environment during the summer of 2002, people continued to evaluate the government on these relatively unfavorable grounds.

Things soon changed. Between September 6, 2002, and the 2002 NES postelection survey, administered in November, trust shot up by 14 percentage points. During this period, the media turned its attention to the congressional debate of a resolution that would allow the president to take the country to war with Iraq. With strong bipartisan support, the resolution passed both houses on October 11, 2002. The focus on Saddam Hussein's threat to the world continued to be a hot topic through the 2002 midterm elections. This was the case for much of late 2002 and early 2003. By February 2003, however, the information environment changed again, and, along with it, so did political trust. Renewed emphasis on the economy, exemplified by such headlines in the *New York Times* as "Hiring in Nation Hits Worst Slump in Nearly 20 Years" (February 6) and "Greenspan Throws Cold Water on Bush Arguments for Tax Cut" (February 12) left only 34 percent of Americans trusting the government a month before the war in Iraq.

Gary Langer (2002) shows that, in 2001–2, trust covaried with the percentage of people identifying war, terrorism, or national security as the nation's most important problem. For example, in the April 2, 2001, ABC News–*Washington Post* survey, only 1 percent of Americans chose war, terrorism, or national security as the most important problem, and only 30 percent of Americans provided trusting responses to the standard trust question. When the late September 2001 *Post* survey showed 64 percent with trusting responses, a Gallup poll taken around the same time showed 64 percent of Americans identifying war, terrorism, or national security as the nation's most important problem. But by January 2002, only 35 percent of Americans identified war, terrorism, or national security as most important, and trust dropped to 46 percent.

This analysis can be extended to include all the polls with a trust question between October 2001 and November 2002.[21] For the surveys taken after the September 11 attacks, when people first started to think about domestic security and the war on terrorism, the correlation between the percentage of trusting responses to the trust question and the percentage of people answering war, terrorism, or national security to the Gallup most-important-problem question is a remarkably high .78. When people think the nation's safety is most important, they trust the government more. When their attention turns elsewhere, trust drops.

Why Concerns about Terrorism Increase Political Trust

This analysis leaves unanswered a fundamental question. Why would the public's focus on the nation's increased vulnerability after September 11 have such a salutary effect on trust in government? Indeed, it seems that such feelings might cause people to feel less warmly about government.

There are two complementary explanations. First, foreign crises generally cause rallies for both the president and institutions (Parker 1995). Hence both threats and rhetoric about threats will cause Americans to rally around the flag. Second, Americans today think increasingly well of the military. If people connect their feelings about the military with their feelings about government, government should be more popular.

Ample evidence exists to support this second point. Since the NES started asking its feeling thermometer questions in 1964, the military has never been as positively evaluated as it was in 2002, with a mean score of 75 degrees. By way of comparison, the mean score in 1980 was 65 degrees. Data on the military gathered by the Gallup organization tell a similar story. In 2002, fully 79 percent of Americans expressed either a "great deal" or "quite a lot" of confidence in the military, compared with only 58 percent in 1975. This increase in positive evaluations of the military runs in stark contrast to evaluations of other institutions. Over the same period, for example, the percentage of people providing positive evaluations of organized religion and Congress fell by 23 and 11 percentage points, respectively, according to Gallup.[22]

Moreover, the median correlation between the military feeling thermometer and trust in government in the 13 NES studies between 1964 and 2002 in which both appear is .09. Most of the correlations range between .06 and .09.[23] In 2002, however, the correlation jumped to .23, more than twice the median.[24] Only the constant media focus on the lead-up to war in Iraq in November 2002, when the NES surveys were taken, can explain such an increase. In sum, concerns about terrorism and domestic security cause people to think about the military. This, in turn, boosts trust in government.

Although the level of political trust recorded in 2003 was the lowest since the September 11 attacks and even a little lower than when Bill Clinton left office, it was still surprisingly high, given just how bad people's perceptions of the economy were in early 2003. In late January 2001, when barely 30 percent of respondents provided trusting responses to the standard trust question, nearly 70 percent of Americans said they thought economic conditions were either good or excellent. In February 2003, with trust at about the same level as January 2001, only 24 percent of Americans said they thought economic conditions were either good or excellent.[25] Such pessimistic views of the economy would ordinarily cause people to trust government much less. It is clear that continued concerns about the war on terrorism and national security, even if somewhat diminished from late-2001 highs, have kept trust from going into freefall.

This analysis suggests that, unless foreign and domestic security permanently takes center stage in the coming decades, trust in government is unlikely to remain very high. Indeed, in the first two years after September

11, political trust has generally held steady around Clinton-era levels, which is higher than most of the prior 20 years but hardly a return to Great Society times. While trust has jumped in response to dramatic events, such as the attacks themselves and the lead-up to the war in Iraq, it has always quickly receded. Absent another military engagement, there will be no natural rally effect, and the correlation between people's feelings about the military and their trust in government will drop back toward its median. Even though the military will likely continue to be popular in a world that it now dominates as never before, the weaker correlation between people's feelings about it and the government means that these positive feelings will contribute less to evaluations of government as a whole. The elements that people typically use to evaluate the government, such as traditional welfare state programs, will again take center stage, which will almost certainly lead to lower sustained levels of political trust absent another exogenous shock.

CONCLUSION

In this chapter, I have defined political trust and discussed some of the merits and shortcomings of the measure that survey researchers use to tap it. Certainly the former outweigh the latter. I have also tracked changes in political trust over time, identifying the factors that have caused it to vary. While most tend to think that political trust started its downward movement due to the deepening morass in Vietnam, I show that this is not the case. Instead, the higher expectations created by the expansion of government's reach in the early Great Society years is a more plausible root cause. The priming theory outlined in this chapter suggests that the redistributive programs created and expanded during the Great Society have become the new criteria that people use to evaluate the government. Since these programs are not particularly popular and people overestimate their cost, government has become less popular. Consistent with the theory, the federal government became more trustworthy to the public after September 11 as the criteria used to evaluate it turned to foreign and domestic security.

Perhaps most importantly, political trust's decline over time has been substantial. Between 1964 and 1994, trust had dropped by more than 30 percent. This provides some evidence that the change in trust has been large enough to effect a fundamental change in public policy outcomes between the 1960s and 1990s. While this review of trust's causes is important, it leaves unanswered an even more important question: what does it matter? I devote the balance of this book to understanding what effect declining political trust has had on American politics since the 1960s.

CHAPTER THREE

Political Distrust, *Not* Conservatism

BILL CLINTON AND Lyndon Johnson share many personal and political characteristics. Both grew up relatively poor southerners who, despite working for progressive Democratic presidential candidates in their youth (Johnson for FDR, Clinton for George McGovern), came to political prominence as moderates. Both held the presidency under favorable political conditions, with sizable Democratic majorities in Congress and a sizable partisan advantage in the electorate. Perhaps most consequentially, both presided over spectacular economic growth. Indeed, reading one year-end summary of 1965 generates at least mild déjà vu: "the American economy displayed unprecedented strength, with a soaring stock market, booming automobile sales, and record personal income and employment."[1]

Despite such striking similarities, Johnson and Clinton ultimately charted vastly different public policy courses. In 1965 alone, the Johnson administration unveiled Medicare, created the Department of Housing and Urban Development, and launched the "War on Poverty." Johnson later dramatically expanded the reach of Aid to Families with Dependent Children (AFDC), made food stamps a permanent program, increased federal aid to education, and pioneered Head Start. On race, Johnson engineered the passage of the Civil Rights Act of 1964 and the Voting Rights Act of 1965, not to mention fair housing and employment statutes. Under Johnson, the federal government, despite a dangerous Cold War and a hot war in Vietnam, capitalized on the favorable political and economic conditions to improve outcomes for the economically disadvantaged.

Nearly 30 years later, Bill Clinton followed a much different path. Even with the many advantages afforded by economic prosperity, Clinton's accomplishments, particularly post-1994, may be described as "bite-sized." After the defeat of comprehensive health care reform, Clinton trumpeted decidedly right-leaning initiatives such as the V-chip, school uniforms, and putting one hundred thousand more police on the street. In fact, perhaps the most significant social policy enacted during the Clinton presidency was the Personal Responsibility and Work Opportunity Reconciliation Act of 1996 (aka the Welfare Reform Act of 1996), which, by terminating AFDC as a federal entitlement program, attacked a key element of Johnson's War on Poverty.

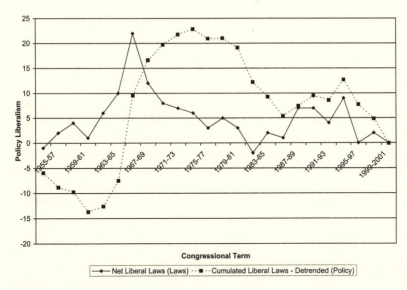

Figure 3.1. Policy Liberalism, 1953–2001. Source: Erikson, MacKuen, and Stimson (2002), from Mayhew's (1991) classification of significant laws, as updated.

Data on policy liberalism bear out this change. Robert Erikson, Michael MacKuen, and James Stimson (2002) calculate two measures of policy liberalism. The first is the difference between the number of liberal and conservative laws of significance passed during each Congress since the 1950s (referred to as *Laws*), and the second is the accumulation of net liberal laws over this period minus the average amount of liberalism for each session of Congress from which these data are taken (referred to as *Policy*). For Laws, a biennium receives a score of 2, for example, if Congress and the president enact three liberal laws of significance and one conservative one. For Policy, the average amount of liberalism during the time series (4.92 for the data used here) is subtracted out from the Laws score for each session of Congress, and this difference is summed over time. This means that for each session of Congress that produced five or more net liberal laws, the Policy measure increases. Fewer than five net liberal laws passed during a biennium produces a decrease. By detrending the net number of liberal laws, this measure provides a snapshot of "policy at any time in comparison to the long-term liberal trend that is driven by societal conditions" (Erikson, MacKuen, and Stimson 2002, 336).

The pattern of policy liberalism by these two measures appears in figure 3.1. As expected, both measures were low during the 1950s. The Laws score reached its maximum at the beginning of the Great Society years and maintained a fairly high level for the decade that followed. It then dropped below five net liberal laws per Congress for the entire Carter administration and all but the last two of the Reagan years. While Laws grew somewhat more liberal again during the late 1980s, it again turned more conservative beginning in the mid-1990s through the end of the decade. As for Policy, it moved above the neutral point for the first time during the 1965–67 session of Congress and continued to rise through the balance of the Nixon administration. Starting in the mid-1970s, however, the government started to produce less liberal legislation than the average in the time series, a trend that continued until the end of Reagan's second term. After a brief upturn in liberal legislation in the late 1980s and early 1990s, it again plummeted beginning with the 104th Congress (1995–97), continuing through the end of the Clinton administration.

Of greatest consequence, both of these measures of policy liberalism are lower during most of the Clinton years than during most of the Republican administrations, and, of course, well below the standard set by the Johnson administration. As a measure of how much politics has changed over the last generation, Richard Nixon emerges as the last great liberal president of the past 30 years, signing twice the amount of liberal legislation into law as did Bill Clinton.

Something fundamental had to change between the Johnson and Clinton presidencies for two such similar men in similar circumstances to lead American public policy on such dissimilar courses. Part of the explanation for Clinton's rightward turn after 1994 is the election of the first Republican congress in 50 years, but something monumental had to produce this Republican tide. Many political observers suggest this "something" is a dramatic right turn in public opinion. In response to the excesses of the Great Society, the conventional wisdom goes, the public has become increasingly conservative and thus unwilling to accept government intervention.

The conventional wisdom is wrong. In actuality, ideology has changed little over the last 30 years. What has changed, and what is responsible for the changed policy environment, is the amount of trust Americans have in their government. Public trust in the federal government has plummeted, and that fact has altered what Americans want their government to do. The result has been a noteworthy shrinkage of the public policy agenda, virtually killing any progressive impulse in American politics.

This chapter dispels the conventional wisdom by demonstrating the fundamental importance of political trust in explaining aggregate policy outcomes. I begin by highlighting the literature that links public opinion and public policy outcomes, and I tie this discussion to the contours of contemporary America's support for big government. Although political rhetoric might suggest otherwise, most Americans support federal involvement in most areas. In fact, there is significantly *more* support for government spending in general today than there was 20 years ago. The only area where public support for federal spending has dried up is redistributive policy. That Americans still support big government in most areas is inconsistent with a conservative revolution, something that I demonstrate has not occurred no matter the measure of public opinion. Instead, I show that policy liberalism over the last 40 years very closely follows changes in political trust. The more Americans trust government, the more progressive the policy course politicians will pursue. Indeed, trust has a larger effect on policy liberalism than any competing explanation. Finally, I demonstrate conceptually and empirically that conservatism and political distrust are two different things.

PUBLIC OPINION AND PUBLIC POLICY

Those who study American public opinion do so, ultimately, because they think it has some impact on political outcomes. This is normatively appealing; the voice of the governed in a democracy ought to have some impact on the decisions made by those who govern them (Dahl 1956; Arrow 1963). Especially in an era so consumed by the use of public opinion data, it also makes good common sense. Officeholders, who always think they are more vulnerable than they really are, want to give their constituents what they want. They will, therefore, most often try their best to follow public opinion (but see Jacobs and Shapiro 2000).

Empirically, political scientists have provided ample evidence that public opinion affects public policy. Benjamin Page and Robert Shapiro (1983) authored the most-cited study suggesting the importance of public opinion to public policy outputs. In examining government outputs between 1935 and 1979, they found that changes in public opinion often led to changes in government policy across a range of important issues. This was particularly true when public opinion on an issue changed dramatically, by Page and Shapiro's definition by more than 20 percentage points. In these cases, government policy followed the direction of public opinion in 90 percent of the cases. Importantly, the opinion and policy changes in this rendering are domain specific. That is, changes in the public's disposition toward racial policy, for example, lead to changes in racial policy.

Taking a somewhat different tack, James Stimson (1999) demonstrates what he refers to as policy moods, which ebb and flow in seemingly conservative and liberal directions over time. In this rendering of public opinion and policy outcomes, the public's general ideological mood about government policies, measured by Stimson as a combination of public policy preferences across a wide range of issues from abortion to race to gun control to general preferences for government intervention, leads to changes in the ideological direction of policy outputs (see also Erikson, MacKuen, and Stimson 2002). Depending upon the public's mood at a certain point in time, leaders may have the opportunity to pursue an aggressive policy course, as Ronald Reagan did in the early 1980s when presented with a conservative policy mood. But policy moods can also constrain elites. Ideologues cannot push too far without risking a reversal. For example, as Reagan continued to push his conservative agenda, the conservative policy mood that had provided his early success turned more liberal, forcing him to be less aggressive.

The importance of public opinion in policymaking shows up on the state level as well. Robert Erikson, Gerald Wright, and John McIver (1993) demonstrate that states with more conservative constituencies provide more conservative policies than states with more liberal constituencies. To anyone who has ever visited both Mississippi and Massachusetts, this should come as no big surprise. On assistance to the poor, for instance, more conservative southern states tend to be the least generous, while more prosperous northern states are the most generous. Citizens of these states share these preferences for state action or inaction.

The Role of Ideology

Each of these treatments of how public opinion affects policy outputs *seems* to have ideology at its core. How liberal or conservative the public is helps to determine how liberal or conservative policy outputs will be. That ideology might play such a central role is somewhat curious, however. If public opinion scholars can agree on one thing, it is that the public is largely "innocent of ideology" (Kinder 1983). Indeed, Philip Converse (1964) found that fewer than 15 percent of Americans organize their thoughts about politics ideologically, and, despite enormous increases in education, ideological thinking has not increased markedly since (Delli Carpini and Keeter 1996). Hence it is difficult to imagine that ideology is at the root of all, or even much, of what the public desires. Indeed, none of the measures of public opinion used by Page and Shapiro; Stimson; and Erikson, Wright, and McIver are measures of philosophical conservatism. Rather, they are either preferences on specific issues or jumbles of public policy preferences combined into a single measure.

Even so, such a focus on ideology is widespread both in scholarly and journalistic circles. After almost every presidential election, and even after some midterm elections like 1994 or 2002, pundits interpret outcomes as though ideology played a central role. However, the sheer frequency of the supposed ideological shifts suggests a different explanation. Ideology is a durable attitude passed along from parent to child early in life (Jennings and Niemi 1968), such that children who grow up with conservative/liberal parents will tend to be conservative/liberal themselves. This means that real changes in Americans' ideological preferences should last far longer than two or four years. Theoretically, adherence to an ideology should be like adherence to a sports team for a lifelong fan. Most do not root for the Yankees one year and the Red Sox the next. Similarly, if people's ideological beliefs carry any meaning, they should not change back and forth willy-nilly nearly each election.

Still pundits press on, suggesting, for example, that 1980 represented an ideological "right turn," with the landslide election and reelection of Ronald Reagan. Stimson's work, however, illustrates that the conservative policy mood was over long before the start of Reagan's second term, leading to the Democrats' recapture of the Senate in 1986. Pundits hailed 1992 as a return to center-left politics with the election of a "new Democrat" and a Democratic Congress. This also seemed plausible until 1994. While the 1994 election was supposed to be the beginning of a conservative revolution, with the right wing of the Republican Party engineering the historic congressional takeover, Bill Clinton thumped Bob Dole only two years later. House Democrats even did well in 1998, gaining seats in a sixth-year midterm election even with their president facing impeachment.

Things were sufficiently good for left-of-center politicians in 2000 that George W. Bush's victory over Al Gore was characterized as a huge upset, but, in 2002, pundits breathlessly heralded a marked conservative turn in the electorate after the Republicans assumed control of both houses of Congress, with the president's party gaining seats in both houses in a midterm election for the first time since 1934.[2] Public opinion may have been driving these outcomes, but the frequency of changes suggests that ideology is not the right aspect of public opinion.

Moreover, measures of philosophical conservatism, as opposed to those of policy mood, reveal another reason why ideology cannot explain the Johnson-Clinton differences. Simply put, much evidence suggests that *people* are not becoming more ideologically conservative even though *policies* are. Excepting social conservatives, whom I will leave aside, traditional conservatives desire less government involvement with just a couple exceptions, namely spending on defense and on law and order. Consider the debate in Congress about who should be responsible for airport security after the September 11 terrorist attacks. Conservatives like House Majority Whip Tom Delay (R-Tex.) and House Majority Leader Dick Armey (R-Tex.) fought hard against federal involvement, a position supported in principle by President George W. Bush. While Bush ultimately compromised by signing legislation that federalized baggage screeners, all three believed that private enterprise would do a better job than the federal government.

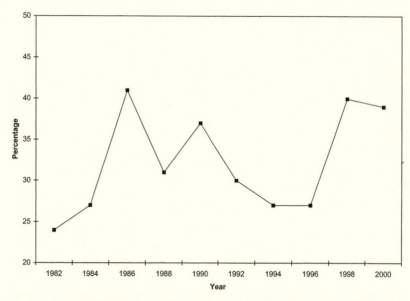

Figure 3.2. Public Support for More Federal Services and Spending, 1982–2000. Source: American National Election Study, Cumulative File, 1948–2000.

In general, conservatives believe that a larger, more intrusive federal government means less freedom and less efficiency, so they resist federal intervention. The strong correlations between spending preferences and measures of conservatism confirm this disposition. According to data from the NES, people's ideological self-identification carries a large negative correlation with preferences for spending on Social Security, the environment, and public schools, in addition to such things as welfare and food stamps (Hetherington 2001). As conservatism increases, support for spending in all these areas ought to decrease. Hence a right turn in public opinion should have increased Americans' preference for spending cuts in almost all areas.

Support for distributive spending programs, however, has remained strong and constant. And support for redistributive spending has fluctuated both up and down over the years, something that a consistent conservative turn would not be able to explain, had one actually occurred. Figure 3.2 demonstrates that Americans do not desire anything close to limited government across the board, which is a hallmark of modern conservatism. Almost all Americans still want the government to build highways, keep food safe, reduce crime, protect the environment and the nation's interests abroad, and keep American students competitive in a global marketplace. Specifically, the NES has asked in each study between 1982 and 2000 the following question:

Some people think the government should provide fewer services, even in areas such as health and education, in order to reduce spending. Other people feel that it is important for the government to provide many more services even if it means an increase in spending. Where would you place yourself on this scale, or haven't you thought much about this?

The interviewer then shows the respondent a seven-point scale with fewer services and spending at one end and more services and spending at the other. The figure tracks the percentage of people who place themselves on the more services and more spending side of the scale's midpoint.

Obviously, this figure does not suggest a consistent rightward drift in public opinion. Whereas only 24 percent of Americans wanted more government services and spending in 1982, 39 percent did in 2000, an *increase* of more than 60 percent in a *liberal* direction. Contrary to the conventional wisdom, public desire for more services and spending increased through most of the Reagan administration as well (see also Stimson 1999). In fact, at no point has a smaller percentage of the public wanted a services and spending increase than in 1982, the year the NES debuted the question. Although there was a marked turn to the right between 1986 and 1996, a marked turn to the left followed it.[3]

While these data only run through 2000, the behavior of Democratic presidential hopefuls for 2004 suggests the trend continues. Several of the candidates have proposed expensive health insurance reform proposals, and most suggest rolling back most of the tax cuts enacted during the George W. Bush years to bridge the budget deficit and to pay for new initiatives. While advocating tax increases is often considered political suicide, the Bush tax cuts were between 15 and 20 percentage points less popular than Ronald Reagan's sweeping tax program 20 years earlier,[4] indicating that people today are significantly less hostile toward government spending. In fact, a Quinnipiac University poll of registered voters taken in April 2003 asked, "What is your preference—to cut taxes or to have the federal government spend more on domestic programs such as education and health care?" Fully 68 percent said that they wanted to spend more on programs, while only 27 percent favored tax cuts.[5]

Support for specific programs varies greatly. In fact, many Americans do support reductions in programs designed to benefit the poor, particularly programs like welfare and food stamps that have been racialized by the mass media and political leaders (Gilens 1999). While this gap between support for antipoverty programs and for programs with larger constituencies is not new (see Free and Cantril 1967), it is substantially wider today than it was 30 years ago (Weaver, Shapiro, and Jacobs 1995), although narrower than it was 10 years ago. Figure 3.3 depicts the gap between support for distributive and redistributive programs. When I use the term *distributive*, I have in mind programs that benefit most, if not all, Ameri-

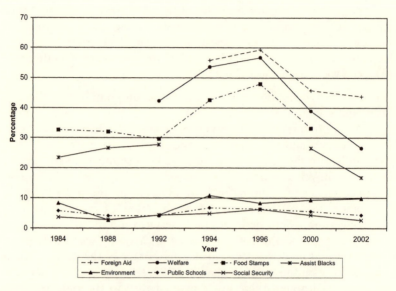

Figure 3.3. Percentage Supporting Federal Spending Cuts on Various Programs, 1984–2002. Source: American National Election Study, Cumulative File, 1948–2000.

cans. In contrast, redistributive programs target specific groups, usually those at the bottom of the socioeconomic ladder. The government takes money from the better off and redistributes it to the less well off.

Since 1984, the NES has asked Americans whether, if they had a say in making the federal budget, they would increase, decrease, or keep spending the same on a range of different programs. They often do not ask the same questions each year, but the pattern of responses over time provides a sense of the contours of public opinion. Since I am interested in people's hostility toward government programs, I present the percentage of people who answer that they would prefer decreased spending.

For the distributive programs, all the lines are clustered at the bottom. Never do as many as 11 percent of Americans want spending cuts on any of these programs. In fact, I cannot even present results for all distributive programs that the NES asks about because it produces so many lines between 5 and 10 percentage points that it renders the figure unreadable. The same lack of desire for federal spending reductions, however, holds for other items like crime reduction, financial aid for college students, and child care. When almost everyone benefits, very few Americans want to reduce the government's role. Of even greater consequence, support for spending on distributive programs has remained constant over time. There is no evidence of a right turn in these data.

When programs do not benefit most people, such as food stamps, welfare, assistance to blacks, and foreign aid, the picture is quite different. More often than not, a plurality of Americans has supported spending cuts on these programs since the mid-1980s. The percentage remained fairly constant from 1984 to 1992 but jumped considerably between 1992 and 1996. Little wonder Bill Clinton thought it was smart to get out of the AFDC business by supporting welfare reform. As public support for federal involvement in redistribution decreased, public policy followed quickly. After 1996, however, the trend reverses. Quite contrary to the notion of a right turn in American public opinion, particularly after the supposed Republican revolution of 1994, taste for spending cuts in all of these areas plummeted. Whereas 48 percent of Americans wanted to see cuts in the federal food stamps program in 1996, only 33 percent did in 2000. Support for spending on welfare, foreign aid, and assistance to blacks took similar turns.

These findings are not just an artifact of question wording. In fact, there is virtually no compelling survey evidence that more Americans have actually embraced conservatism since the 1960s (see also Stimson 1999; Mayer 1992). In each presidential election year between 1984 and 2000, the NES has asked people to place themselves on seven-point scales that reflect their preferences on the government's role in providing health insurance, aid to minorities, guarantees of employment and standard of living, women's rights, the proper level of services and spending, and defense spending. I combine people's responses to these six items additively and take the mean. The line tracking opinions to these items over time, labeled "Issue Scale," appears in figure 3.4. The mean at the end of the time series is a paltry three percentage points higher than at the beginning.

Perhaps most of the right turn took place before 1984. Most of the issue placement questions debuted in the 1980s, so I may be missing the critical period. Fortunately, the NES has asked the government-guaranteed-job and standard-of-living question since 1972, which should capture the ideological drift if one occurred. As is also clear from figure 3.4, however, responses to this question provide no evidence of a right turn. In fact, the estimated mean is *exactly* the same in 1976, 1988, and 1996.

People do not behave as ideological conservatives. Surprisingly, they do not even increasingly see themselves as such. Every election year, the NES asks people to place themselves on a seven-point scale ranging from extremely liberal at one end to extremely conservative at the other. Moderate, or middle of the road, represents the scale's midpoint. Figure 3.4 also reflects how the average score to this item, which I label "Conservatism," has changed over time.[6] The line is essentially flat. Comparing the beginning and ending points of the series, conservatism has increased by a mere

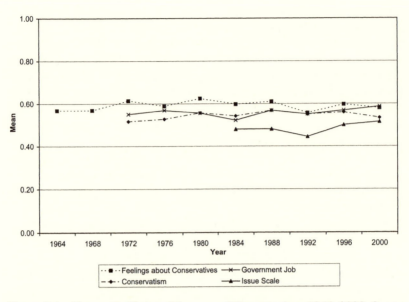

Figure 3.4. Changes in Various Measures of Conservatism, 1964–2000. Source: American National Election Study, Cumulative File, 1948–2000.

two percentage points. Such modest movement could not explain why Johnson and Clinton pursued such different paths.

In fact, people do not even seem to like conservatives much more than they did in the 1960s. Since 1964, the NES has asked people to rate "conservatives" on the feeling thermometer scale, ranging from 0 (cold) to 100 (warm). The final line in figure 3.4 tracks this item over time. While it has varied a little more than the others, the average response to the feeling thermometer is still very flat. Only in 1980 did the mean increase by as much as five percentage points over its 1964 mean, and, in 1992, people actually felt less warmly about conservatives than they did during the Johnson administration. In comparing the endpoints, positive affect toward conservatives has increased by just under two percentage points, again a substantively very small change.

SOLVING THE PUZZLE

This public opinion landscape provides us a puzzle in need of a solution. American policy is increasingly conservative; Americans, by nearly all measures, are not. Americans today express more support for spending cuts on redistributive programs than they did in the 1960s (Weaver, Shapiro, and Jacobs 1995). But they are neither more nor less supportive of spending cuts for programs that benefit everyone. Therefore, to the extent that the gap between support for distributive and redistributive spending has widened, it is completely a function of changes in support for redistributive spending. Complicating matters, this gap has not remained uniform in size over the last 20 years. It was considerably larger in the early to mid-1990s than it was in the 1980s or the early twenty-first century. What explains this pattern of opinion, which will, public opinion scholars assure us, affect policy outcomes?

WHY POLITICAL TRUST SHOULD AFFECT PUBLIC POLICY

I argue that political trust solves this puzzle. Empirically speaking, it is a prime suspect. Unlike conservatism, it has changed significantly and in the proper direction. Recall from chapter 2 the pattern of political trust's change over time. It dropped precipitously from the high recorded in the early Johnson years through the end of the Carter presidency. It rebounded briefly during Ronald Reagan's first term, then dropped again from the mid-1980s through the mid-1990s. Since 1994, however, political trust has steadily crept up with each election study. In fact, in 2002, trust reached a level not seen since the Nixon administration. Moreover, the recent rebound in political trust coincides with the recent increase in support for government services and spending in general, depicted in figure 3.2 and for the various redistributive spending programs depicted in figure 3.3.[7]

Moreover, political trust is correlated with support for spending on redistributive programs but not for support for spending on distributive ones, which is critical because support for the former has varied, while support for the latter has remained constant. In 2000, for example, the NES asked people whether they supported increased, decreased, or constant levels of spending for 13 different programs. Among spending preferences for programs with a redistributive character, and particularly those with a racialized beneficiary group (e.g. "spending on welfare programs," "to assist blacks," and "food stamps"), political trust always carries a significant correlation. This is true of spending on foreign aid as well. People who trust government more are willing to spend more in these areas. In contrast, when people are asked about their preferences for spending on more universal programs, such as spending on highway construction, Social Security, public schools, crime prevention, and preventing illegal immigration, the average correlation with political trust is a paltry .02.

The Theoretical Case for Trust

These empirical properties are certainly nice and seem to suggest we are onto something. However, there are other explanations that are empirically pleasing yet theoretically unsound. A correlation between two phenomena does not imply that one causes the other. For example, in every presidential election since 1944, the incumbent party's presidential candidate has won on the Tuesday following a victory by the Washington Redskins in their last home game before the election; the out party has won after each Redskins loss. The correlation is perfect, but this does not mean that the Redskins won the presidency for Bill Clinton in 1996 and lost it for Al Gore in 2000.

Theoretically speaking, trust should affect public policy opinions and, hence, outcomes. The reasoning is straightforward. People can easily connect the federal government with federal programs. If they do not trust the federal government, then they will want it to do less. But a lack of trust ought to affect public support for some programs but not others. Someone who distrusts government should have little quarrel with programs that provide or promise benefits. Perhaps a distrustful person believes that the government is inefficient and unethical, but that ought to matter less when a monthly check arrives in the mail.

Contrast that with programs that offer no discernible, immediate benefit and that may demand sacrifices. Political trust should be very necessary for people to support them. When people know for certain that they will not readily or materially gain from a program but that they will have to help pay the costs, it is essential that they trust the agent asking such sacrifice. In the case of spending on welfare, for instance, nonrecipients will need to trust the government if they are to support generous spending. Nonrecipients only pay the costs and receive no direct benefit. Although a society with less poverty will be healthier, a nonrecipient has to believe that government spending will actually effect this outcome, something a politically trustful person will be more likely to believe than a politically distrustful one.

In other words, when someone perceives that self-interest or group interest is at stake, he or she will need to trust the government to support a government-sponsored policy. I should note that scholars have consistently shown that the effects of self-interest on policy preferences pale in comparison to those of symbolic attitudes such as partisanship, ideology, and racial attitudes that are developed early in life through preadult socialization (e.g., Kinder and Sears 1981; Sears et al. 1978). These findings make sense because early experiences build these attitudes that people use for the rest of their lives. This means that symbolic attitudes will be well developed and easily accessible, making them good candidates to guide other opinions and behaviors.

I am offering a bit of a twist regarding political trust. Political trust is another symbolic attitude (Krosnick 1991), albeit a more malleable one, and it should *interact* with self-interest. In other words, policies requiring sacrifice ought to activate political trust, with the magnitude of trust's effect dependent upon the degree to which a person perceives that a policy encroaches on his or her self-interest. Therefore, policies that everyone benefits from, such as environmental spending or national defense, will not activate political trust. No one's self-interest is at stake. In the case of spending on the poor, however, the nonpoor will need to trust the government to support generous spending on antipoverty programs because the nonpoor only pay the costs and receive no direct benefit.

Trust in government should be particularly important when a person perceives that a measure of risk is involved and that only the government is in a position to mitigate this risk. Consider the interaction between trust and risk in everyday life. Except for people who lived through the Great Depression, most will deposit funds in their local bank without needing much trust in it. Even if the bank closes, deposit insurance will cover the losses (thanks to the federal government). Perceived risk approaches zero, making trust unnecessary. In contrast, people must have a good deal of trust in their stockbroker. Stock portfolios can go up and down, and brokers provide nothing in the way of an insurance policy if investments go awry. Obviously, there is much greater risk in investing in the market than depositing in a bank, which increases the need for trust.

This reasoning dovetails nicely with work that political scientists have recently borrowed from evolutionary psychologists (see Hibbing and Theiss-Morse 2002; Hibbing and Alford 2004 for a review of this literature). Quite different from the rational choice literature, which suggests that individuals seek to maximize their personal utility, evolutionary psychology emphasizes the importance of fairness in understanding how people react to outcomes. The ultimatum bargaining game is the vehicle most often employed in these studies. In this game, experimental subjects meet an experimenter who has $20 and is allowed to divide it with the subject as he wishes. The subject can then decide to accept the share of the $20 he is offered, or he can decline the offer. No matter what, the subject is assured at least $1 if he accepts the experimenter's offer. If the subject declines the offer, however, neither the experimenter nor the subject keeps any money. The results of these games suggest that fairness is more important to most people than is material gain. Subjects that receive offers well below $10 are overwhelmingly likely to decline the offer, thus punishing the experimenter and themselves. To avoid feeling like they are being played for suckers, people, on average, would rather have nothing at all rather than a few dollars.

Hibbing and Theiss-Morse (2002) show this is a major reason why people dislike Congress. They fear that elites will waste their money on junkets and favors for their friends, which ordinary voters feel they can do little to stop. People plausibly feel the same way about programs that they pay for but do not benefit from. Recipients are in a position to play them for suckers. However, if people trust that government can intervene to make certain taxpayers will not be played for suckers, they are likely to perceive less unfairness and will be more supportive of such government programs as a result.

The Information Environment and Political Trust

Information-processing theories further suggest that trust should be important in understanding policy outcomes, particularly in the present political context. These theories hold that at least two criteria must be met for an attitude to be of consequence. First, people must actually possess the attitude. This seems an easily met criterion, but it is less so than one might guess. Decades of survey research demonstrate that people provide answers to survey questions, whether or not they really have an opinion, merely because they don't want to appear ill-informed. In fact, to avoid the risk of seeming uninformed, people even provide opinions about political issues that do not exist. In 1978, a group of researchers at the University of Cincinnati asked a random sample of Cincinnati residents whether they would support or oppose the repeal of the 1975 Public Affairs Act. Of course, there never was a Public Affairs Act of 1975, but more than 30 percent of respondents gave their opinion (see Bishop et al. 1980).[8]

While this is an extreme example, the political science literature is littered with more subtle ones. Philip Converse (1964) coined the term nonattitude to describe the tendency of people to answer survey questions one way at one point in time and then give a completely different answer to exactly the same question a couple months or years later. If people had true attitudes, Converse argued, they would not change their opinion so radically. More likely, they had no real opinion at either time (or at least during one of the interviews) but wanted to respond to avoid seeming uniformed.

The more difficult the concept, the more likely survey researchers are to find nonattitudes. For example, if you ask someone whether he or she is a Republican, a Democrat, or an independent, you will find few nonattitudes because people recognize and understand these labels. However, if you ask someone whether they are a liberal, a conservative, or a moderate—terms that many people recognize but do not understand as well—

you will find a significant number of nonattitudes. In fact, when the NES asks its ideological self-placement question every two years, more than 20 percent of Americans always, and more than 30 percent sometimes, say that they don't know or haven't thought enough about it to provide an answer. In all likelihood, a similar percentage provides responses without really knowing what ideology is.

Like party identification, trust in government is a simple concept, about which almost all people will express true attitudes. Although people update how much they trust the government based on new information, their baseline feelings are arrived at on a gut level. In that sense, trust is more affective (feeling) than cognitive (thinking). This is of consequence because affective attitudes are more likely than cognitive ones to drive political change. For instance, racial issues, which people reason about on the gut level as well, forged a new set of party alignments in the 1960s (Carmines and Stimson 1989).[9] Such a reordering of preferences would not have occurred over inflation policy. Indeed, it was the affective character of party identification that caused the University of Michigan researchers in the 1950s to identify it as the central attitude in Americans' political belief systems (see Campbell et al. 1960). While it might be normatively better to have a polity occupied by thinkers rather than feelers, ample research suggests that the American public is dominated by feelers.

Very little political expertise is required to know whether you trust or do not trust the government, which is good for my purposes because a host of studies attest to Americans' inattentiveness to politics and inability to organize political beliefs within a coherent framework (e.g. Converse 1964; Luskin 1987; Delli Carpini and Keeter 1996). Instead, we know that Americans rely on heuristics, or shortcuts, to help them make decisions (Popkin 1994; Sniderman, Brody, and Tetlock 1991). People have neither the time nor the interest to become political experts, so they look for cues in the political environment to help them reason things out. For example, rather than gathering all the relevant information about welfare reform to determine a position, a Republican might decide to support it simply because most Republicans in Congress do. In this case, party serves as a heuristic (see Popkin 1994 for a host of other colorful examples).

Trust in government is another attractive shortcut. Trust can act as a simple decision rule for supporting or rejecting government activity. When confronted with a policy proposal, whether or not they know much about it, people could simply ask themselves whether and to what degree the government will be involved. Other things equal, if people perceive the architect of policies as untrustworthy, they will reject its policies; if they consider it trustworthy, they will be more inclined to embrace them.

The second criterion that an attitude must meet is to be accessible when people express their preferences. In other words, people must be able to find the attitude in their brain to use it. The political environment makes different attitudes more and less accessible depending upon how politics is presented. The mass media's behavior should make trust particularly accessible in today's political climate. Indeed, media references to trust in government are ubiquitous. Television news, the public's most important information staple, is disproportionately negative (Patterson 1993). Regular features like the *Fleecing of America, Reality Check,* and *Your Money, Your Choice,* all of which uncover some form of government waste or malfeasance, cut to the core of what political trust means. The dominant game schema reporting style, moreover, regularly portrays politicians' motives as disingenuous, further encouraging people to question those in the political world (Capella and Jamieson 1997). Furthermore, government powerlessness is among the dominant news frames used on network news today (Neuman, Just, and Crigler 1992). Since government effectiveness is one component of political trust, media portrayal of government and leaders as incapable of confronting political challenges should make trust accessible.

In a broader sense, both the news and popular culture present politics today as a game of deception perpetrated by officeholders on ordinary citizens (Hart 1994). For those who avoid political news, anti-Washington messages are pervasive elsewhere in the media. A recent Pew Foundation study reports that better than 10 percent of Americans say that they receive at least some political information from late-night talk shows, and close to half of those under age 30 do.[10] Those turning in to these and other pop culture outlets find talk show hosts like Jay Leno and David Letterman constantly questioning the ability and ethics of those in political life. Rarely, if ever, do they make positive references about politicians or the government. Although these portrayals are often very entertaining, they will, at best, serve to keep trust on the tops of people's heads, and, at worst, further undermine public confidence.

In short, trust meets both criteria needed for an attitude to affect public opinion and political behavior. Since it is easily developed, almost everyone has real attitudes about government trustworthiness. Moreover, trust is easy to use, making it all the more attractive as an explanation for the political behavior of an underinformed public. Finally, it is large part of the information environment. The political discourse encourages people to think about politics and policies in terms of how much they trust the federal government.

Not surprisingly, ample empirical evidence suggests that trust of various sorts affects opinions and behaviors profoundly. For example, trust plays a prominent role in the social psychology literature, with trusting relationships facilitating cooperation between individuals (for a review, see Putnam 2000). Such findings in psychology can be used in political research as well. Starting from the notion that trust causes individuals to cooperate with each other, Robert Putnam (1993) shows that more trusting societies provide their institutions similar cooperation and support.

Trust's role in organizational theory is also applicable to the political realm. Herbert Simon (1947) and Chester Barnard (1958) posited the importance of trust in gaining workers' acceptance of decisions made by organizational authorities, and Tom Tyler and Peter Degoey (1995) provide empirical support for these propositions. In fact, they find that perceived trustworthiness has a large effect not only on people's willingness to voluntarily accept management decisions, but also to accept the decisions of family and political authorities. Once government has earned the trust of its citizens, it follows that it will receive more leeway to pursue policy goals.[11] If the government has lost this trust, however, it will be more difficult for it to gain policy support, especially when proposed policies involve at least perceived sacrifice and risk. Hence the decline of political trust between the Johnson and Clinton presidencies ought to be of fundamental import in understanding why public policy has taken the turn that it has.

POLITICAL TRUST AND POLICY LIBERALISM IN THE AGGREGATE

My case would be even more compelling if I could show a correspondence between the government's policy liberalism and the public's level of trust in government over time. Since much of what distinguishes liberal from conservative public policy revolves around redistribution, periods of liberal policymaking should be preceded by periods of high trust, and periods of conservative policymaking should be preceded by periods of low trust. Trust should, in turn, increase or decrease public support for specific redistributive programs, which elected officials could easily observe with public opinion data (consistent with Page and Shapiro 1983). In addition, officeholders might be able to deduce such general feelings from the public through trips home to the district.

The data in figure 3.5 suggest exactly this story. Changes in political trust tend to lead changes in policy liberalism enacted by the government. Policy liberalism here is the Laws measure developed by Erikson, MacKuen, and Stimson (2002), which is presented in figure 3.1. It is the net number of liberal laws passed in a given session of Congress. Specifically, the figure contains data for political trust measured in a given election year, such as 1964, and policy liberalism from the session of Congress after the election year, such as the 1965–67 session of Congress.[12] The correspondence between the two trends is remarkable. When political trust is high, as it was at the beginning of the time series, politicians provide more liberal public policy. When political trust is low, as it was after the Carter presidency, for instance, politicians provide more conservative public policy. In fact, the

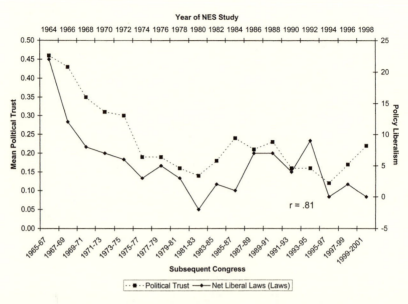

Figure 3.5. Political Trust and Policy Liberalism, 1964–2001. Sources: American National Election Study, Cumulative File, 1948–2000; David Mayhew's (1991) classification of significant laws, as updated.

correlation between political trust in a given election year and policy liberalism in the succeeding congress is an extraordinary .81. Levels of political trust, it appears, may be driving public policy.

Of course, competing explanations exist. My case that trust is a cause of how liberal public policy outputs are would be even more convincing if I demonstrated that it had an effect even after taking account of competing explanations. A good starting point for such an analysis is Erikson, MacKuen, and Stimson's (2002) recent work linking an alternative measure of public opinion, Stimson's policy mood, with measures of policy liberalism. The first dependent variable I will use is Laws. Erikson, MacKuen, and Stimson (2002) used data from the 1953–55 session of Congress through the 1995–97 session, and I have updated this measure to run through the 1999–2001 session.[13]

The first column of table 3.1 replicates Erikson, MacKuen, and Stimson's baseline analysis with the updated data. I explain variation in Laws and later Policy using regression analysis, explained in chapter 2. The explanatory variables in the first regression model are the net number of liberal laws in the prior session of Congress ($Laws_{t-1}$) and policy mood lagged by one biennium ($Mood_{t-1}$). Both have positive and statistically significant effects. Most important, the positive sign on policy mood

TABLE 3.1
Measures of Policy Liberalism as a Function of Political Trust, Policy Mood, and the Partisan Composition of Government, 1953–2001

Variable	Laws Para. Est. (SE)	Laws Para. Est. (SE)	Policy Para. Est. (SE)	Policy Para. Est. (SE)	Δ Policy Para. Est. (SE)	Δ Policy Para. Est. (SE)
Constant	−21.796 (11.164)	−32.692 (7.689)	−34.457 (12.573)	−15.265 (7.708)	−30.153 (11.262)	−16.819 (8.405)
Laws $_{t-1}$	0.387* (0.181)	−0.306* (0.131)	—	—	—	—
Policy $_{t-1}$	—	—	0.990* (0.086)	0.751* (0.071)	—	—
Mood $_{t-1}$	0.410* (0.190)	0.397* (0.130)	0.571* (0.203)	0.105 (0.122)	0.580* (0.186)	0.319* (0.146)
Democratic president $_t$	—	3.466* (1.053)	—	2.497* (0.875)	—	2.919* (1.188)
Number of Democratic houses of Congress $_t$	—	3.437* (0.746)	—	3.773* (0.647)	—	2.992* (0.834)
Political trust $_{t-1}$	—	38.943* (6.965)	—	24.126* (5.240)	—	30.198* (6.785)
Adj. R_2	0.38	0.87	0.85	0.94	0.28	0.82
N	24	18	24	18	24	18

Sources: American National Election Study, 1948–2000; Mayhew's (1991) Significant Laws, as updated; and Stimson's (1999) Policy Mood, as updated from http://www.unc.edu/~jstimson/mood2k.txt.
* $p < .05$. One-tailed tests.

means that the more liberal the public's policy mood, the larger the net number of liberal laws enacted during the next Congress. Erikson, Mac-Kuen, and Stimson's measure of public opinion affects policy outputs by the government. But is policy mood the best measure of public opinion for predicting policy liberalism?

In fact, a more fully specified model demonstrates that the effect of policy mood on Laws is much smaller than the effect that political trust has.[14] The results from this analysis appear in the second column in table 3.1. In addition to the lagged dependent variable and lagged policy mood, I also add other explanatory factors that should affect policy liberalism, including the presence of a Democratic president, the number of houses of Congress controlled by the Democrats in a given biennium (see also Erikson, MacKuen, and Stimson 2002), and, most importantly, political trust measured the year before the beginning of a new Congress (Political Trust$_{t-1}$). All should have a positive effect on policy liberalism. That is, a Democratic president, a Democratic Congress, and more political trust should all increase policy liberalism.

And, in fact, all do. Each variable is positively signed and statistically significant, with the exception of the lagged dependent variable. The interpretation of the partisan control of government variables is most straightforward. Other things being equal, the presence of a Democrat in the White House increases the net number of liberal laws by about three and a half laws (the estimated effect of 3.466 suggests this). Similarly, each house of Congress controlled by the Democrats increases the net number of liberal laws by about three and a half laws. If the Democrats control both houses, it increases policy liberalism by about seven laws (3.437 x 2 = 6.874).

The interpretation of the effects of political trust and policy mood is a little more complicated. The estimated effect of policy mood is .397. The best way to calculate its effect relative to the other variables is to multiply its estimated effect by the amount that policy mood changed over the time period (13.84 points), a calculation called a *first difference* (see King 1989). This yields a first difference of 5.49 laws, which is larger than the effect of a Democratic president but smaller than that of Democratic control of both House and Senate.

The relative effect of political trust can be calculated the same way. Its estimated effect is 38.943. Its minimum, achieved in 1994, is .119, and its maximum, achieved in 1964, is .461. Multiplying trust's estimated effect by the amount that it changed over the period yields a first difference of 13.32 laws, which is more than twice as large as that of policy mood and more than three times that of having a Democratic president. Although policy mood is influential, political trust is much more so.

In fact, the effect of political trust is more impressive than that of policy mood no matter how policy liberalism is measured. Take, for example, the Policy measure, which was depicted along with the net number of liberal laws in figure 3.1. Recall that this is the accumulation of liberal laws relative to the trend in liberalism over time. The third and fourth columns in table 3.1 contain the results from parallel analyses using this dependent variable. Again, in the simplest form of the model, with a lagged measure of Policy (Policy$_{t-1}$) and a lagged measure of policy mood (Mood$_{t-1}$) as explanatory variables, the estimate for policy mood is positively signed and statistically significant. But, in the more fully specified model, which includes these two variables along with a lagged measure of political trust (Political Trust$_{t-1}$) and the partisan makeup of the government variables, the effect of policy mood evaporates.

Again, trust emerges as the better measure of public opinion in explaining policy liberalism. Increasing trust from its minimum to its maximum during the time series increases the relative liberalism of the detrended policy course by more than 8 laws (24.126 x .342 = 8.251). This is not to suggest that policy mood has no effect. Erikson, MacKuen, and Stimson (2002) demonstrate that it significantly affects the partisan composition of the federal government. Since both a Democratic president and the number of Democratic houses exert significant effects, policy mood has indirect effects on Policy. However, the magnitude of this indirect effect pales in comparison to the direct effect of political trust on the nation's relative policy liberalism over time.

Finally, trust has a larger effect on how much policy changes from session to session than does policy mood.[15] The dependent variable here is Policy at time t (a particular Congress) minus Policy at time $t - 1$ (the Congress before it), which I call ΔPolicy, or change in policy. Hence, a positive score means policy liberalism has increased between the two congresses, and a negative score means policy has grown more conservative. With ΔPolicy as the dependent variable and lagged policy mood as the lone explanatory variable, policy mood exerts the familiar positive and significant effect. In the more fully specified model, which includes all the other explanatory variables, policy mood continues to influence the dependent variable, along with the partisan makeup of government variables and political trust. But, again, political trust has, by far, the largest effect of all the explanatory variables. In moving from its minimum to its maximum in the time series, political trust produces an increase of 10.32 laws, other things being equal. In contrast, policy mood, also moving from its minimum to its maximum, increases the number of liberal laws by 4.41 laws, less than half as much as trust.

Furthermore, changes in political trust cause changes in policy mood (Chanley, Rudolph, and Rahn 2000). When the public trusts the government more, the policy mood swings to the left. When the public is distrustful, the policy mood swings to the right. So, even the effect that policy mood has on policy liberalism is indirectly the result of changes in political trust. This set of relationships is depicted in figure 3.6. It suggests that political trust is the real catalyst for change in public policy.

Although I am using a lagged measure of political trust (Political Trust$_{t-1}$) to predict policy liberalism (lets say, Laws$_t$), which helps establish the true causal order of the two variables, some might still wonder whether the reverse causal order is more accurate. That is, does lagged policy liberalism (let's say, Laws$_{t-1}$) predict political trust (Political Trust$_t$)? Indeed, there does seem to be some impressionistic evidence to suggest this causal order. The two most pronounced recoveries in political trust since the 1960s occurred during periods characterized by con-

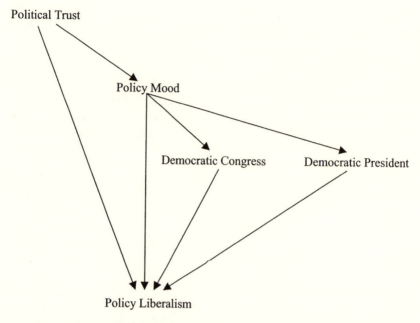

Figure 3.6. The Causes of Policy Liberalism.

servative public policy—the Reagan revolution in the early 1980s and Clinton's post-1994 turn to the right. If a systematic relationship between lagged policy liberalism and contemporaneous political trust emerges, it would throw my entire analysis into question.

Fortunately, I can test this possibility by estimating a regression model with contemporaneous political trust (Political Trust$_t$) as the dependent variable and lagged political trust (Political Trust$_{t-1}$) and lagged Laws (Laws$_{t-1}$) as independent variables. The results are reassuring. The effect of lagged Laws does not approach statistical significance. In other words, I find no systematic evidence that more conservative government leads to increases in political trust.

As an alternative explanation to the Reagan and Clinton era increases in trust, recall that both the early 1980s and middle to late 1990s were characterized by rapid economic expansion. I can test whether there is systematic evidence over the period that a better economy increases political trust. To do this, I include change in the gross domestic product recorded in the year that political trust was measured as an explanatory variable in the regression model explained in the previous paragraph. It carries a positive sign and is statistically significant, while lagged policy liberalism remains statistically insignificant. In other words, economic performance affects political trust, as decades of literature suggests (see Weatherford 1984; Citrin and Green 1986; Hetherington 1998), but the liberalness of policy outputs in the prior session of Congress does not. Economics, not conservative public policy, explains why trust increased in the early 1980s and middle to late 1990s.

In sum, how much people trust government in the aggregate exerts the largest direct effect on the public policy course that elected officials follow in the aggregate. As I hypothesized, the more people trust government at a given point in time, the more liberal policies that officeholders attempt to enact in the next session of Congress. The government's policy liberal-ism does not affect political trust. These results are normatively appealing in that elected officials have done well translating public opinion into pub-lic policy over the last several decades. In 1964, with public optimism about government at an all-time high, the Johnson administration along with Congress implemented more liberal laws in the 1965–67 session than any other time in the last 40 years. In contrast, after trust in government reached a low point in 1980, Ronald Reagan and the Ninety-seventh Con-gress implemented the most conservative policy course.

Indeed, as a measure of public opinion, political trust should be quite useful to politicians. It must be difficult for elites to determine how conser-vative or liberal their constituents are because ordinary Americans do not think in such terms. People are much better at expressing how they *feel* about government. Political trust can be thought of as a measure of such feelings. It seems that politicians try to understand how much the public trusts them, and they use this information to decide how much govern-ment to provide them. While political scientists have long argued that policy follows opinion, the measure of public opinion that I use is different and more realistic than the one most often considered in the literature. In setting the nation's policy course, politicians follow how much Americans trust government, not their difficult-to-gauge, and often contradictory, ideological preferences.

The data also suggest that it is important for elites to pay close attention to political trust in setting a policy course. The public may punish them if they provide policy inconsistent with aggregate levels of political trust. The most striking case is the beginning of the Clinton presidency. With political trust at a fairly low point relative to the time series, Clinton and the Democratic Congress pressed a very liberal policy course in the suc-ceeding legislative session, passing a net nine liberal laws. The public made them pay for their excesses. In 1994, a politically distrustful public turned congress over to the Republicans for the first time since the 1950s.

Of further note, these data suggest that the public would have allowed Clinton to govern substantially further to the left than he did during his last years in office, with political trust increasing markedly after 1994. Of course, his close identification with the health care debacle likely put this initiative out of reach. However, support for other liberal initiatives was increasing as a consequence of increasing trust in government. The data in figures 3.2 and 3.3 make this clear. Clinton, however, did not risk a move leftward. He and his advisors thought they had been swamped by a conservative tide that would last for at least the duration of his presidency, when, instead, it was a distrustful one that quickly ebbed. By misinterpreting public opinion, Bill Clinton missed an opportunity to contribute to a progressive legacy.

ARE DISTRUST AND CONSERVATISM THE SAME THING?

While, at first blush, it seems that those who are distrustful and those who are conservative would both want the government to do less, more careful consideration reveals an important distinction. Conservatism is a *philosophy* that has at its core the virtues of limited government in most areas. Conservatives would want any government, no matter whether it was perfectly effective, to be as minimally involved as possible.

Political distrust is not a philosophy, per se, and is thus much more flexible. People who are guided by political distrust have no problem with the government being involved in things from which they benefit. In addition, they do not necessarily have a problem with government intervention in areas where they receive no direct benefit but have to make sacrifices for others, provided they believe that the government will be effective. While the distrustful distrust *this* government and thus want to minimize its involvement in certain areas, they might embrace government involvement in these same areas if they trusted it would do a good job. This is not true of conservative ideologues. Outside of national defense and law and order issues, they oppose government on philosophical grounds, no matter its quality.

As an empirical matter, the measures of conservatism that I use and my measure of political trust are only weakly correlated. For example, the correlation between trust and ideological self-placement over the nine election studies taken between the 1984–2000 period is, on average, .05.[16] They are clearly not the same thing.

That political distrust and conservatism are two distinct concepts has important implications for those on the political left in American politics. To increase public support for their initiatives, progressives do not need to change people's ideology, a complex set of attitudes at the core of their political belief systems, which is good news because such ideological changes have happened only rarely in American political history (e.g. Burnham 1970). Instead, liberals need to resuscitate the image of the federal government, the delivery system for most federal programs. While this will not be easy either, given how ingrained political distrust is in the post-Watergate political culture, it happens more frequently than changes in ideology. The last 40 years have taught us that Americans' political trust responds favorably to sustained economic success, a policy direction in tune with the public's preferences, overt use of patriotic symbols, and strong presidential leadership. This is true despite the fact that even the most successful political leaders utter few kind words about the things government does well.

Conclusion

In this chapter, I have demonstrated that a fundamental change in American politics occurred between the Johnson and Clinton presidencies. Rather than fighting a war on poverty with government-sponsored initiatives as Johnson did, Clinton, at times, worked to roll back Johnson-era programs. A change in public opinion is the cause. Although most political commentators point to an ideological right turn in American politics, no evidence for one exists. Not only have measures of ideology failed to move to the right, people's preferences for government intervention do not square with an ideological change. A significant percentage of Americans only wants less government in the area of redistribution, not for programs from which everyone or almost everyone benefits. Conservative ideologues, on the other hand, want less government across the board. This division between redistributive and distributive preferences squares better with an increasingly distrustful public. Political trust should only affect preferences for programs that require sacrifice, exactly the programs for which support has deteriorated over time.

In addition, political trust and policy liberalism are strongly correlated. This suggests that politicians sense how politically trustful or distrustful the public is. They, in turn, provide policies that reflect how much faith the public has in its government. When people are trustful, policy grows more liberal. When people are distrustful, policy turns more conservative.

Political trust has changed significantly and in the correct direction; it is correlated with the right preferences for government involvement (those for which support has varied over time) but not the wrong preferences (those for which support has remained constant); it makes good theoretical sense; and it temporally precedes, and tracks closely, changes in policy liberalism. In fact, it exerts a larger effect on policy liberalism than all other competing explanations. Taken together, it seems that declining political trust helps explain what many have erroneously referred to as a conservative turn in American politics.

CHAPTER FOUR

The Dynamic Importance of Political Trust

ON THE MORNING of April 19, 1995, Timothy McVeigh pulled a rented
Ryder truck packed full of explosives in front of the Murrah Federal Building in Oklahoma City, OK. By eight-thirty, McVeigh had set the fuse and
left the area. At 9:04, he detonated the bomb, killing 168 people, 19 of
them children, a group he would later refer to as collateral damage.

In the days following the attack, most speculated that Islamic extremists
were the perpetrators. It shocked most to find that it was an American. In
the months that followed, McVeigh made it clear that his grievance was
against the federal government. He was so offended by the botched efforts
of federal law enforcement during the siege of the Branch Davidians' com-
pound in Waco, Texas, in 1993 that he felt compelled to send a message
to Washington, carrying out his attack on the second anniversary of the
dénouement of the Waco standoff. The destruction of the Murrah Federal
Building was America's worst act of terrorism until September 11, 2001.

It is not hard to guess where Timothy McVeigh would score on the
NES's trust in government scale. While this book is not about the causes
of domestic terrorism, the story serves an important purpose. Even if most
people's negative feelings about government are subtler than his,
McVeigh's actions demonstrate that feelings about government can have
a profound impact on behavior. If McVeigh had felt positively, or even a
little less negatively, toward the government, he would not have carried
out his attack. His hatred of government, among other things, caused his
behavior.

Surprisingly, the notion that political trust might have measurable effects on political behavior and public opinion runs counter to the scholarly
conventional wisdom. The dramatic decline in political trust between the
mid-1960s and the mid-1970s motivated scholars to focus attention on
why. But, in doing so, they lost sight of the implications of trust's decline.
For trust to be worth studying, however, it must have some consequences
for normatively important opinions and behaviors.

I have provided a theory that explains why political trust ought to be
influential, when it ought to be influential, and on what it might exert its
influence. I have also provided support for the theory in the aggregate. I
next need to test the theory with individual-level data to support these
aggregate-level findings. In other words, do politically distrustful individ-

uals behave differently from politically trustful ones in a way consistent with the aggregate-level patterns I have shown?

In this chapter, I explain why scholars ignored the consequences of declining trust soon after they first identified the onset of its decline. I identify two problems: scholars were looking in the wrong places, and they were improperly assigning cause and effect. To remedy the second problem, I fashion and test a theory that specifies the changing causal dynamics of political trust over time. I show that using 1970s reasoning about causal sequence today would lead to an inaccurate interpretation of how the political world works.

WHY SCHOLARS MISSED THE CONSEQUENCES OF DECLINING POLITICAL TRUST

That Americans express little trust in government sounds bad. But does it matter? Since scholars have focused on explaining variation in political trust, the dominant strain for years in the political science literature is that distrust is largely a ritualistic reaction to the present political discourse (Citrin 1974). This view is not without merit. Many things that one might think would suffer from low political trust have not suffered. As trust plummeted, elections continued to occur without incident, presidents continued to send the military to faraway places like Kuwait, Somalia, and Bosnia with little public recrimination, the size of government continued to grow incrementally, and, even in the very angry-seeming 1990s, Bill Clinton achieved the highest second-term approval ratings of any president in the survey era.

In fact, a report from the Pew Foundation (1997) entitled *Deconstructing Distrust* concluded, "It is difficult to pinpoint the specific negative behavioral or attitudinal consequences of distrust. It has not diminished Americans' sense of patriotism, nor has it created a climate of opinion that is conducive to acceptance of illegal anti-government activities. . . . For the most part, Americans remain open-minded about government" (12–13). While it seems that trust in government should affect politics, the supporting evidence has been thin.

Two reasons explain these null findings. First, political scientists have, in some cases, offered explanations for political trust's decline that are more likely consequences than causes of it. For example, around the time that political trust began to drop, presidential approval also dropped. Dwight Eisenhower, John F. Kennedy, and Lyndon Johnson (at first) typically achieved approval ratings 10 to 15 percentage points higher than their successors (Brody 1991). Finding a correlation between presidential approval and political trust, scholars concluded that dissatisfaction with the president had caused political trust to decline (Citrin 1974).

However, a stronger theoretical argument can be made that declining political trust caused increasing dissatisfaction with the president. Psychologists find that, when people make judgments, they tend to reason from the general to the specific. Consider the use of stereotypes. General stereotypes about a particular racial group inform feelings about specific members of that group much more than experiences with specific group members affect the stereotypes. If a person does not like African-Americans as a group, he or she is unlikely to like individual African-Americans, because the stereotype is working as a shortcut. The same general-to-specific reasoning holds in politics as well. If a strong Democrat is introduced to a Republican politician and knows nothing else, the strong Democrat is more likely to evaluate the Republican poorly than if the politician were a Democrat. Hence general feelings about the government (political trust) should affect feelings about specific parts of the government (the president). At a minimum, the two attitudes ought to be arrived at together.

Causal analysis of presidential approval and political trust demonstrates that each causes the other, but political trust has a much larger effect on feelings about the president than feelings about the president have on political trust (Hetherington 1998). Moreover, the effect that political trust has on presidential approval is politically significant because it explains why contemporary presidents are less popular than their predecessors. If we take into account the amount that political trust declined since the 1960s, Ronald Reagan's outgoing approval ratings become indistinguishable from Dwight Eisenhower's, and Bill Clinton's midpresidency approval ratings bear a striking resemblance to those of Lyndon Johnson's at the same point in his presidency (see Hetherington 1998 for details). In short, declining political trust has undermined presidential approval, something scholars missed by treating approval as a cause of trust instead of a consequence.

The second reason that scholars have underestimated the importance of declining political trust is that they have been looking for effects in the wrong places. Since voter turnout was declining at the same time as trust, political scientists naturally placed a lot of emphasis on measures of participation when exploring trust's potential implications. However, low political trust does not cause people to stay home on Election Day (Citrin 1974). The absence of a relationship between political trust and participation appears to be another key reason that scholars dismissed the importance of declining political trust.

This is unfortunate because one could make a strong argument that low trust encourages participation and high trust discourages it. Those who are most dissatisfied with government have the largest incentive to change it. If someone loses her job and believes the government is responsible, she may be encouraged to participate to bring about political change. In contrast, those who are satisfied with government tend to be complacent. Indeed, much research suggests an asymmetry in the effect of presidential approval at midterm elections, with disapprovers voting at significantly higher rates than approvers (Kernell 1977). This happens because human beings, risk averse by nature, are more motivated by the negative (Kahnneman and Tversky 1974).

The discussion about trust and participation tracks closely the scholarly debate on the effect of negative advertising. While some have suggested that negative ads depress turnout because people do not like them (Ansolabehere and Iyengar 1995), others, using different data, have found the reverse. Indeed, negative advertising may increase turnout (Freedman and Goldstein 1999; for a review see Wattenberg et al. 1999). At a minimum, the potentially positive and negative effects of negative advertising may cancel each other out, producing no relationship between it and voter participation (Finkel and Geer 1998). The relationship between trust and participation likely follows the same pattern.

An Individual-Level Theory of Political Trust's Causal Dynamics

Much of the scholarly literature about political trust centers on what affects it, although more recent efforts detail what it affects (Scholz and Lubell 1998; Hetherington 1998, 1999; Tyler and Degoey 1995). In the social science vernacular, when is political trust a dependent variable and when is it an explanatory variable? When we treat something as a dependent variable, we are trying to explain what causes it to change. When we treat something as an explanatory variable, we are trying to understand what it causes to change.

The research that treats political trust as a dependent variable, detailed in chapter 2, shows us convincingly that perceptions of government performance, particularly regarding war, scandals, and the economy, have large and consistent effects on trust. These findings are, of course, consistent with my definition of political trust. People have clear expectations about government in these three areas. Government ought to be ethical, win wars, and keep the country prosperous. When people are not getting these things from government, they trust it less.

It is less clear, however, how trust is causally related to functions that go beyond the minimum expectations that people have of government. While almost everyone agrees that government should provide its citizens peace and prosperity, many disagree about how much aid government ought to provide poor people or how aggressively it ought to redress outcomes for historically discriminated-against groups. The conventional scholarly wisdom suggests that dissatisfaction with the government's performance in such areas might undermine trust (see Miller 1974). In contrast, my work suggests that a lack of political trust causes people to want less government action in these areas.

Resolving this question is important. Generally speaking, the statistical methods used by social scientists cannot *determine* what causes what. Regression is the tool used by most political scientists to estimate the effect that an explanatory variable has on a dependent variable. In fact, I used this tool in the last chapter to show that political trust has a larger effect than policy mood on policy liberalism. With regression analysis, the researcher specifies which is the dependent variable and which is the explanatory variable(s) based on a theory of how the world works. The theory is of paramount importance because it determines how the results are interpreted.

For example, most research shows that partisanship affects vote choice (e.g. Campbell et al. 1960). That is, Republicans tend to vote for Republican candidates and Democrats tend to vote for Democratic candidates. Using regression, we can estimate how large the effect of partisanship is on vote choice. However, regression is just a tool. If the data are all collected at the same time, as is the case with cross-sectional surveys, the most commonly used surveys in the field, the causal ordering of variables is not altogether clear. For that reason, we could also use regression to estimate the effect of vote choice on partisanship even though the causal ordering specified here is opposite to how the world really works. A less careful reader might erroneously conclude from the latter results that voting for Democrats causes people to identify as Democrats. Getting the causal ordering of variables right is fundamentally important. Otherwise, one runs the risk of interpreting the political world backwards.

The Babysitter Analogy

An analogy helps illustrate how I hypothesize political trust is causally related to support for government programs that require risk or sacrifice. Any new parent can tell you that deciding on a babysitter is difficult business. Your child is precious, and this decision carries a high degree of risk. If you choose poorly, the consequences could be catastrophic. Hence you need to have significant trust to leave your baby with another person. In all likelihood, you will choose someone that you have had some previous experience with, whether it be a friend, or, more helpful for my purposes, someone who has done other work for you in the past.

Let's assume that your prospective babysitter is a teenager who has done a very conscientious job with your yard work. Past experience increases your trust in her, which, in turn, increases the probability that you will hire her as your babysitter. Trust has played two roles to this point. First, trust is a dependent variable explained by your assessment of the potential sitter's performance with yard work. Next, it is an explanatory variable, explaining whether you hire her as a babysitter.

Let's further assume that you make the hire and go out for dinner and a movie. After you return home, your perception of the sitter's performance causes you to update your trust in the sitter. Trust is again a dependent variable, and your perception of her performance as a babysitter is the explanatory variable. If you come home and all is well, then your trust in the babysitter may increase. However, if you come home and your child is awake three hours after bedtime because his arm is hanging loosely from his shoulder socket, then you update your trust of the sitter downward dramatically.

Based on this updated evaluation, you decide whether you will hire her again. If performance met expectations, other things being equal, you will, and, if not, you will not. In this final part of the sequence, trust again acts as an explanatory variable, explaining whether or not you hire the sitter again.

Political trust ought to work much the same way with new programs that require perceived sacrifice or entail some risk. Similar to the trust that develops from a job well done with lawn care, trust in government may develop from government doing well with duties like providing peace and prosperity. Trust starts as a dependent variable explained by past performance. Trust is important because it generates support for new programs from which most will not benefit. At this point, trust becomes an explanatory variable, explaining support for the new programs. Once the legislation is passed and government gets involved in these new areas, people then update their political trust based on their perceptions of how well the government is doing with these new programs. Trust is again a dependent variable. Finally, based on their updated levels of political trust, people decide whether they want the government to remain involved in this area or get involved with new areas involving risk or sacrifice. Trust again becomes an explanatory variable. Figure 4.1 provides a schematic of the hypothesized causal sequence.

The Great Society's rise and fall nicely tracks the temporal contours that I have explicated. Johnson could launch his programs because government had generally performed at a high level on issues of peace and prosperity in the preceding two decades, placing political trust at a high level. Indeed, political trust was at its survey-era high when Johnson began to move his agenda. The first arrow in figure 4.1 suggests this part of the story. A

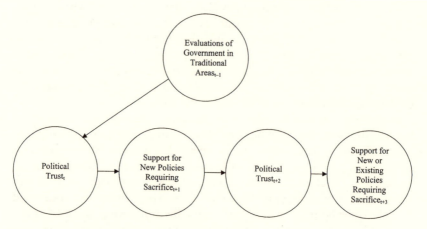

Figure 4.1. The Causal Dynamics of Political Trust in Temporal Sequence.

decade of what many perceived as negative experiences with race-targeted and antipoverty programs, however, caused people to trust the government less. For example, neither whites nor blacks were particularly satisfied with urban race riots, busing students out of neighborhood schools, and racial tensions in newly integrated neighborhoods. These all contributed to the decline in political trust, which is represented in figure 4.1 as the arrow between support for new policies requiring sacrifice at time $t + 1$ and political trust at time $t + 2$. The new, more negative assessment of the government's trustworthiness, in turn, undermined support for federal involvement in the future. Of course, this link is represented as the last arrow in figure 4.1.

To return to the analogy of the babysitter, many Americans today perceive that they have come home to an injured child and are, therefore, reluctant to rehire the babysitter. This does not mean that they do not want the erstwhile sitter to do the things that she has demonstrated proficiency for in the past. Sure, she can still rake the yard. But babysitting or picking up the dry cleaning in your brand new car is probably out.

A Test of the Theory

In the early to middle 1960s, the federal government got involved in a new area that would require at least a perceived sacrifice on the part of many Americans. Specifically, the Johnson administration and the federal courts emphasized the need for federal race-targeted initiatives. In the second and third years of his presidency, Johnson engineered the passage of and signed the Civil Rights Act of 1964 and the Voting Rights Act of 1965. These laws, landmarks in the decades-long civil rights struggle, ensured the civil and voting rights of all Americans regardless of skin color. Later, Johnson signed Fair Housing and Fair Accommodations statutes to further protect the rights of racial minorities. His administration also took the first steps to racially integrate schools consistent with the *Brown v. Board of Education* decision, which eventually got the country involved in the politically charged issue of busing.

In addition, Johnson championed need-based programs that aided African-Americans disproportionately. For example, he created the Department of Housing and Urban Development and guided a new housing act through Congress with $7.8 billion to finance housing programs for low-income families. Spending on Aid to Families with Dependent Children, the federal government's largest welfare program, expanded dramatically during the Johnson years and the several years that followed, with the number of recipients reaching its apex and benefits for recipients nearly quadrupling (see Gilens 1999, 19).

Since policy of this sort was a new domain for the federal government, it allows a test of my theory about the causal dynamics of political trust and policy preferences at the individual level. To recap my expectations, when the government gets involved in a new area and people assess its performance, the theory suggests that trust is a dependent variable as people evaluate performance in the new area. At this point in the causal process, people's satisfaction with racial policy affects their political trust, just as parents' evaluation of a first-time babysitter affects their trust in the sitter. As time passes, this updated trust evaluation becomes an explanatory variable, helping to explain support for efforts in this new policy realm.

The best way to distinguish cause from effect with individual-level data is to use panel studies. Panel studies differ from the usual cross-sectional studies in that the same people are asked the same questions a minimum of two different times. If an attitude like political trust measured at an earlier time has an effect on racial policy preferences measured at a later time, trust is a cause of racial policy preferences. The reverse is true as well. If racial policy preferences measured at an earlier point in time have an effect on political trust at a later time, then racial policy preferences are a cause of political trust.

Panel studies are rare but, fortunately, the NES conducts them every so often, including one in which the same people were asked questions in 1972, 1974, and 1976. The timing is important because the federal role in racial policy was still relatively new to Americans, which means that their racial policy preferences should influence their levels of political trust and not vice versa. I use these data to estimate what statisticians refer to as *cross-lagged models*. Panel respondents' political trust scores and opinions on racial policies at time t are dependent variables, and these same opinions measured two years earlier (which I refer to as *lagged variables*) are explanatory variables.[1] If a lagged variable is a significant predictor of another attitude at a latter point in time, it is a cause of that variable. Conversely, if a lagged variable fails to achieve statistical significance, it is probably not a cause.[2]

The NES provides two suitable racial policy preferences in its 1972–76 panel.[3] Respondents were asked the following two questions:

> 1. Some people feel that the government in Washington should make every effort to improve the social and economic position of blacks. Others feel that the government should not make any special effort to help blacks because they should help themselves. Where would you place yourself on this scale, or haven't you thought much about this?
>
> 2. There is much discussion about the best way to deal with racial problems. Some people think achieving racial integration of schools is so important that it justifies busing children to schools out of their own neighborhoods. Others think letting children go to their neighborhood schools is so important that they oppose busing. Where would you place yourself on this scale, or haven't you thought much about this?

In both cases, people are asked to place themselves on a seven-point scale between the poles specified in the questions. Since I am interested in the effect of political trust in areas that require perceived sacrifice or involve perceived risk, I confine my analysis to white respondents. In the realm of racial policy, it is generally whites who are being asked to sacrifice their tax dollars or their societal advantage to increase racial equality.

The results of these cross-lagged models appear in figure 4.2. In all four models, the lagged effect of the racial policy preferences on political trust is statistically significant, supporting the theory that dissatisfaction with racial policies soon after their implementation helped drive trust downward. When race-targeted policies represented a relatively new area of government involvement, people updated their trust in government based on how they thought the government was doing with these policies.

By the 1990s, race-targeted policies were no longer new. My theory suggests that the causal dynamics should have, therefore, reversed. To return to the babysitter analogy, people already know whether or not they trust the babysitter based on past performance. This new evaluation of the babysitter's trustworthiness will, in turn, affect their decision to hire her again. Hence, trust now should affect support for race-targeted polices rather than the reverse.

To test the theory, I replicate the 1970s cross-lagged models using data from the 1990–92 and the 1992–94 NES panel studies. The NES did not ask exactly the same racial policy questions in the 1990s panels as the 1970s panels, but this actually helps me make my case. Even though peo-

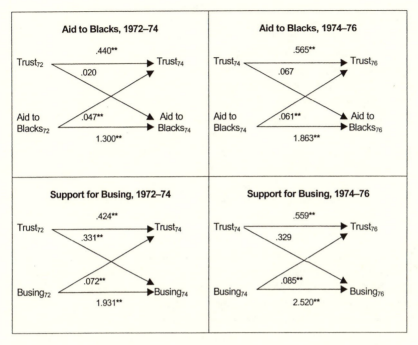

Figure 4.2. Cross-Lagged Models: Political Trust and Racial Policy Preferences, 1972–76, White Respondents, OLS and Ordered Probit Estimates. Source: American National Election Study, 1972–76 Panel Study.

ple's concerns with racial policy in the 1960s and early 1970s might have concerned programs like busing, their perceptions of federal failure in the racial policy domain more broadly construed should undermine support for other racial policy initiatives in the future. The questions asked in the 1990s are the following:

1. Some people say that because of past discrimination, blacks should be given preference in hiring and promotion. Others say that such preference in hiring and promotion of blacks is wrong because it discriminates against whites. What about your opinion—are you for or against preferential hiring and promotion of blacks? Do you favor/oppose preference in hiring and promotion strongly or not strongly?

2. Some people say that because of past discrimination it is sometimes necessary for colleges and universities to reserve openings for black students. Others oppose quotas because they say quotas give blacks advantages they haven't earned. What about your opinion—are you for or against quotas to admit black students? Do you favor/oppose quotas strongly or not strongly?

3. Some people say that the government in Washington should see to it that white and black children go to the same schools. Others claim that this is not the government's business. Have you been interested enough in this question to favor one side over the other? How do you feel? Should the government in Washington see to it that white and black children go to the same schools, or is this not the federal government's business?

4. Some people feel that the government in Washington should make every effort to improve the social and economic position of blacks. Others feel that the government should not make any special effort to help blacks because they should help themselves. Where would you place yourself on this scale, or haven't you thought much about this?

5. If you had a say in making up the federal budget this year, for which of the following programs would you like to see spending increased and for which would you like to see spending decreased? Should federal spending be increased, decreased, or kept about the same on programs that assist blacks?

Again, I confine my analysis to white survey respondents.

The results presented in figure 4.3 suggest that political trust has, as expected, emerged as the causal force. The various lagged racial policy preferences exert a statistically significant effect in explaining political trust only once—school integration in the 1992–94 panel. And in this case, trust also affects support for a federal role in school integration, suggesting these opinions are arrived at together. In the other seven cross-lagged models, lagged racial policy preferences are statistically insignificant in predicting trust. In contrast, lagged trust is statistically significant in four of the eight equations predicting racial policy preferences, and approaches significance in a fifth. As predicted, people's distrust of the government, born in part of their dissatisfaction with racial policy outcomes in the 1960s and 1970s, now undermines their support for federal intervention on race.

Beyond providing empirical support for my theory, these results also hint at the general nature of political trust's significance. American politics tends to experience periods of rapid change, like the New Deal and Great Society eras, when significant policy innovation occurs. In the wake of these periods, political trust is a dependent variable as people evaluate how the government is doing with its new responsibilities. Such periods of rapid change, however, are quite rare. Instead, American politics is noteworthy for its continuity. During periods of stasis, political trust explains whether people want government involved in new tasks or how much people want government involved in certain old ones. Hence, most of the time scholars should be considering what effect political trust has on support for policies rather than what effect support for these policies has on political trust.

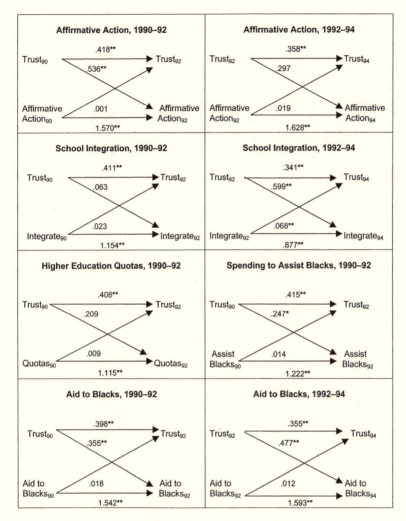

Figure 4.3. Cross-Lagged Models: Political Trust and Racial Policy Preferences, 1990–94, White Respondents, OLS and Ordered Probit Estimates. Source: American National Election Studies, 1972, 1992, 1994.

CONCLUSION

Until recently, scholars have provided precious little evidence that political trust has any consequential effect on American politics. In this chapter, I have discussed reasons for the null findings. By focusing on participatory behaviors, something trust does not affect, scholars, it seems, were looking in the wrong places. Instead, political trust affects preferences for government policy that might require sacrifices, or which many people perceive to be risky.

In addition, I have provided evidence of the causal dynamics of political trust over time. When policies are new, people's evaluation of them affects political trust and not vice versa because people are using their evaluation of government's performance on these new programs to update their evaluations of government. After these programs have become established parts of the political landscape, however, the degree to which people trust government affects how strongly they support these policies.

CHAPTER FIVE

Political Trust and Public Support for Government Spending

IN AN ERA dominated by widespread skepticism about the federal government, it is not surprising that the Republican Party, with its philosophy of limited government, has dominated the White House since political trust began to deteriorate, winning six of the nine elections between 1968 and 2000. Of even greater consequence, during the 12 years that Democrats have occupied the White House, neither Jimmy Carter nor Bill Clinton much embraced the federal government or federal programs either. Carter felt that "the government has almost become like a foreign country, so strange and distant," and, Clinton rhetorically brought the era of big government to a close in his 1995 State of the Union Address.

As Michael Nelson (2001) has noted, the last president to champion a relatively progressive domestic policy agenda was actually a Republican, Richard Nixon. Nixon promised Americans "full prosperity in peacetime," a safe and clean environment, and universal health insurance. His version of welfare reform was to provide modest income guarantees, not to expunge people from the rolls after two years, Bill Clinton's method. Nixon even backed a quotas-based approach to increase the number of African-Americans working on federal construction projects. In addition, he extended the Voting Rights Act of 1965 for five years and, for the first time, made it apply to states outside the South. He signed the first Clean Air Act in 1970 and the Consumer Product Safety Act of 1972, which, respectively, made efforts to reduce auto emissions and provision for the enforcement of safety standards. Nixon was also a big spender. He allocated more than two billion dollars for public-service jobs, the most ambitious such program since the New Deal. And he signed no fewer than three major increases in Social Security benefits, ultimately indexing the program for inflation in 1972 (Mayhew 1991).

Nixon cared about domestic policy in part because it would help him secure reelection (Reeves 2001). Nixon clearly believed that supporting this wide range of progressive programs and policies would win him votes, and his landslide victory in 1972 over George McGovern indicates that he was right. Although his divisive use of race in the 1970 midterm elections shows he was no liberal, Nixon governed relatively far to the left on many issues, at least by contemporary standards.

In this chapter, I explain why Nixon governed as he did. I first show that, while antipoverty measures were relatively popular when Nixon was president, they became increasingly unpopular in the 20 years after his presidency. I next explain why they became less popular, with political trust the main culprit. Trust had this effect because political leaders, especially Ronald Reagan, connected these sacrifice-requiring programs with stories of government incompetence. As evidence, I estimate a series of models using individual-level data that demonstrate the effect of political trust on public preferences for redistributive spending. Consistent with expectations, its effect is particularly strong when people perceive that investment in such programs carries with it substantial risk. In contrast, political trust has no effect on people's preferences for spending on programs that do not require sacrifice or carry risk.

Decreasing Support for Redistribution

The main reason that no president since Nixon has shown his progressive impulse on issues like redistribution is that such programs have become a political liability, with support drying up considerably since the Nixon years. Given the paucity of survey questions asked about welfare programs in the late 1960s and early 1970s, it is hard to measure exactly how steep the drop-off has been, but the limited evidence suggests a stark deterioration.

In May 1972, the Potomac Association asked a national sample the following question.

> Now again, let me read off the names of some other programs the federal government in Washington is helping to finance and ask whether you think the amount of tax money now being spent for each of these purposes should be increased, kept at the present level, reduced, or ended altogether. . . .
>
> Welfare programs to help low income families . . .

33 percent of Americans thought welfare spending should be increased, 42 percent thought it should be kept about the same, and 24 percent thought it should either be reduced or ended altogether (Weaver, Shapiro, and Jacobs 1995). In 1984, the NES started to ask a similar question about food stamps. Even though Americans are generally about 10 percentage points more supportive of government spending when asked about food stamps, specifically, than welfare programs in general, only 21 percent of Americans favored an increase in 1984, 46 percent favored current spending levels, and 33 percent wanted to cut spending. Clearly, a substantial increase in the percentage of Americans who sought cuts in the nation's social safety net occurred between the early 1970s and the mid-1980s.

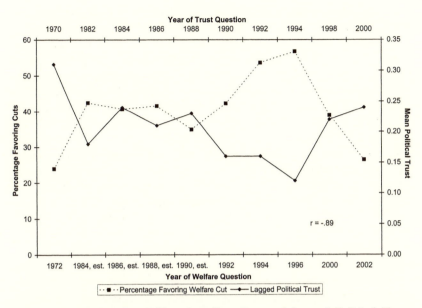

Figure 5.1. Support for Welfare Spending Cuts and Lagged Political Trust, 1970–2002. Sources: American National Election Study, Cumulative File, 1948–2000; 1972 welfare data from Potomac Association.

In 1992, the NES started to ask people about their spending preferences for "welfare programs." Despite a floundering economy that increased the number of people in need, only 17 percent favored a spending increase, while 43 percent favored cuts. Figure 5.1 tracks the public's desire for spending cuts on welfare over time. Between 1972 and 1984, support for spending cuts on welfare programs nearly doubled, from 24 percent to 43 percent, and, by 1996, nearly 60 percent of Americans favored cutting the program.[1] When Nixon was president, strong public demand for spending cuts was largely absent, but, by the 1990s, the opinion environment changed dramatically. As a result, political elites turned against welfare spending.

Martin Gilens (1999) demonstrates that, as welfare took on a black face during this period, support for the program dropped. Political trust is another likely root cause of increasing hostility toward welfare spending. Unlike conservatism, which remained constant during this period, political trust had yet to take its steepest drop until after 1972, as the Watergate scandal came to light, the economy headed toward stagflation, and the war in Vietnam came to an unhappy end. Trust again dropped after 1992, reaching its low point in the time series in 1994. These are both periods when support for welfare spending dropped as well. After that, however, trust began to increase, and the public's hostility toward welfare spending also began to ebb.

Indeed, the correspondence between changes in trust and changes in the public's desire to cut welfare is remarkable. Figure 5.1 plots a lagged measure of political trust along with the percentage of people supporting welfare spending cuts. By a lagged measure of political trust, I mean a measure of it taken at some point in time before the measure of support for welfare cuts was taken. In this case, the period of the lag is two years because the NES studies are taken at two-year intervals. I have hypothesized that changes in political trust cause changes in support for programs like welfare. Using a lag allows me to impose some causal order to the variables, since the measure of the hypothesized cause (political trust) comes before the hypothesized outcome (support for welfare spending cuts). So, for example, I correlate the percentage favoring welfare spending cuts in 1996 with the mean trust score in 1994, since 1994 is the last time the NES asked the trust question prior to the 1996 survey.

Since more trust should provide more support for redistributive programs, the correlation between trust and the desire for welfare spending cuts should be negative. Indeed, it is. In fact, the correlation is a remarkably strong −.90. In other words, increases/decreases in political trust were consistently followed by decreases/increases in support for cuts in welfare programs two years later. Similar to the correspondence between the amount of trust in government and the degree of policy liberalism presented in chapter 3, this is an impressive finding on the aggregate level.

The connection, even though theoretically plausible, might be spurious or just a coincidence. For example, Martin Wattenberg (1984) found that the decline of party identification in the electorate occurred at the same time that political trust began to decline. Hence, there was a strong correlation between the two on the aggregate level. However, using individual-level data, he found that less trustful people were not more likely to see themselves as independent from the parties. The absence of an individual-level connection calls into question the aggregate-level pattern. Therefore, I need to show a link on the individual level as well. Are distrustful people less supportive of welfare spending than trustful ones?

POLITICAL TRUST AND WELFARE POLICY

Through his frequent use of anecdotes, Ronald Reagan did much to cement the connection between feelings about government and feelings about redistributive spending. In his first run for president in 1976, Reagan introduced Americans to a Chicago "welfare queen" who turned out to be a woman named Linda Taylor. According to Reagan, Taylor had bilked the system out of $150,000 worth of welfare, food stamps, and Medicaid benefits by using 80 aliases and numerous Social Security numbers. Taking full advantage of the federal government's incompetence, she even managed to get herself around town in a new white Cadillac. The story resonated well with the public—never mind that Taylor was ultimately convicted of using only four names to obtain eight thousand dollars worth of benefits.[2] The connection that Reagan made between a federal program and the government's inability to administer it well is more important than the details.

Early in his first term as president, Reagan told another story that highlighted the incompetence of government rules and enforcement regarding welfare policies. He informed an audience that "a person yesterday, a young man, went into a grocery store and he had an orange in one hand and a bottle of vodka in the other, and he paid for the orange with food stamps and he took the change and paid for the vodka. That's what's wrong [with the system]." Americans were understandably outraged that government would allow such abuses. It hardly mattered that government rules actually forbade such a transaction. Ultimately Reagan's assistant secretary of agriculture, Mary C. Jarratt, corrected Reagan publicly some weeks later, stating that events depicted in the president's story likely did not occur.[3] The veracity of the story, however, is secondary. When people hear stories like this, particularly from political leaders they are inclined to believe, a connection develops between welfare abuse and the inability of the government to stop it.

Importantly, the nature of Reagan's attacks against the federal government represented a departure from his predecessors on the right. Reagan did not argue that certain programs were beyond what the federal government *ought* to do, as Barry Goldwater did in 1964. Goldwater was not a racist, but his deeply held philosophical belief that power should reside in the states caused him to reject federal involvement in racially integrating the South. He did not think the federal government was incapable, just inappropriate. The key principle for Goldwater was philosophy, not ability. In contrast, Reagan argued that the federal government was *incompetent* to carry out its tasks. Although Reagan, like Goldwater, was a philosophical conservative, he often couched his objection to federal power in performance as opposed to philosophical terms. Hence, while Goldwater's approach engaged only people's philosophical conservatism, Reagan's engaged people's distrust of government in addition to their philosophical conservatism.

Moreover, recent survey evidence suggests his efforts were effective. During the 1990s, various survey organizations have asked Americans, "When the government in Washington decides to solve a problem, how much confidence do you have that the problem actually will be solved: a lot, some, just a little, or none at all?" Never have as many as 10 percent of Americans said "a lot," but never fewer than 10 percent have said "none at all." Moreover, better than half the sample always chooses either the "just a little" or "none at all" option, and, in most cases, it is about 60 percent.[4] Among those who say they have little or no confidence, the ABC News polling unit has asked a follow-up question: "Is it because those problems often are very difficult to solve, or is it because the government often is incompetent?" Responses of government incompetence always far outnumber difficult problems, sometimes by as many as three and a half to one ("Low Grades" 1998). While, unfortunately, such questions were not asked prior to Ronald Reagan's appearance on the national political stage, it seems likely that public assessments of government competence deteriorated as leaders like Reagan gave people reason to believe that government was incompetent.

Whether based in fact or not, Reagan's attacks were successful because they played on two widely held beliefs. First, those receiving public assistance would rather take advantage of the system than make an honest living. Even though recipients spent, on average, a little over a year on public assistance during this period (with a third on welfare for less than a year and more than three-quarters less than five years), a 1994 Harvard University–Kaiser Family Foundation poll found that a plurality thinks recipients are basically lifers.[5] Second, most Americans believe that government is incompetent to fix the problem. Since most Americans pay for but do not benefit from welfare programs, this combination should make political trust, which was low and dropping after the Nixon and Carter presidencies, influential in understanding people's decreasing support for them. In this chapter, I demonstrate that declining political trust undermines Americans' support for spending not only on welfare but on a range of programs that do not benefit them directly, particularly when they do not think much of the group that they perceive receives the lion's share of the benefits.

EXPLAINING SUPPORT FOR GOVERNMENT SPENDING

In chapter 3, I contrasted the distributions of support for government spending between different types of policies and how these distributions have changed over time. Americans want the federal government to be less generous in redistributing income, a desire that increased markedly between the early-1970s and mid-1990s, a period when political trust dropped significantly. In 2000 and again in 2002, however, hostility toward redistributive spending decreased markedly, a turn that coincided with a significant increase in political trust. In short, changes in spending preferences on redistribution over time closely track changes in political trust.

TABLE 5.1

Percentage Supporting Cuts in Federal Spending on Various Programs by Levels of Political Trust

Variable	Below Trust Midpoint	Above Trust Midpoint	Difference
Programs requiring sacrifice			
Welfare programs	58	52	+6
Food stamps	50	37	+13
Foreign aid	63	43	+20
Universal programs			
Protecting the environment	8	6	+2
Social Security	6	6	0

Source: American National Election Study, 1996.

But is political trust actually the cause of this fluctuation? The descriptive evidence is compelling. Using data from the 1996 NES, I divide the sample into people scoring at or above the political trust midpoint and people scoring below it. I then compare their preferences for cutting spending on a number of programs, some requiring at least perceived sacrifice and others not. The results appear in table 5.1. For the programs that require sacrifice of most Americans—welfare, food stamps, and foreign aid—those scoring at or above the political trust midpoint are significantly less inclined to favor spending cuts than those who score below. In fact, on foreign aid, the difference is a whopping 20 percentage points and on food stamps it is more than 10. In contrast, I find no significant difference between trusters and distrusters in their support for spending cuts for programs that distribute benefits widely.

While these results are suggestive, I also need to identify and control for other factors that shape individuals' preferences for government spending on different policies to make certain that the relationship between trust and spending preferences is not spurious. The scholarly literature suggests the importance of many factors.

Although an entire research tradition in political science proposes that people are primarily self-interested, attitudes learned early in life exert a much larger effect on spending preferences than self-interest does. Specifically, ideology (Jacoby 1994; Kluegel 1990; Pan and Kosicki 1996) and partisanship (Converse and Marcus 1979; Elliot, Seldon, and Regens 1997; Page and Jones 1979) profoundly affect spending preferences, with those on the political left more inclined to support spending and those on the right more inclined to oppose it.

How people feel about the group that they perceive will benefit from government spending affects preferences as well. Feelings about racial groups are particularly influential. Zhongdang Pan and Gerald Kosicki (1996) find that feelings about blacks have a significant effect on support for spending on federal programs to assist blacks (see also Kinder and Sanders 1996), and Martin Gilens (1999) finds that antiblack stereotypes are the most significant predictor of support for spending on redistributive programs like welfare and food stamps. Racial stereotypes affect support for need-based, as opposed to race-based, programs because Americans erroneously tend to perceive that blacks are the major beneficiaries of such spending (Gilens 1999).

Self-interest is important, albeit to a much lesser degree than these symbolic attitudes. For example, members of certain racial groups (Pan and Kosicki 1996), urban residents (Elliot, Seldon, and Regens 1997; Howell and Laska 1992), and older Americans (Rhodebeck 1993) are more supportive of spending when they perceive that it will benefit them (see also Sears et al. 1980). In addition, the importance of self-interest is reflected in that those with high incomes support redistributive spending less than those with low incomes, but high-income people are more supportive of programs that might benefit them (Evans 1992; Inniss and Sittig 1996). Others have also shown that gender and education can affect spending preferences (see Elliot, Seldon, and Regens 1997; Pan and Kosicki 1996).

In addition, economic evaluations can influence spending preferences. When people perceive that the economy has improved, they are sometimes more supportive of government spending (Rhodebeck 1993; Wlezien 1995) and assistance to those in need (Skitka and Tetlock 1992). Still, one can imagine that people might believe that the poor should be able to take advantage of good economic times, reducing support for redistributive spending when the economy is good.

In attempting to isolate the effect of political trust, I must account for each of these alternative explanations. Otherwise I run the risk of attributing their effects to political trust. In figure 5.2, an arrow diagram of my model explains people's spending preferences. A person's spending preference on a given program is the dependent variable, and each of the variables with arrows pointing toward it is a potential explanation.

Of course, I have also suggested that political trust's effect is conditioned by perceived sacrifice and risk. When people perceive either or both to be high, trust matters more. For programs like public schools, for example, political trust should be most necessary to the people who are paying costs but not receiving benefits. Specifically, I have in mind those who do not have school-aged children.[6] Trust should theoretically be less necessary for

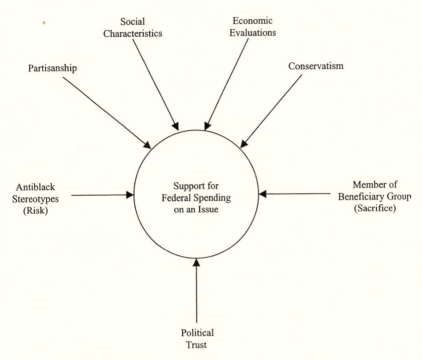

Figure 5.2. Spending Preferences as a Function of Political Trust, Symbolic Attitudes, Risk, and Sacrifice.

people who receive the benefits, in this case those who do have school-aged children. My hypothesis suggests an interaction between political trust and whether the respondent is a potential beneficiary of federal spending.

Similarly, people need to trust the government more when they perceive that their investment in a federal program carries significant risk. If people believe that the recipients of government spending are undeserving and thus likely to waste whatever government money they receive, then they will perceive a substantial risk to spending in these areas. They might be played for suckers. To support continued spending, such people would have to believe that government can monitor recipients effectively. Trust is less necessary for people who think well of the beneficiary group, since effective monitoring by the government would be unimportant.

The need for trust, then, ought to be contingent on how people feel about the perceived beneficiaries of government spending. As Martin Gilens (1999) convincingly demonstrates, public support for programs like welfare and food stamps is largely a function of people's negative stereotypes about African-Americans. When people have negative stereotypes

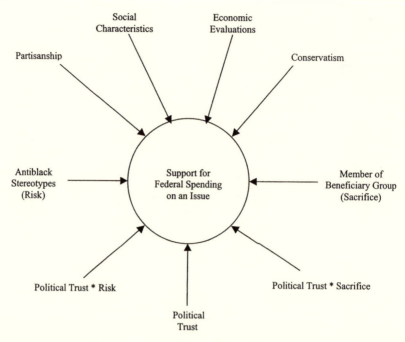

Figure 5.3. Spending Preferences as a Function of Political Trust, Symbolic Attitudes, Risk, and Sacrifice, and Appropriate Interactions.

about blacks' work ethic, the specter of risk is raised, requiring people to trust the government to support spending on programs they perceive benefit blacks. This suggests an interaction between political trust and risk, measured here as the rejection of antiblack stereotypes for implicitly or explicitly racial programs.

The models including these interactions appear as an arrow diagram in figure 5.3.[7] This model is the same as that presented in figure 5.2 except that it includes the interactions between trust and risk and sacrifice, respectively.[8]

DATA

To test my hypotheses, I use data from the 1992, 1994, and 1996 NES. Over these years, the NES asked nearly two dozen questions to tap Americans' spending preferences. Due to space considerations, I cannot present analyses for all these items. Instead, I confine the material that I present to questions that have been asked in multiple studies or those that speak

TABLE 5.2
How Political Trust Should Affect Support for Different Spending Programs

	Risk Low	*Risk Potentially High*
Benefits distributed universally (no sacrifice)	Social Security Crime prevention Protect the environment (Trust should have *no effect*)	
Benefits distributed widely (some people sacrifice)	Financial aid Public schools Child care (Trust should have *some effect*, but only for the few making the sacrifice)	
Benefits distributed narrowly (many people sacrifice)	The poor (Trust should have a *substantial effect*, but only for those making the sacrifice)	Food stamps Welfare Assistance to blacks (Trust should have a *substantial effect* for those making the sacrifice, particularly those who perceive the beneficiary is high risk)
Benefits distributed outside the U.S. (everyone sacrifices)		Soviet Union Foreign aid (Trust should have a *universally strong effect*)

centrally to my hypotheses. So, for instance, I do not present the results from a 1992 model explaining support for spending on science and technology because it was neither asked more than once by the NES nor bears directly on my hypotheses.[9] I do, however, use the question on spending to assist blacks, asked only in 1992, because who the beneficiaries and sacrificers are is very clear. I include the following spending preferences in my analysis: spending on Social Security, crime prevention, environmental protection, financial aid for college students, public schools, child care, the poor, food stamps, welfare, assistance to blacks, foreign aid, and the former Soviet Union.

Table 5.2 breaks the programs into a typology with expectations about how large political trust's effect on support for them should be. The magnitude of trust's effect is a function of perceived sacrifice and perceived risk. As they increase, so, too, should the need for political trust. When programs distribute benefits universally, as with spending on the environment or to prevent crime, no one is asked to make a sacrifice and no real risk is involved. Trust should, therefore, have no effect.[10]

When government spends money on specific groups at the expense of other groups, the importance of political trust rises among those who pay the costs but do not reap the benefits. Hence trust should become more influential as fewer people benefit from the program, especially when people think ill of the beneficiary group. With small, generally ill-thought-of beneficiary groups, the risk of spending on such programs among nonrecipients becomes higher because the perceived probability that money will be wasted increases. Many Americans might view spending on food stamps, welfare, and assistance to blacks in this way, in addition to spending on foreign aid.

As for the measurement of the dependent variables, the NES asks respondents, "If you had a say in making up the federal budget this year, for which of the following programs would you like to see spending increased and for which would you like to see spending decreased. Should federal spending on ___ be increased, decreased, or kept about the same?" I code responses advocating an increase as 1, those advocating a decrease as 0, and those advocating keeping spending the same as .5.

To ease interpretation, I map all variables onto (0, 1) intervals. The estimated effects can be interpreted as the percentage change in the dependent variable caused by moving an independent variable from its minimum to its maximum. For example, if political trust has an effect of .100, it means that, on average, a person with the highest trust score will be 10 percent more supportive of spending on a program than someone with the lowest trust score, other things being equal. As was the case the past two chapters, I estimate each of the models using OLS regression.[11] Since all the variables measured are on the same (0, 1) interval, I can compare the relative size of their effects. For example, if political trust has an effect of .100 and partisanship has an effect of .150, it means that the effect of partisanship is .050 larger than that of political trust.

RESULTS

I first present the results for programs that distribute benefits universally. Political trust should have no effect on support for spending on programs like Social Security, crime prevention, and environmental protection because pretty much everyone does or will benefit. The results presented in table 5.3 confirm my expectations. Never does political trust have a statistically significant effect on support for any of these programs. Since political trust has declined markedly over time and since support for spending in these areas has remained relatively constant, it would have been a problem if trust affected these spending preferences. Fortunately for my theory, it does not.

In contrast, conservatism is most often statistically significant, with those who are more conservative much less supportive of spending than those who are less so. The exception is spending on crime prevention, for which conservatism often carries a positive sign indicating that greater conservatism encourages a preference for more spending. Since conservatives often advocate more spending on defense and law and order, this is predictable. More important, however, conservatism carries a negative sign for spending on Social Security in 1994 and to protect the environment in all years. This is a problem for conservatism as an explanation for changing preferences for government spending over time. If public opinion had, in fact, become more conservative, these results suggest that a significant reduction in support for spending on Social Security and the environment should have occurred as well. Since no such reduction has occurred, it provides further evidence that conservatism is not the key to understanding the dynamics of recent public opinion change.[12]

I move now to programs that require sacrifice of some people but with beneficiary groups that are either large and inclusive or favorably perceived. The programs that I have in mind are spending on financial aid for college students, public schools, child care, and the poor.[13] The results appear in table 5.4. As expected, the effect of political trust is either relatively small or indistinguishable from zero, achieving statistical significance in only 5 of 10 cases. In contrast, conservatism always exerts a large negative effect. Again, this means that, had conservatism increased significantly over time, support for these popular programs would have dropped significantly, which, of course, has not occurred.

Trust and Perceived Sacrifice

That political trust has some effect in certain cases is consequential. If perceived sacrifice makes political trust important, it should have a significant effect on the preferences of people who pay the costs but do not benefit from these programs. The models with the interactions between trust and beneficiary group will tell the story. For financial aid, public schools, and child care, trust should have a significant effect on spending preferences among those who do not have children but not among those who do. For spending on the poor, trust should have a significant effect on the nonpoor's preferences, but not for those who are poor.

TABLE 5.3
Benefits Distributed Universally, No Sacrifice (parameter estimates)

Variable	Social Security			Crime Prevention			Protect Environment		
	1992	1994	1996	1992	1994	1996	1992	1994	1996
Intercept	0.872***	1.017***	0.855***	0.867***	0.942***	0.851***	1.010***	0.943***	0.945***
	(0.026)	(0.034)	(0.038)	(0.026)	(0.034)	(0.039)	(0.027)	(0.040)	(0.040)
Political trust	-0.004	-0.011	0.002	0.025	0.036	0.014	0.011	0.035	0.019
	(0.029)	(0.033)	(0.034)	(0.028)	(0.033)	(0.034)	(0.030)	(0.038)	(0.036)
Partisanship	-0.094***	-0.061**	-0.143***	-0.041*	-0.032	-0.100***	-0.081***	-0.108***	-0.113***
	(0.022)	(0.023)	(0.028)	(0.021)	(0.024)	(0.028)	(0.022)	(0.028)	(0.029)
Conservatism	-0.001	-0.124***	-0.042	0.107***	-0.061*	0.102*	-0.182***	-0.340***	-0.339***
	(0.033)	(0.039)	(0.044)	(0.033)	(0.038)	(0.045)	(0.035)	(0.045)	(0.047)
Economic evaluation	-0.067*	-0.125***	-0.131**	-0.117***	0.004	-0.002	-0.067*	0.031	-0.066
	(0.029)	(0.030)	(0.053)	(0.029)	(0.030)	(0.054)	(0.030)	(0.035)	(0.056)
Age	-0.076**	-0.054*	-0.011	-0.061*	-0.079**	-0.025	-0.108***	-0.180***	-0.076*
	(0.027)	(0.030)	(0.034)	(0.026)	(0.030)	(0.035)	(0.028)	(0.035)	(0.035)
Race	0.095***	0.086***	0.112***	0.042*	0.033	0.005	-0.018	-0.045*	0.068**
	(0.020)	(0.023)	(0.026)	(0.019)	(0.023)	(0.026)	(0.020)	(0.027)	(0.026)
Gender	0.077***	0.065***	0.052***	0.018	0.053***	0.006	-0.002	0.000	-0.043**
	(0.013)	(0.014)	(0.015)	(0.012)	(0.014)	(0.016)	(0.013)	(0.016)	(0.016)
Education	-0.191***	-0.274***	-0.244***	-0.099***	-0.121***	-0.068*	-0.020	-0.035	-0.024
	(0.025)	(0.029)	(0.032)	(0.025)	(0.029)	(0.032)	(0.026)	(0.034)	(0.033)
Income	-0.079**	-0.023	-0.070*	0.030	0.047	-0.002	-0.089**	0.042	-0.039
	(0.027)	(0.031)	(0.031)	(0.027)	(0.030)	(0.031)	(0.028)	(0.035)	(0.032)
Adjusted R^2	.13	.15	.16	.03	.03	.01	.06	.10	.11
N	1,907	1,536	1,369	1,899	1,540	1,373	1,902	1,542	1,370

Source: American National Election Studies, 1992, 1994, 1996
Note: Standard errors are given in parentheses.
*$p < .05$.   **$p < .01$.   ***$p < .001$. One-tailed tests.

TABLE 5.4
Benefits Distributed Widely, Sacrifice Asked of a Small Group of People (parameter estimates)

Variable	Financial Aid		Public Schools			Child Care			Poor	
	1992	1996	1992	1994	1996	1992	1994	1996	1992	1996
Intercept	0.925***	0.922***	0.982***	1.079***	1.074***	0.948***	1.038***	1.059***	1.053***	1.008***
	(0.032)	(0.043)	(0.028)	(0.037)	(0.038)	(0.032)	(0.040)	(0.042)	(0.027)	(0.043)
Political trust	0.055	0.031	0.077**	0.049	0.081**	0.084**	0.072*	0.010	0.058*	-0.008
	(0.035)	(0.038)	(0.031)	(0.035)	(0.034)	(0.035)	(0.037)	(0.037)	(0.031)	(0.037)
Partisanship	-0.104***	-0.163***	-0.110***	-0.096***	-0.170***	-0.154***	-0.112***	-0.173***	-0.185***	-0.214***
	(0.026)	(0.031)	(0.022)	(0.025)	(0.027)	(0.025)	(0.027)	(0.031)	(0.023)	(0.030)
Conservatism	-0.144***	-0.142***	-0.127***	-0.290***	-0.169***	-0.234***	-0.351***	-0.402***	-0.138***	-0.276***
	(0.040)	(0.049)	(0.035)	(0.041)	(0.043)	(0.040)	(0.045)	(0.049)	(0.036)	(0.049)
Economic evaluation	-0.052	0.046	-0.072**	-0.015	0.066	-0.041	0.033	0.022	-0.102***	-0.038
	(0.034)	(0.058)	(0.030)	(0.031)	(0.052)	(0.034)	(0.034)	(0.059)	(0.031)	(0.058)
Age	-0.197***	-0.225***	-0.173***	-0.215***	-0.245***	-0.243***	-0.215***	-0.109**	-0.092***	-0.121***
	(0.035)	(0.038)	(0.031)	(0.034)	(0.034)	(0.035)	(0.037)	(0.038)	(0.028)	(0.038)
Race	0.088***	0.133***	0.058**	0.053*	0.091***	0.076***	0.097***	0.146***	0.071***	0.178***
	(0.023)	(0.028)	(0.020)	(0.025)	(0.025)	(0.023)	(0.027)	(0.028)	(0.021)	(0.028)
Gender	0.012	0.016	0.035*	0.056***	0.049***	0.055***	0.051***	0.018	0.043***	0.011
	(0.015)	(0.017)	(0.013)	(0.015)	(0.015)	(0.015)	(0.016)	(0.017)	(0.013)	(0.017)
Education	0.052*	0.036	-0.048*	-0.075**	-0.095**	0.026	-0.130***	-0.051	-0.145***	-0.171***
	(0.030)	(0.035)	(0.027)	(0.031)	(0.032)	(0.030)	(0.033)	(0.035)	(0.027)	(0.035)
Income	-0.041	0.005	-0.028	0.065*	0.024	-0.129***	0.053	-0.072	-0.093**	-0.023
	(0.033)	(0.034)	(0.029)	(0.032)	(0.030)	(0.033)	(0.035)	(0.034)	(0.031)	(0.039)
Beneficiary group	-0.005	0.020	0.028*	0.016	0.017	0.022	0.015	0.014	0.030	0.003
	(0.016)	(0.022)	(0.014)	(0.016)	(0.020)	(0.016)	(0.017)	(0.020)	(0.021)	(0.024)
Adjusted R^2	.07	.11	.09	.13	.16	.15	.15	.22	.16	.21
N	1,767	1,367	1,777	1,540	1,372	1,766	1,520	1,361	1,889	1,365

Source: American National Election Studies, 1992, 1994, 1996

Note: Standard errors are given in parentheses.

*$p < .05$.   **$p < .01$.   ***$p < .001$. One-tailed tests.

TABLE 5.5
Benefits Distributed Widely, Sacrifice Asked of a Small Group of People, with
Interactions (parameter estimates)

Variable	Financial Aid	Public Schools	Child Care	Poor
Political trust	0.102*	0.075*	0.088*	0.085**
	(0.047)	(0.042)	(0.047)	(0.034)
Beneficiary group	0.027	0.027	0.024	0.063*
	(0.022)	(0.020)	(0.022)	(0.028)
Political trust × beneficiary group	−0.103*	0.004	−0.009	−0.132*
	(0.065)	(0.061)	(0.069)	(0.075)

Source: American National Election Studies, 1992.
Note: Standard errors are given in parentheses.
*$p < .05$.   **$p < .01$.   ***$p < .001$. One-tailed tests.

Despite the fact that my measures of the beneficiary group are necessarily crude, I generally find this pattern of results, presented in table 5.5. In all four cases, the effect of political trust is statistically significant among those making the sacrifice, either those without children under 18 or those who make more than $15,000 a year. Moreover, the sign on the interaction between trust and the beneficiary group is almost always negative, indicating that the effect of political trust is less among beneficiaries of federal spending than among nonbeneficiaries.

I show what the interaction between political trust and being a beneficiary of federal spending looks like in figure 5.4, using support for financial aid as an example. Among those without children under 18, the slope of the line in figure 5.3 is relatively steep, indicating that as political trust increases, support for spending on financial aid increases. In this case, a person who is most trustful is about 10 percent more supportive of financial aid spending than a person who is most distrustful. Since those who do not have young children pay for but do not benefit directly from such spending, support for spending requires trust. Among those who do have children under 18, however, the line is flat. Political trust does not affect support for spending on financial aid among those who might benefit from it.

Trust and Perceived Risk

Thus far, my theory has held up fairly well. When sacrifice is required of some people, trust is important for them. Extending this reasoning, I

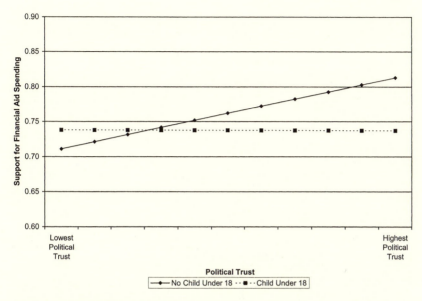

Figure 5.4. The Effect of Political Trust on Support for Spending on Financial Aid, Parents vs. Nonparents.

should find that political trust has larger effects on support for spending on programs that have beneficiaries relatively small in number and not well thought of, because more people will be asked to make sacrifices and more people will likely perceive risk in these investments.

Among the items that the NES asked in the years that I am examining, spending on welfare, food stamps, and assistance to blacks fit this category. The results for these dependent variables appear in table 5.6. Again, they conform to expectations. Over the three years of study, the NES asked these three items on seven total occasions, and political trust significantly explains people's spending preferences in six of the seven cases. In addition, political trust's median effect is .099, nearly twice as large as that for programs with more numerous beneficiaries who are better thought of.

The careful reader might have noted that the estimated effect of conservatism is most often quite a lot larger than that of political trust and, thus, might be tempted to conclude that conservatism is more important than trust in understanding why support for redistributive programs has declined over time. However, the effect of conservatism (or any other variable) over time is calculated by multiplying its estimated effect by the amount that it has changed over the period in question. Mathematically, the equation is

TABLE 5.6
Benefits Distributed Narrowly, Sacrifice Asked of a Large Group of People (parameter estimates)

Variable	Food Stamps			Welfare			Assistance to Blacks
	1992	1994	1996	1992	1994	1996	1992
Intercept	0.475***	0.410***	0.479***	0.489***	0.438***	0.505***	0.441***
	(0.037)	(0.040)	(0.048)	(0.039)	(0.044)	(0.049)	(0.035)
Political trust	0.042	0.099**	0.137***	0.060*	0.153***	0.100**	0.089**
	(0.036)	(0.037)	(0.038)	(0.036)	(0.040)	(0.039)	(0.035)
Rejection of antiblack stereotypes	0.174***	0.133***	0.106**	0.215***	0.179***	0.128**	0.300***
	(0.037)	(0.027)	(0.043)	(0.039)	(0.030)	(0.044)	(0.036)
Partisanship	-0.087***	-0.120***	-0.126***	-0.121***	-0.108**	-0.140***	-0.132***
	(0.026)	(0.026)	(0.030)	(0.028)	(0.026)	(0.031)	(0.026)
Conservatism	-0.202***	-0.115***	-0.254***	-0.266***	-0.220***	-0.275***	-0.211***
	(0.041)	(0.044)	(0.049)	(0.043)	(0.048)	(0.050)	(0.040)
Economic evaluation	-0.028	-0.035	-0.028	-0.050	-0.063*	-0.082	-0.014
	(0.035)	(0.033)	(0.058)	(0.038)	(0.036)	(0.060)	(0.035)
Age	-0.011	-0.022	0.016	-0.048	-0.033	-0.019	0.019
	(0.033)	(0.034)	(0.038)	(0.035)	(0.038)	(0.039)	(0.032)
Race	0.081***	0.100***	0.123***	0.071**	0.038	0.100***	0.285***
	(0.025)	(0.027)	(0.029)	(0.026)	(0.029)	(0.030)	(0.024)
Gender	0.028	0.006	-0.007	0.031	0.024	-0.008	0.015
	(0.015)	(0.016)	(0.017)	(0.016)	(0.017)	(0.018)	(0.015)
Education	0.021	-0.064*	-0.004	-0.051	-0.094**	-0.028	0.098***
	(0.031)	(0.033)	(0.035)	(0.033)	(0.037)	(0.036)	(0.030)
Income	-0.093**	-0.025	-0.016	-0.106**	-0.040	-0.081*	-0.087**
	(0.036)	(0.038)	(0.039)	(0.038)	(0.042)	(0.040)	(0.033)
Beneficiary group	0.115***	0.137***	0.122***	0.109***	0.108***	0.101***	See above (race)
	(0.024)	(0.023)	(0.025)	(0.026)	(0.026)	(0.026)	
Adjusted $R2$	.11	.15	.16	.14	.15	.16	.22
N	1,810	1,512	1,320	1,808	1,516	1,322	1,795

Source: American National Election Studies, 1992, 1994, 1996.
Note: Standard errors are given in parentheses.
*p < .05.   **p < .01.   ***p < .001. One-tailed tests.

TABLE 5.7
Benefits Distributed Narrowly, Sacrifice Asked of a Large Group of People, with
Interactions (parameter estimates)

Variable	Food Stamps	Welfare	Assist Blacks
Political trust	0.213**	0.181*	0.302***
	(0.088)	(0.094)	(0.087)
Rejection of antiblack stereotypes	0.250***	0.269***	0.394***
	(0.051)	(0.055)	(0.051)
Political trust × rejection of antiblack stereotypes	−0.332**	−0.236	−0.413**
	(0.157)	(0.167)	(0.154)

Source: American National Election Studies, 1992.
Note: Standard errors are given in parentheses.
*p < .05.   **p < .01.   ***p < .001. One-tailed tests.

Conservatism's contribution to change over time =
    effect of conservatism × amount
conservatism has changed over time. (1)

The data presented in chapter 3 clearly show that conservatism has remained constant over time, which means that the last part of the equation,
amount conservatism has changed over time, is equal to zero. Since anything multiplied by zero equals zero, conservatism's contribution to
change over time is zero.

Since, in contrast, political trust has changed over time and since it
has a consistently significant effect on these spending preferences, it has
contributed to changes in these preferences over time. In short, I have
now shown a connection on both the aggregate and individual levels. In
the aggregate, changes in trust lead to changes in spending preferences
on redistribution. And, importantly, trustful individuals are more supportive of this type of spending than distrustful individuals.

In table 5.7, I present evidence that, as expected, perceived risk conditions the effect of political trust on the racialized redistributive policies.
Gilens (1999) demonstrates that people desire less spending on these programs largely because they perceive the beneficiary group to be black and
they perceive blacks to be lazy. Hence I include interactions between political trust and the degree to which people believe that African-Americans are
lazy or hardworking, my measure of risk. Among those carrying negative
stereotypes about blacks' industriousness, spending presumably entails risk.
Unless the proper authorities can intervene capably, these people will tend
to believe that government spending on an undeserving group will be
wasted. Hence trust in government should be very necessary to people who

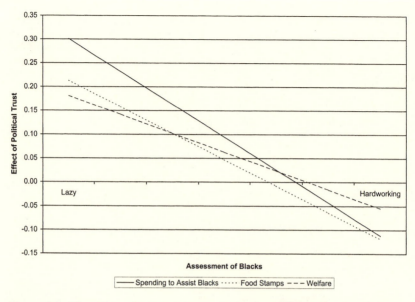

Figure 5.5. The Effect of Political Trust on Support for Racialized Spending Programs, Conditional on Racial Attitudes.

think blacks, the *perceived* beneficiary group, are lazy. In contrast, if respondents think blacks are hardworking, trust should be less necessary.

I find exactly this pattern of results. For each of the racialized spending items included in the 1992 study, the estimated effect for political trust itself is positive and statistically significant. This means that, when the rejection of antiblack stereotypes variable is near 0 (when people think blacks are lazy), political trust's effect is very large. As an example, consider preferences for federal spending to assist blacks. Political trust's effect of .302 means that, among those who rate blacks as most lazy (Rejection of Antiblack Stereotypes = 0), a person who scores the maximum on the political trust scale will be about 30 percent more supportive of government spending on blacks than someone who scores at the minimum on the trust scale, other things being equal.

The negative sign on the interaction is important as well. That it is always negative and almost always at least approaches statistical significance means that, as people take an increasingly positive view of blacks' industriousness, the effect of political trust diminishes. I show these effects graphically in figure 5.5. As people reject the stereotype that blacks are lazy, the effect of political trust becomes insignificant in understanding support for

TABLE 5.8
Benefits Distributed Narrowly, Sacrifice Asked of a Large Group of People, with Interactions, by Beneficiary Group (parameter estimates)

Variables	Food Stamps		Welfare		Assistance to Blacks	
	Nonpoor	Poor	Nonpoor	Poor	Nonblack	Black
Political trust	0.235**	0.114	0.200*	0.075	0.316***	0.045
	(0.098)	(0.210)	(0.103)	(0.235)	(0.097)	(0.224)
Rejection of antiblack stereotypes	0.264***	0.146	0.286***	0.134	0.415***	0.242**
	(0.056)	(0.131)	(0.059)	(0.146)	(0.059)	(0.098)
Political trust × rejection of antiblack stereotypes	−0.375*	−0.171	−0.273	−0.100	−0.426**	−0.130
	(0.177)	(0.352)	(0.187)	(0.392)	(0.180)	(0.319)
N	1,538	268	1,539	269	1,567	228

Source: American National Election Studies, 1992.
Note: Standard errors are given in parentheses.
*$p < .05$. **$p < .01$. ***$p < .001$. One-tailed tests.

spending on food stamps, welfare, and assistance to blacks. In other words, those who think highly of blacks do not need to trust the government to support spending on this group, just as I hypothesized.

Finally, if *both* perceived sacrifice and perceived risk are important, trust's effect should be larger and trust's interaction with a measure of perceived risk should be stronger among those making the sacrifice for the programs than among those benefiting from them. This proposition can be tested by splitting the sample into two groups: those who are poor and those who are not, in the case of spending on food stamps and welfare, and into those who are black and those who are not black for spending to assist blacks. The estimated effects for both political trust and its interaction with the rejection of antiblack stereotypes should be larger among the nonpoor and nonblack, respectively, because they are paying the costs and not receiving the benefits.

The results of this analysis appear in table 5.8 and show the expected pattern. For both food stamps and welfare, the effect of political trust among the nonpoor is more than twice as large as among the poor. And for spending to assist blacks, the effect of trust among nonblacks is seven times larger than among blacks. In addition, the effect of the interaction is quite a lot larger among those who are paying the perceived costs than those receiving the benefits. That is, antiblack stereotypes are much more important in conditioning the effect of political trust among nonbeneficiaries than among

Figure 5.6. The Effect of Political Trust on Support for Spending to Assist Blacks, Conditional on Sacrifice and Risk.

beneficiaries. This squares nicely with my theory because perceived risk should be much stronger for the sacrificers than the beneficiaries.

Figure 5.6 illustrates what these effects look like for one of the items, spending to assist blacks.[14] The left side of the figures depicts people who hold antiblack stereotypes. Here the line tracking the effect of trust for nonblacks is well above the line tracking the effect of trust for blacks. This means that the effect of trust is much larger for nonblack people. In addition, the slope of the line for nonblacks is steeper than for blacks, demonstrating that the importance of perceived risk is larger for those making the sacrifice than for those receiving the benefit. In short, the effect of trust is largest among those who would not benefit from government spending and who both have the most stereotypically negative view of blacks.

Finally, I have not made much of support for federal spending outside the United States, but it could provide further support for my theory. Since spending abroad does not directly benefit many Americans at home, it requires at least perceived sacrifice of just about everybody. Moreover, most Americans likely view this type of spending as risky, although measuring risk in this case is not possible. With the money going outside the nation's borders, Americans have a hard time evaluating how it is being spent. This should make political trust particularly influential.

TABLE 5.9
Benefits Distributed outside the U.S., Sacrifice Is Universal (parameter estimates)

Variable	Soviet Union 1992	Foreign Aid 1994	Foreign Aid 1996
Intercept	0.292***	0.124***	0.203***
	(0.034)	(0.038)	(0.039)
Political trust	0.120***	0.225***	0.285***
	(0.038)	(0.037)	(0.035)
Partisanship	0.052*	−0.023	0.041
	(0.028)	(0.027)	(0.028)
Conservatism	−0.107**	−0.117***	−0.131**
	(0.044)	(0.044)	(0.045)
Economic evaluation	0.168***	0.123***	0.073
	(0.038)	(0.034)	(0.055)
Age	0.057	0.087**	0.039
	(0.035)	(0.034)	(0.035)
Race	−0.060**	0.008	0.106***
	(0.026)	(0.026)	(0.026)
Gender	−0.063***	−0.056***	0.014
	(0.017)	(0.016)	(0.016)
Education	0.156***	0.173***	0.033
	(0.033)	(0.033)	(0.033)
Income	−0.016	0.057*	−0.074*
	(0.036)	(0.034)	(0.032)
Adjusted R^2	.05	.09	.07
N	1,872	1,532	1,362

Source: American National Election Studies, 1992, 1994, 1996.
Note: Standard errors are given in parentheses.
*$p < .05$.   **$p < .01$.   ***$p < .001$. One-tailed tests.

Indeed, the results in table 5.9 confirm my hypotheses. Among the three foreign spending items available in the NES (spending on the Soviet Union in 1992 and spending on foreign aid in 1994 and 1996), the median effect of political trust is .225, which is more than twice the effect that it had on even the racialized programs. Indeed, these results suggest that no variable has a consistently larger effect on such spending preferences than does political trust. Although conservatives have consistently criticized U.S. efforts at foreign aid, the effect of conservatism is about half that of political trust in the two foreign aid equations. In short, these results further demonstrate the importance of political trust when sacrifice is necessary and perceived risk is high. In practical terms, when political trust is relatively low, Americans are significantly less generous to other nations, in addition to poor people at home, than when they trust their government more.

It is also significant to find an individual-level link between trust and spending preferences on foreign aid spending. In chapter 3, I showed that public hostility toward foreign aid spending was very high in 1994 and 1996, with more than 55 percent of Americans advocating spending cuts both years. In 2000 and 2002, with political trust on the increase, the percentage of Americans advocating spending cuts fell below 45 percent. It seems clear that the recent increase in political trust has also contributed to less hostility toward foreign aid spending, a particularly important finding, given the government's need to spend more abroad in its efforts to combat terrorism.

Conclusion

Public support for spending to help those in need has deteriorated significantly since the Johnson and Nixon eras, while support for spending on programs that benefit most or all Americans has remained high. My results suggest that declining political trust explains this gap. While political trust has little or no effect on support for programs that have remained popular over time, it has a substantial effect on programs whose popularity has varied, specifically those requiring most Americans to make sacrifices for others. This tendency is even stronger when people do not think highly of blacks, the group that most whites think receives the lion's share of redistributive spending. These results provide individual-level evidence for the aggregate-level trends shown previously. Taken together, trust emerges as an attractive explanation for why it *seems* that the political center has shifted to the right since the 1960s. Conservatism has not increased, but declining trust makes it seem as though it has.

The implications of these findings are also problematic for those at the bottom of the socioeconomic ladder. A strong economy generally increases trust in government, and higher levels of political trust increase public support for redistribution. Politicians, in turn, tend to heed the public's wishes. However, a good economy makes redistribution somewhat less important. Although it does not cause all boats to rise, more boats rise than when the economy is bad. Hence when poor people are in greatest need, political trust is generally low, which undermines public support for spending that would benefit them.

CHAPTER SIX

Political Trust and the Racial Policy Preferences of Whites

SINCE THE CIVIL rights era ended along with the 1960s, many whites believe that the race problem in the United States has been solved. They argue that, since laws were passed to ensure voting rights and ban active discrimination, Americans no longer discriminate. With all the talk of racial profiling by police, large and persistent wage gaps between white and black workers, and the significant underrepresentation of blacks in elective office, the record seems to suggest otherwise.

In 1991, ABC's *PrimeTime Live* produced one of the few memorable moments from a network news division over the last 20 years, fundamentally challenging the view that white America is now colorblind. Host Diane Sawyer took the show to St. Louis, Missouri. With hidden cameras and microphones, the show followed two trained fair housing testers through a number of different tasks that people face in their everyday lives. Among other things, the men each tried to rent an apartment, apply for a job, and secure financing for a car. To obtain these services, they always went to exactly the same places and dealt with the same people when possible. Both in their thirties with similar socioeconomic backgrounds, the two men were identical in every way except their race: one was white, the other black.

The hidden cameras showed that people consistently treated the two men differently no matter whom they encountered first. The owner of a dry cleaners provided a job application to the white man, but told the black man no job was available. A landlord with an apartment to rent showed it to the white man, but told the black man that it had already been rented. A used car salesman offered a lower price and a more attractive financing deal to the white man than the black man. Even when caught on film, these people denied that race had played a role in guiding their behavior. The moral of the story is that, even with laws designed to prevent racial discrimination, it still occurs routinely in American life.

Situations such as these are difficult to police, but the report suggests the need for continued, if not increased, intervention. People are not policing themselves, likely because most do not see their response to race as a problem. Indeed, if each of the people that the *PrimeTime* fair housing testers came in contact with were asked whether or not they supported racial equality, they would likely reply that they did. Such attitudes are important. If people do not perceive that a problem exists, they will do little to solve it.

Historically speaking, only the federal government has shown much willingness or ability to protect racial minorities from discrimination. Although its efforts have been imperfect, even taking steps back in some areas in the 1990s, those efforts are certainly more effective than doing nothing. For example, only 2 percent of black students in the South attended majority white schools in 1964, but, only three years after the passage of the Civil Rights Act of 1964, which provided federal enforcement power for the Supreme Court's 1954 *Brown v. Board of Education* decision, 13 percent did. This percentage would grow as high as 43 percent by 1988 (Frankenberg, Lee, and Orfield 2003, 47). Such change is inconceivable absent federal intervention. Since many whites are reluctant integrationists, federal involvement is, perhaps, even more important.

For government to be successful in protecting minority interests, however, it must have the public's trust. In this chapter, I show that only then will whites support government intervention in an area that is not necessarily consistent with their perceived self-interest. Specifically, whites must trust that, when the government gets involved, it will not provide an unfair advantage to racial minorities. Since government has lost much of this trust since the 1960s, support for race-targeted policies has either declined or held steady. Given that support for the principle of racial equality has skyrocketed over the same period, support for federal efforts to ensure fair treatment should have increased. Instead, a decline in political trust has offset any potential gains.

THE PRINCIPLE-IMPLEMENTATION GAP

Public opinion, in the aggregate, tends to move glacially if at all (Page and Shapiro 1992). Neither party identification nor ideology has changed much since the 1960s. In the study of American public opinion, stability is the rule. However, two political attitudes stand out as exceptions: political trust and support for *the principle* of racial equality. I have made much of political trust's rapid decline since the 1960s, but increases in support for racial equality this century have been even more dramatic. Although political scientists rightly question how much professed support results from people's desire to be socially appropriate, there can be little doubt that racial tolerance in principle has increased greatly. Everyone cannot be lying to survey interviewers.[1]

Consider the following survey marginals. When the National Opinion Research Center first asked Americans in 1942 whether or not they supported black and white children attending the same school, only 42 percent expressed support. By the mid-1990s, more than 95 percent did. In 1942, only 46 percent supported desegregated public transportation. By the early 1970s, that figure had increased to 88 percent. Although this question has not been asked for decades, resistance to integrated transportation is surely almost nonexistent today. An even more significant change has occurred in support for equal access to jobs. In 1944, 55 percent of whites endorsed the idea that whites ought to get jobs first. By 1972, only 3 percent did (Schuman et al. 1997).

Changes in public opinion of this magnitude almost always have at their root a change in elite behavior. In the case of race, both scientists and politicians played a role. Starting in the 1920s and 1930s, the scientific community started to dismiss arguments that suggested innate biological differences between the races, findings that ultimately filtered into the public domain. Racial attitudes improved as biological racism ebbed, making people much less likely to traffic in racial stereotypes (Kinder and Sanders 1996; but see Herrnstein and Murray 1994 to suggest biological racism still lives). In addition, the Democratic Party changed course on the race issue in the early 1960s, sending a message to its identifiers that they should support racial equality (Carmines and Stimson 1989). Indeed, the most rapid change in the marginals described above took place in the early to mid-1960s. Generational replacement has since solidified these gains in racial tolerance (Firebaugh and Davis 1988).

While public support for racial equality in principle has increased markedly, support for the programs designed to bring it about has lagged well behind, creating what political scientists and sociologists refer to as the "principle implementation" gap (e.g., Bobo 1988; Bobo and Kluegel 1993; Kinder and Sears 1981; Sniderman and Piazza 1993). Many of the same people who say they support equality between blacks and whites do not support government-sponsored initiatives designed to make equality a reality. For example, while 95 percent of Americans supported integrated public schools in 2000, only 34 percent thought the federal government should work to ensure this outcome.[2] Similarly, while almost everyone now thinks that blacks and whites should compete for the same jobs, only 35 percent of Americans in 2000 thought that the federal government ought to ensure that the competition is fair.[3] Such differences represent the principle-implementation gap.

The gap exists in all areas, including income. Almost no one would support, in principle, persistent differences in the earning power between racial groups. However, since the Current Population Survey has been keeping data for the Census Bureau, racial differences have been stark. In 1970, for instance, African-Americans made about 58 cents on the dollar compared with whites. In 2000, African-Americans still only made 65 percent of what whites did. While the narrowing is encouraging, the gap is still six-sevenths of the way from being closed even after thirty years.

One program that would help narrow the income gap is affirmative action, especially in higher education. William G. Bowen and Derek Bok (1998) convincingly demonstrate that graduating from college, particularly an elite college, does much to narrow the wage gap between the races. Since African-Americans, on average, score lower than whites on college entrance exams, however, they tend to be underrepresented at both. Providing African-Americans with a preference in college admissions, then, can do much to reduce income inequality.

Despite the demonstrated success of using racial preferences, an overwhelming percentage of white Americans oppose such policies.[4] According to data from the 1992 NES, for example, 72 percent opposed the use of affirmative action in higher education, while only 28 percent supported it. The use of preferences in hiring decisions is even less popular, with more than 80 percent of white Americans typically expressing opposition.[5] In fact, when presented with evidence that a company has a history of discriminating against black job applicants, fewer than 50 percent of whites in the 2002 NES thought that a company should be required to provide blacks any preference in hiring.[6]

Many whites oppose affirmative action because they perceive that it is a form of reverse discrimination that substantially and unfairly disadvantages them. Bowen and Bok (1998), however, demonstrate that very few whites are actually harmed, at least in higher education. During the period of their study, they found that eliminating racial preferences would have increased the likelihood of admission for white undergraduate applicants from 25 percent to 26.5 percent, a miniscule difference. Clearly, perceptions are much more influential than reality in forming whites' opinions about affirmative action.

The Widening of the Principle-Implementation Gap

The gap between principle and implementation has grown even wider over the last 40 years, mostly because public support for federal race-targeted policies (the implementation part) has either deteriorated or remained constant, while support for the principle of racial equality has increased. This is surprising given that those who believe in racial equality in principle are, on average, significantly more supportive of race-targeted policies than those who do not (Kinder and Sanders 1996). This suggests that the enormous increases in support for racial equality in principle, not to mention the marked improvement in whites' racial attitudes, should have substantially increased support for race-targeted policies.

The distributions of support for the federal government playing a role to ensure school integration and fair treatment in jobs demonstrate otherwise. The NES has not asked these questions every year but has done so periodically since the mid-1960s. The starting and ending points reflect a noteworthy *deterioration* in public support for a federal role in these areas. In 1964, 41 percent favored federal involvement to ensure school integration and 39 percent favored federal involvement to ensure fair treatment in jobs. By 2000, these percentages had declined to 34 and 35 percent respectively. In fact, in the early to mid-1990s, only 28 percent wanted the federal government to play a role in school integration and 26 percent in ensuring fair treatment in jobs.

Some might be tempted to conclude that part of the reason for the decline in public support for a federal role is that these problems are not as big as they once were, and, as a result, Americans may believe that government should focus its attention elsewhere. This interpretation is incorrect on two levels. First, school segregation is a *bigger* problem at the beginning of the twenty-first century than it was 10 years before. According to Erica Frankenberg, Chungmei Lee, and Gary Orfield (2003), the United States has experienced a significant resegregation since the early 1990s. While desegregation for African-Americans in public schools increased continuously from the 1950s through the 1980s, particularly after the passage of the Civil Rights Act of 1964, the trend reversed itself after 1988. In fact, the percentage of white students encountered by the average black student was lower in 2000 than it was in 1970, the year before Court-ordered busing to achieve integration was first employed (Frankenberg, Lee, and Orfield 2003, 30). The backsliding is particularly pronounced in the South. For example, the average black student in Alabama had 38 percent whites in his or her school in 1980, up from zero percent before 1960. By 2000, however, this percentage had dropped to 30 percent (Frankenberg, Lee, and Orfield 2003, 10). Such trends toward segregation are evident in a range of different data, including the percentage of schools with more than 50 or 90 percent black students or the percentage of black students in majority white schools.

Scholarly research suggests that this trend toward resegregation is problematic for racial minorities. For example, according to a 1997 Department of Education report titled "The Social Context of Education," more segregation tends to produce schools with higher concentrations of poverty, which, in turn, undermines student achievement on many levels.[7] In fact, the achievement gap between the races decreased dramatically during the 1970s and 1980s, but it began to increase again after resegregation took hold in the 1990s (Grissmer, Flanagan, and Williamson 1998).

Second, although most Americans probably have no idea that segregation in public schools has recently increased, they still report being more

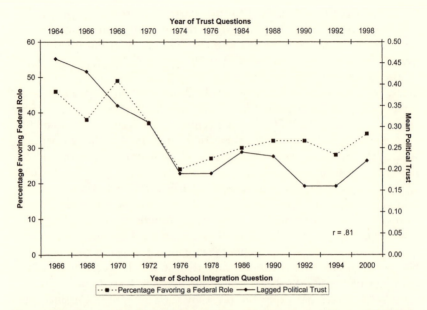

Figure 6.1. Support for a Federal Role in School Integration and Lagged Political Trust, 1964–2000. Source: American National Election Study, Cumulative File, 1948–2000.

concerned about the issue than in the recent past. A 1999 Gallup Poll found that 59 percent of Americans thought more needed to be done to integrate schools, up from 37 percent in 1988.[8] Importantly, however, the public has barely become more supportive of the federal government playing a role in such efforts over this same period. Although in 1988 the NES did not ask its question on the federal role in school integration, it did in 1986 and 1990, with 30 and 32 percent favoring a federal role. By 2000, the percent in favor had only increased to 34 percent. Whereas the percentage of Americans who thought more needed to be done on school integration increased by a whopping 22 points between the late 1980s and the 1990s, the percentage who thought the federal government ought to play a role in this process increased by only a couple points.

Although it is not clear who the public thinks ought to oversee school integration, figure 6.1 provides some insight into why it has not embraced the federal government for this role. Americans do not trust government enough to support its involvement. The figure shows that the now familiar lagged measure of political trust closely tracks changes in public support for a federal role in school integration over time. Support for a federal role was high in 1966, at least relative to the rest of the time series, and, of course, political trust was also at its maximum in the 1964 NES study. The public's desire for a federal role in school integration, however, plummeted after 1970, reaching its minimum for the time series in 1976 at 24 percent. Part of the reason for the decline can be attributed to political events. Most importantly, the NAACP began to file and win lawsuits to ban school segregation in nonsouthern cities. As the specter of court-ordered busing rose in the non-South, support for federal efforts among nonsoutherners plummeted.[9]

In addition, political trust was also dropping rapidly during this period because of Watergate, deepening economic problems, and the nation's ultimate failure in Vietnam. As trust recovered to some degree during the 1980s, so, too, did support for a federal role in school integration, with 32 percent favoring it by the end of the decade. The 1990s witnessed two turns. As political trust was reaching toward its time series minimum in the early 1990s, support for a federal role dropped along with it. But with trust on the upswing at the end of the 1990s, public support for government intervention in school integration reached 34 percent, its highest level since 1972. Indeed, the correlation between lagged political trust and the percentage of Americans favoring federal involvement is a remarkable .81.[10] I should add that this relationship is no anomaly. The correlation between lagged political trust and the percentage of Americans favoring federal involvement in ensuring fair treatment in jobs is also a very robust .72.[11]

The relationship between racial equality in principle and programs designed to ensure it is reminiscent of the relationship between education and voter turnout. Any study of voter turnout shows that those who are better educated are much more likely to vote. Since education rates have skyrocketed over the last 40 years, voter turnout should have increased substantially since the 1960s, other things being equal. Instead, turnout has declined. Other factors that also affect turnout must have changed in such a way to offset the positive effect of increasing education. Steven Rosenstone and Mark Hansen (1993) demonstrate elegantly that the parties' declining ability to mobilize voters has done exactly that. Taking a similar tack, Robert Putnam (2000) shows that the rapid decrease in Americans' social involvement with one another is the major culprit.

Similarly, dramatic increases in support for the principle of racial equality should have increased support for race-targeted policies since the 1960s. However, declining political trust, like the parties' declining ability to mobilize voters and Americans' declining social capital, has offset those gains. In short, one main reason that whites today do not support race-targeted policies is that they do not trust the federal government to implement them well or fairly. Given that, historically, the federal government has done the most to ensure fair outcomes for racial minorities, declining political trust is of fundamental import.

POLITICAL TRUST AND RACE-TARGETED POLICIES

Similar to last chapter, I have presented aggregate-level evidence of a link between political trust and a variable of normative import, in this case racial policy preferences. As political trust in the electorate decreases/increases, the percentage of Americans who advocate a federal role in dealing with racial policies decreases/increases. To make the most compelling case available, I must again show that individuals who trust government are more supportive of these racial policies than those who do not.

There is ample reason to think that political trust might play this role among white Americans. Just as parents who distrust their teenagers may wish to restrict their activities, those who distrust government may wish to restrict its activities. Both parents and citizens differentiate among activities, however, imposing the greatest restrictions on those that are unsupervised and costly. Political trust, therefore, should affect support for policies that concentrate benefits on a political minority while imposing perceived or real costs on a majority. The majority does not realize a direct benefit from the policy and therefore has both less personal incentive to support it and little or no personal experience with which to evaluate it. Hence they will need to trust the agent that implements such programs, in this case the federal government.

Many whites plausibly view racial policies this way. With affirmative action, for example, whites forfeit certain advantages in the name of future racial progress. If whites possess a fair amount of political trust, they may be more inclined to accept that these programs work on their behalf even if it is not readily apparent that they do. If, however, they are distrustful, they have little reason to believe that such programs take their needs into account while addressing the problems of others.

The magnitude of trust's effect should depend upon the degree to which people perceive a policy encroaches on their self-interest. In general, trust will affect whites' racial policy preferences because these programs require them to make sacrifices for less tangible goals. Following the same reasoning, political trust's influence should vary according to the specific policy. Arguing that there is no one race issue, Paul Sniderman and Thomas Piazza (1993) group policies into three broad categories: the race-conscious, social welfare, and equal treatment agendas. Though I expect political trust to be significant in predicting white preferences across all three agendas, it should be most influential for the race-conscious agenda, when policies require the most highly tangible and publicized sacrifices.

Specifically, I consider affirmative action in hiring and college admissions part of the race-conscious agenda. If the government proposes whites' children be denied college admission in favor of those perceived to be objectively less qualified applicants, the cost is obvious, the burden substantial, and the benefit, future racial progress, less clear. Although the federal government itself is not the root of all affirmative action programs, it was originally a federal initiative and disputes regarding it are often settled in federal jurisdictions. Moreover, the federal government could, if it chose, end such programs. As a result, many whites surely perceive that the federal government is the engine for affirmative action programs.[12]

Trust should still have a sizable, albeit somewhat smaller effect, on general racial spending issues, or, collectively, the social welfare agenda. Since Americans' tax dollars fund federal government initiatives and since funding for racial policy initiatives will not benefit whites directly, the degree to which whites trust the government should affect how much they want to spend. The cost, however, is somewhat more diffuse and less visible than for race-conscious policies. Whites, for instance, do not earmark a certain percentage of their taxes to programs designed to benefit blacks.

Trust should have a smaller effect on equal treatment policies, such as equal treatment in hiring and school integration, since, by supporting these policies, whites must only sacrifice their societal advantage. Indeed, as the category's name suggests, programs of this sort guarantee that blacks receive only the same rights as other citizens. To the degree that trust affects support for policies in the equal treatment domain, however, it is particularly important. Because of racial prejudices, government intervention has often been necessary to ensure equal treatment. For instance, many southern whites were not willing to guarantee voting rights or integrate schools, transportation, or accommodations without government involvement. Given that the federal government has most often been an important player in ensuring civil rights, it would be particularly troubling to find that Americans have lost such faith in their government that it undermines their support for ensuring even basic rights for all citizens. Of course, the aggregate-level evidence has already suggested this troubling likelihood.

Explaining Racial Policy Preferences

Again, I must account for other potential causes of support for racial policies to avoid attributing the effects of other variables to political trust. The scholarly literature is rich with competing explanations.

Some scholars emphasize psychological explanations, centering, not surprisingly, on racial prejudice. While overt racism still lingers and manifests itself in opposition to race-targeted policies, a new type of symbolic racism or "racial resentment" has emerged (e.g., Kinder and Sanders 1996). Invidiously, such racism cloaks dislike of blacks behind commitment to American values of hard work and self-reliance. Whites who rate blacks' industriousness unfavorably believe that blacks, as a group, violate American standards of hard work. They should, therefore, be less likely to support racial policies.

In contrast, other scholars argue that opposition to racial policies may reflect a principled objection to the policies, rather than their beneficiaries (Sniderman and Piazza 1993). This approach suggests that scholars should study what people think the government should do in general instead of what the government should do for specific racial groups (Sniderman and Carmines 1997). Such principled objections ought to manifest themselves in attitudes such as partisanship and conservatism. Since ordinary Americans tend to mirror the opinions of partisan and ideological elites with whom they identify (Zaller 1992), the current partisan cleavage suggests that Democrats and liberals will be more inclined to support racial policies, while Republicans and conservatives will be more likely to oppose them.

Still others suggest that opposition may be rooted in threat, either to one's material or personal interests or to the interests of his or her group. Whites oppose policies, such as busing, or support racist candidates, such as George Wallace or David Duke, when they feel that they or their group are economically or politically threatened by black advances (Bobo 1983, 1988; Key 1949), although the locus of this threat, whether realistic or psychological, is still at issue (Oliver and Mendelberg 2000; Voss 1996). While it is difficult to tap self-interest in this area, previous research uses income as a proxy, finding that higher-income individuals are somewhat less supportive of explicitly and implicitly racial policies (Gilens 1995). In addition, economic evaluations might also be important expressions of self-interest. During downturns, people may be less generous in assisting disadvantaged groups (Wilson 1987), so more negative perceptions should predict less support for racial policies.

The emphasis a person places on equality should affect his or her support for policies designed to ensure it (Kinder and Sanders 1996). In addition, previous research suggests that education affects racial policy preferences, heightening support for some items (Sniderman, Brody, and Tetlock 1991) and diminishing it for others (Tuch and Hughes 1996). Given the legacy of segregation, those living in the South might continue to resist race-targeted policies (Kuklinski et al. 1997). Finally, white respondents often express more support for racial policies when blacks interview them (Kinder and Sanders 1996). I present the proposed model graphically in figure 6.2.

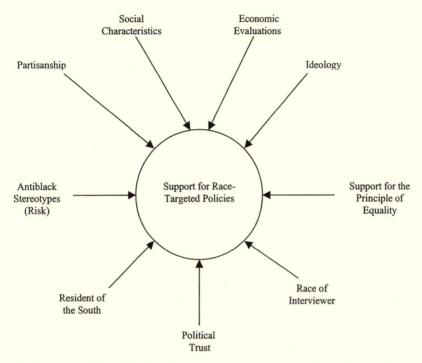

Figure 6.2. Racial Policy Preferences as a Function of Political Trust, Other Symbolic Attitudes, and Social Characteristics.

DATA

I employ the 1990, 1992, and 1994 NES to assess the effect of political trust on racial policy preference among whites, and I use OLS regression to estimate the models.[13] The 1990–94 NES surveys feature a host of racial policy items, which I define as programs targeted explicitly to racial minorities. In all, I incorporate six different racial policy preferences as dependent variables, classifying them into the aforementioned race-conscious, social welfare, and equal treatment agendas. The items include support for affirmative action and the use of racial quotas in college admission, both part of the race-conscious agenda, support for government aid to blacks and spending to assist blacks, part of the social welfare agenda, and support for government ensuring school integration and equal treatment in hiring, part of the equal treatment agenda. Each of the dependent variables is arrayed so that least-supportive responses are at their scales' low end and most supportive at the high end.

TABLE 6.1
Percentage Supporting Various Racial Policies by Levels of Political Trust, 1992

Variable	Below Trust Midpoint	Above Trust Midpoint	Difference
Affirmative action	12	18	+6
Higher-education quotas	23	32	+9
Federal role in school integration	25	39	+14
Federal role in fair treatment in jobs	32	39	+7
Maintaining or increasing spending to assist blacks	67	74	+7

Source: American National Election Study, 1992.

RESULTS

The results presented in table 6.1 hint that political trust has the hypothesized effect among whites. Using data from white respondents from the 1992 NES, I divide the sample by whether a person scored at or above the midpoint of the trust scale or below the midpoint. I then calculate the percentage of respondents who registered support for the various racial policies. The differences between trusters and distrusters are striking. Though affirmative action is unpopular for all respondents, 18 percent of those scoring at or above the trust midpoint support it, while only 12 percent below the trust midpoint do. Even larger gaps exist for the other items. For example, those scoring at or above the trust midpoint are 14 percentage points more supportive of the federal government playing a role in school integration than those below it. Similarly, those at or above the midpoint are 9 percentage points more supportive of using quotas in higher-education admissions than those below. Since the average respondent scored above trust's midpoint in 1964 but near the minimum in the 1990s, these results suggest that race-targeted programs would be much more popular in the present day had trust not declined so dramatically.

To test whether there is a causal connection between political trust and racial policy preferences at the individual level, I estimate the model explicated in figure 6.2. If I find that political trust affects racial policy preferences and is positively signed and substantively large, then, coupled with the aggregate-level findings, I have strong support that political trust explains the persistence, or even widening, of the principle-implementation gap.[14]

The results appear in tables 6.2–6.4 and are categorized by policy agenda, with the race-conscious items in table 6.2, the social welfare items

TABLE 6.2
Whites' Support for Race-Conscious Agenda, 1990–94 (parameter estimates)

Variable	Affirmative Action			Education Quotas	
	1990	1992	1994	1990	1992
Intercept	0.230**	0.089*	0.054	0.102	0.086*
	(0.085)	(0.043)	(0.048)	(0.094)	(0.050)
Political trust	0.156***	0.176***	0.076*	0.156**	0.181***
	(0.051)	(0.037)	(0.034)	(0.057)	(0.042)
Partisanship	0.004	−0.001	−0.052*	−0.009	−0.070**
	(0.036)	(0.026)	(0.024)	(0.040)	(0.029)
Conservatism	−0.097	−0.113**	−0.065	−0.014	−0.086*
	(0.067)	(0.042)	(0.041)	(0.073)	(0.048)
Economic evaluation	0.033	−0.074	0.018	0.238***	0.027
	(0.073)	(0.045)	(0.045)	(0.080)	(0.051)
Racial attitudes	0.168***	0.098**	0.127***	0.233***	0.198***
	(0.041)	(0.039)	(0.027)	(0.045)	(0.044)
Support for equality	0.282***	0.226***	0.224***	0.494***	0.367***
	(0.071)	(0.039)	(0.042)	(0.079)	(0.044)
Income	−0.174***	−0.110***	−0.004	−0.078	−0.133***
	(0.047)	(0.033)	(0.030)	(0.052)	(0.038)
Education	−0.075	0.014	−0.057*	−0.047	−0.039
	(0.048)	(0.031)	(0.030)	(0.052)	(0.036)
South	0.019	−0.002	0.005	−0.023	−0.041*
	(0.027)	(0.017)	(0.015)	(0.030)	(0.020)
Race of interviewer	0.244**	0.273***	−0.008	0.214*	0.100
	(0.093)	(0.063)	(0.020)	(0.102)	(0.070)
Adj. R^2	.12	.09	.09	.16	.14
N	711	1,442	1,289	700	1,415

Source: American National Election Studies, 1990, 1992, 1994.
Note: Standard errors are given in parentheses.
*$p < .05$. **$p < .01$. ***$p < .001$. One-tailed tests.

in table 6.3, and the equal treatment items in table 6.4. For 13 of the 14 items, political trust does have the hypothesized effect, the lone exception being aid to blacks in 1992.

Also consistent with expectations, I find variation in trust's impact on the different race agendas, although the pattern does not fit my expectations perfectly. Since all variables are measured on the same (0, 1) interval, I can compare the size of trust's effect in the various models. Again, the

TABLE 6.3
Whites' Support for Social Welfare Agenda, 1990, 1992, 1994 (parameter estimates)

Variable	Aid to Blacks			Spending on Blacks	
	1990	1992	1994	1990	1992
Intercept	0.395***	0.112**	0.114**	0.542***	0.243***
	(0.067)	(0.038)	(0.045)	(0.074)	(0.048)
Political trust	0.068*	0.047	0.136***	0.085*	0.090*
	(0.041)	(0.033)	(0.032)	(0.045)	(0.040)
Partisanship	−0.057*	−0.062**	−0.086***	−0.057*	−0.112***
	(0.029)	(0.023)	(0.023)	(0.031)	(0.028)
Conservatism	−0.074	−0.083	−0.043	−0.137*	−0.120**
	(0.054)	(0.053)	(0.039)	(0.060)	(0.046)
Economic evaluation	0.025	−0.031	−0.040	0.011	−0.030
	(0.058)	(0.040)	(0.042)	(0.065)	(0.049)
Racial attitudes	0.242***	0.263***	0.230***	0.226***	0.246***
	(0.033)	(0.035)	(0.025)	(0.037)	(0.043)
Support for equality	0.361***	0.306***	0.382***	0.413***	0.363***
	(0.057)	(0.034)	(0.039)	(0.064)	(0.043)
Income	−0.093**	−0.076**	−0.012	−0.159***	−0.040
	(0.037)	(0.029)	(0.028)	(0.042)	(0.036)
Education	0.042	0.132***	0.044	0.004	0.035
	(0.038)	(0.028)	(0.028)	(0.042)	(0.034)
South	−0.058**	−0.043**	−0.005	−0.036	−0.028
	(0.022)	(0.015)	(0.014)	(0.024)	(0.019)
Race of interviewer	0.177*	0.085	−0.015	0.168*	0.178**
	(0.085)	(0.053)	(0.019)	(0.084)	(0.066)
Adj. R^2	.25	.20	.27	.22	.16
N	682	1,342	1,262	722	1,428

Source: American National Election Studies, 1990, 1992, 1994.
Note: Standard errors are given in parentheses.
*$p < .05$.   **$p < .01$.   ***$p < .001$. One-tailed tests.

estimates in the tables are the effects that the independent variables have across their ranges.

Political trust has the largest impact on support for the race-conscious agenda, as expected, where the median effect is .156. This number means that, on average, a person with the lowest score on the political trust index is about 15 percent less supportive than a person with the highest trust score. In the equal treatment domain, trust's effect is only a little smaller,

TABLE 6.4
Whites' Support for Equal Treatment Agenda, 1990–94 (parameter estimates)

Variable	Equal Treatment in Hiring (1992)	School Integration 1990	1992	1994
Intercept	0.168** (0.057)	0.462*** (0.102)	0.179*** (0.057)	0.314 (0.070)
Political trust	0.112* (0.048)	0.150** (0.061)	0.249*** (0.048)	0.121** (0.050)
Partisanship	−0.043 (0.034)	−0.035 (0.043)	−0.059* (0.034)	−0.104** (0.036)
Conservatism	−0.121* (0.056)	−0.229** (0.082)	−0.057 (0.056)	−0.169** (0.061)
Economic evaluation	0.033 (0.059)	0.041 (0.087)	−0.023 (0.059)	0.134* (0.066)
Racial attitudes	0.134** (0.051)	0.183*** (0.049)	0.133*** (0.051)	0.077* (0.140)
Support for equality	0.500*** (0.051)	0.365*** (0.086)	0.448*** (0.051)	0.323*** (0.062)
Income	−0.103** (0.044)	−0.062 (0.057)	−0.101** (0.043)	−0.045 (0.044)
Education	0.122** (0.041)	−0.003 (0.057)	0.015 (0.041)	−0.054 (0.044)
South	0.019 (0.023)	0.050 (0.033)	0.001 (0.023)	0.011 (0.022)
Race of interviewer	0.083 (0.082)	−0.112 (0.110)	0.100 (0.082)	−0.043 (0.030)
Adj. R^2	.12	.10	.11	.10
N	1,475	739	1,467	1,319

Source: American National Election Studies, 1990, 1992, 1994.
Note: Standard errors are given in parentheses.
*$p < .05$.   **$p < .01$.   ***$p < .001$. One-tailed tests.

with a median effect of .135. Somewhat surprisingly, trust is less influential in the social welfare domain, with a median effect of only .085. Still, the most important consideration is that the effect of political trust is significant no matter the racial policy.

Though attitudes like partisanship and conservatism receive much more attention from political scientists than political trust does, political trust is the only variable from the political realm that exerts such a consistently significant effect. Partisanship and conservatism achieve statistical significance in only two of the five race-conscious equations, respectively. Though partisanship fares somewhat better for the remaining policy agendas, particularly social welfare, its effect is generally smaller than that of trust. For its part, conservatism is only significant in half of the 14 models.

Both racial attitudes and support for the principle of equality consistently exert among the most substantial effects on racial policy preferences. Those who feel more positively toward blacks and those who value equal opportunity more are, not surprisingly, more supportive of race-targeted policies. These results are important because they confirm that improvement in whites' racial attitudes in addition to their increasing support for principles of equality over time should have brought about a dramatic increase in support for race-targeted policies. Of course, I have shown that this has not occurred. Since none of the other individual-level explanations exert consistently strong effects, it suggests that the decrease in political trust over time has offset the effects of improving racial attitudes and increasing support for the principle of equality. The fact that Americans do not trust their government helps maintain the principle-implementation gap. If trust were higher, the gap would be smaller.

Trust and Perceived Sacrifice

I have argued that political trust affects whites' support for racial policies because these policies require whites to make sacrifices today on the belief that such programs will benefit society in the future. Without trusting the government to administer such programs well or fairly, whites may feel their sacrifices are pointless, even punitive.

If I am right, trust should be more influential for whites who feel directly threatened by racial policies than those who do not. The higher-education quotas item provides an ideal test. Trust should be significantly more important in predicting support among whites with children than among whites without children. White parents might perceive education quotas as harmful to their children's future, while those without children face no direct threat.[15] In the former case, trust should be necessary. In the latter case, trust should be less so.

To test these hypotheses, I make two minor changes to the baseline model used so far. I add a dummy variable indicating whether the respondent reports having children or not and create an interaction between it and political trust.

The interpretation of this interaction requires some explanation. The estimate for political trust will reflect its effect among those with no children, while the estimate for the interaction between having children and

TABLE 6.5
Testing the Sacrifice Hypothesis, Education Quotas, 1992

Variable	Parameter Estimate (SE)
Political trust	−0.015
	(0.085)
Has child	−0.047*
	(0.028)
Political trust × Has child	0.257**
	(0.097)
Adj. R^2	.14
N	1,415

Source: American National Election Studies, 1992.
*$p < .05$.   **$p < .01$.   ***$p < .001$. One-tailed tests.

political trust will reflect how much larger or smaller trust's effect is among those who have children relative to those who do not. According to my theory, the interaction should be positively signed and significant, indicating that trust's effect is larger for those with children because they are more likely to perceive a direct threat from the program.

The results using the 1992 data appear in table 6.5.[16] Supportive of the sacrifice hypothesis, the effect of trust for those without children (those not required to make a perceived sacrifice) is insignificant, but the effect for those with children (those required to make a perceived sacrifice) is, as expected, significantly larger.

The interaction is shown graphically in figure 6.3. Among whites with children, the line reflecting political trust's effect is positively sloped and steep. This means that those who trust the government least are unsupportive of higher-education quotas, other things being equal. But as trust increases to its maximum, support for this policy increases by more than 25 percent, a very substantial gain. In fact, only support for the principle of equality exerts a stronger effect on support for higher-education quotas than does political trust among white parents. In contrast, the line reflecting the effect of political trust for white nonparents is flat. This means that knowing how trustful a respondent is tells us absolutely nothing about how supportive he or she is of higher-education quotas.

In sum, these results support the sacrifice hypothesis. When whites perceive that a racial policy affects them directly, political trust becomes important in understanding their support or opposition. However, trust

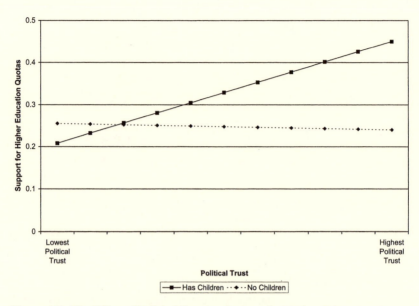

Figure 6.3. The Effect of Political Trust on Support for Higher-Education Quotas Conditional on Having a Child.

does not influence policy preferences among those who are unlikely to perceive a direct threat.

Trust and Perceived Risk

If I am correct that perceived risk also makes political trust important, trust's effect should be largest among those who have negative feelings about the group benefiting from the government program. Since the programs are all race-targeted, trust should have a large effect among those with negative racial attitudes and a much smaller effect among those with positive racial attitudes. For the former group, investing preferences, funds, or government intervention in a group that they view as undeserving represents a risky investment. To support such an investment, these people will have to trust the government, the only player in the process that could mitigate this risk.

To test this hypothesis, I make one minor change to the model. I add an interaction between political trust and people's perceptions of blacks' industriousness. Again the interpretation of the effects requires some explanation. The estimate for political trust will reflect its effect among those

TABLE 6.6
Testing the Risk Hypothesis, White Respondents, 1992 (parameter estimates)

Variable	Affirmative Action	Education Quotas	Aid to Blacks	Spending to Assist Blacks	School Integration	Equal Treatment in Hiring
Political trust	0.340***	0.352***	0.236**	0.324***	0.441***	0.180
	(0.095)	(0.109)	(0.088)	(0.104)	(0.125)	(0.126)
Racial attitudes	0.173***	0.276***	0.344***	0.352***	0.220***	0.165*
	(0.056)	(0.063)	(0.049)	(0.060)	(0.073)	(0.074)
Political trust x Racial attitudes	−0.338*	−0.351*	−0.382*	−0.479**	−0.393*	−0.140
	(0.179)	(0.205)	(0.165)	(0.197)	(0.237)	(0.238)
Adj. R^2	.10	.14	.20	.16	.11	.12
N	1,442	1,415	1,342	1,428	1,467	1,475

Source: American National Election Studies, 1992.
Note: Standard errors are given in parentheses.
*$p < .05$.   **$p < .01$.   ***$p < .001$. One-tailed tests.

who have the most negative racial attitudes (blacks are most lazy), while the estimate for the interaction between racial attitudes and trust will reflect how much more or less political trust matters as people's racial attitudes improve. Since those with the most negative racial attitudes should require trust the most, the effect of political trust alone should be positive and significant. This taps when racial attitudes equals zero. Since trust should matter less as people's feelings about blacks improve (in other words, as the racial attitudes variable increases toward 1), the effect of interaction should be negative. Since all the policies under review are explicitly racial in character, the pattern of results should hold for all items.[17]

The results presented in table 6.6 suggest very strong support for the risk hypothesis. For five of the six items, the effect for political trust is positive and statistically significant, while the effect of the interaction is negatively signed and statistically significant. In the case of equal treatment in hiring, the only exception to the expected pattern of findings, the signs are still in the proper direction.

Figure 6.4 shows how these interactive effects work. Take the affirmative action item, for example. Among those who describe blacks as most lazy on the seven-point scale, the effect of political trust on support for the program is about .35. This means that those who are most trustful are about 35 percent more supportive of affirmative action than those who are least trustful, other things being equal. For those whose opinion about blacks' industriousness is at the median, which, in this case, is the

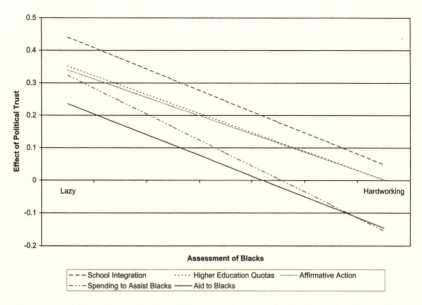

Figure 6.4. The Effect of Political Trust on Support for Various Race-Based Programs Conditional on Antiblack Stereotypes.

midpoint of the scale, the effect of trust is about .17, or about half its effect among people who think blacks are most lazy. Among people who describe blacks as most hardworking, trust has no effect on support for affirmative action.

The conditional effect of trust is greatest for school integration. Among those who think blacks are most lazy, the most trustful respondents are nearly 45 percent more supportive of a federal role in school integration than those who are least trustful. Among those at the median of the racial attitudes scale, the most trustful are about 25 percent more supportive than those who are distrustful. And, again, the effect of trust is negligible when whites rate blacks as hardworking.

In sum, I find strong support for the risk hypothesis. The more negatively whites feel about blacks, the greater the risk they will tend to perceive in programs designed to benefit them. And, when people perceive greater risk, it increases the importance of trust in explaining preferences for these policies. These results provide individual-level support for the aggregate-level case presented at the beginning of the chapter. Political trust has an effect among exactly the individuals that the theory suggests it should.

CONCLUSION

Federal policies are the final products of a process involving the federal government. I have hypothesized that, if people distrust the federal government, other things being equal, they oppose its policies when they perceive that their share of policy costs is high and their benefits slight. These results provide further evidence. Political trust has a large effect on whites' racial policy preferences. Consistent with my expectations, the effect is largest when whites perceive that a program directly affects their interests, as with parents and affirmative action in higher education. Furthermore, trust's effect also increases dramatically when people think negatively about the beneficiary group.

If these results are applied longitudinally, they speak to a larger question as well. Without doubt, whites' racial attitudes have become more tolerant over the last three decades (Schuman et al. 1997). Hence, the gap between professed support for racial equality and the programs designed to effect it should have shrunk considerably. It has not. The principle-implementation gap still persists and in some areas has widened. Declining trust in government is a particularly compelling explanation. The results suggest that many whites simply do not trust the government enough to implement and administer the programs designed to make racial equality a reality. This is true of controversial programs, such as affirmative action, but it is also true of initiatives that most Americans support, such as school integration. In the case of school integration, I have demonstrated that people have recently become increasingly concerned about the issue, but their distrust of the federal government means that they do not want it involved in the solution. Since school resegregation has developed its greatest momentum in the South and since southern state governments are particularly unlikely to take action, it is unclear what set of institutions might confront this problem.

CHAPTER SEVEN

Political Trust and the Demise
of Health Care Reform

ON AUGUST 9, 1994, Minority Leader Bob Dole (R-Kans.) took to the Senate floor to debate Bill Clinton's health care reform plan. Judd Gregg (R-N.H.) had recently forwarded to Dole a constituent letter, and Dole read from it at length.

> Recently my 10-year-old son was the victim of a near-drowning. Thanks to the intervention of people at the scene, he survived the initial incident and was transported to a nearby hospital where he received superb care and treatment, was stabilized and then sent to Children's Hospital in Boston, about an hour away from where we were. With God's help and the outstanding care and treatment that he received in the intensive care unit at Children's, my son is awake, alert and sitting up in his room, surviving with virtually all his physical and mental faculties intact.
>
> After the initial crisis had passed, I sat in quiet reflection over the entire episode, and it dawned on me with chilling clarity that had the Clinton health plan been in effect, the outcome could have been drastically different. In the scheme of things that the president proposed, we would not have been able to send our son to Boston. We would have been relegated to some other hospital, if any. And the penalty for going against the plan would be a $10,000 fine and possible jail sentence.
>
> I have no feelings of rancor; just fear that events could have been taken out of my control and put in the hands of some unseen, uncaring, bean-counting bureaucrat whose only concern was compliance to a government policy that only leads to mundane mediocrity.
>
> The choice comes down to a simple question. If you were in my place, would you want the freedom to determine your child's care and outcome, or would you rather be forced to accept what the government will give you?

Dole concluded his remarks by asserting that politics in Washington boiled down to this decision. How intrusive would an incompetent government be in the lives of ordinary Americans? When presented this way, it is little wonder Clinton's health care plan met with a decisive defeat in Congress and, soon after, the Republicans assumed the majority in both houses of Congress for the first time in nearly 50 years.

As an opponent of the Clinton plan, Dole was smart to couch his objections in antigovernment terms. In doing so, he caused people to think about health care reform in terms of how they felt about government. And, in 1994, those feelings were particularly negative, with political distrust at its highest point since public opinion polls began tracking it in the 1950s—even higher than during Vietnam, Watergate, or Jimmy Carter's crisis of confidence. Dole's statement was neither partisan, nor ideological. It was simply anti-Washington. Carried out by "[u]nseen, uncaring, bean-counting" bureaucrats, policies featuring government involvement inevitably lead to "mundane mediocrity." Moreover, these allegedly poorly administered, wasteful policies often demand that citizens who are content with the status quo make large sacrifices for others. Such policies demand that the public have at least a moderate amount of political trust. Given the opinion environment in 1994, the Clinton proposal was doomed to failure.

In this chapter, I track how public opinion turned against health care reform and outline the various modes of attack used against it. I demonstrate that the key to its defeat was that the public came to identify it too closely with the federal government. I next show which strategies used by opponents caused people to think about health care reform in this way. Many attempted to paint the plan as ideologically extreme or too closely identified with a flawed president, but such attacks did not work. Instead, appeals tying the reform effort to people's distrust of government drove public perceptions of the plan outside the mainstream. Moreover, not only did decreasing political trust defeat health care reform, it was instrumental in bringing about the Republican sweep of the House just months later, which, in turn, fundamentally changed elite dialogue about what government might hope to accomplish.

ATTACKING HEALTH CARE REFORM

Bob Dole, of course, was not alone in attacking the Clinton health care initiative by attacking Washington. Most notably, the Health Insurance Association of America, a trade association representing the interests of the nation's health insurance providers, spent more than $10 million on their Harry and Louise television ads, using themes similar to Dole's. Harry and Louise were two 40-something white yuppies who apparently spent their days studying and discussing the potential effects of the Clinton health care reform initiative.

In March 1994, the following ad began airing, mostly on CNN and in large eastern media markets.

Setting: A living room. Louise is on the couch reading a paperback version of an early draft of the Clinton plan. Harry has just sent teen son Matt off to do homework after a basketball game.

Harry: Health care reform again, huh?

Louise: This plan forces us to buy our insurance through these new mandatory government health alliances.

Harry: Run by tens of thousands of new bureaucrats.

Louise: Another billion-dollar bureaucracy.

Harry: You know, we just don't need government monopolies to get health coverage to everyone.

Like Dole's letter, this ad attacks inefficient government bureaucracy. Worse, according to Harry and Louise, Clinton-style health care reform would increase by tens of thousands of new employees the size of what most Americans perceive to be an already bloated federal bureaucracy.

A second Harry and Louise spot, which invoked both bureaucratic incompetence and the need for sacrifice under the Clinton plan, began airing about the same time.

Announcer: The government may force us to pick from a few health care plans designed by government bureaucrats.

Louise: Having choices we don't like is no choice at all.

Harry: They choose.

Louise: We lose.

Even if they regularly choose the same options, Americans still love their choices whether it be McDonalds or Burger King, Coke or Pepsi, or a menu of potential doctors. By advising viewers that those presently happy with their coverage might forfeit the right to make such choices, Harry and Louise make clear that some people will have to make sacrifices under the Clinton reform plan. According to my theory about political trust and policy preferences, this tactic should make how much people trust the government very influential in deciding whether they support or oppose this new government initiative, good news for Clinton's opponents, with trust at its lowest point ever.

Although most Americans never saw these ads when they aired because media buys were concentrated in the Washington–New York corridor, they learned of them through the news media. After Hillary Clinton assailed the ads as "cynical distortions," they became fair game for review, providing them added publicity. Similar to George Bush's Willie Horton ad in 1988 and Lyndon Johnson's Daisy ad in 1964, both of which aired infrequently (the Daisy ad only once), Harry and Louise received most of their attention through discussion by political elites. Such elite-level discussion not only provides the ads free air time, it also increases their credibility (Jamieson 1992).

The Harry and Louise ads were only a small part of a bigger effort to discredit health care reform. By one estimate, opponents spent more money attempting to defeat the Clinton plan in 1994 than all three major presidential candidates did running for election in 1992 (Johnson and Broder 1996). These efforts were stunningly successful. Prior to the campaign against the Clinton plan, taxpayer-funded systems of various sorts consistently registered better than 55 percent support from the public and often higher than 60 percent (Jacobs and Shapiro 2000). The Clinton plan, specifically, enjoyed 60 percent support when launched in September 1993, maintaining similar backing as late as February 1994. Harry and Louise came on the scene in March, and, by July, support had dried up considerably, with only 40 percent supporting the Clinton proposal. As one might expect, the percentage of Americans expressing opposition also jumped during this period, from 33 percent in September 1993 to 56 percent in July 1994 (Jacobs and Shapiro 2000).

While the numbers clearly demonstrate that the attacks took their toll, less clear is *why* these attacks worked so well. Not surprisingly, given the nature of the attacks, many Americans began to perceive that the core problem with health care reform was an overreliance on government. Larry Jacobs and Robert Shapiro (2000) show that, in the first months of 1994, 40 percent of Americans feared it would involve government too much. By April, this percentage had increased to 47, an enormous change in such a short period. Although survey organizations stopped asking this question in April, this number likely jumped much higher as the summer progressed and support waned.

In short, concerns about big government appear to be the root cause of public dissatisfaction with Clinton-style health care reform. As opponents framed their attacks in antigovernment terms, people began to evaluate the president's plan in terms of their negative feelings about the federal government. The defeat of health care reform is a textbook example of how to use public distrust of government to undermine public support for a new government-run program.

THE HEALTH CARE REFORM DEBATE OF 1994

While political trust was important in the attack on the Clinton plan, opponents did more than bash the government. Amy Fried and Douglas Harris (2001) analyzed the debate about health care reform in the *Congressional Record*, finding that attacks were essentially three-pronged. The most common set of criticisms involved big government, including references to "health care bureaucrats," "Washington bureaucrats," and "government-run health care." Opponents implied that big government had proven in other areas to be more a hindrance than a solution, so its involvement in health care might jeopardize the availability and quality of present services.

Moreover, opponents using the antigovernment approach suggested that those who were satisfied with their insurance would have to make sacrifices. For example, the Harry and Louise ads said that, under the Clinton plan, people would face a limited choice of providers and might not be able use their present family doctors. Others claimed that the Clinton plan would ration health care, such that services would at best be delayed and at worst denied. Based on my theory about the importance of trust when people are asked to make sacrifices, such attacks should make political trust influential.

According to Fried and Harris (2001), the second prong of the attack was ideological. Opponents used terms like "socialized medicine," "a socialistic system," "overly liberal," "embarrassingly liberal," and various derivatives to criticize the plan. Those employing this approach commonly likened the Clinton plan to the British and Canadian systems.

Critics using this tack were trying to take advantage of what they perceived to be a conservative turn in the public's ideology. Given the success of George H. W. Bush in 1988 and subsequent Republican candidates who saddled their opponents with the liberal label, engaging ideology seemed like a winning strategy as well. Even if Americans were not becoming significantly more ideologically conservative, opponents could still be successful if they could increase the importance of ideology in people's minds. Ever since the NES started asking the public about ideology in 1972, conservatives have always outnumbered liberals, so simply activating conservatism could potentially defeat the Clinton plan.

Finally, the third prong of the attack attempted to tie Bill Clinton's personal unpopularity to the reform effort. By painting Clinton as personally flawed, opponents hoped that people would view his plan as flawed. This approach made good sense, too. Although presidents usually enjoy a honeymoon period that lasts several months at the beginning of their presidency, Clinton was less popular than his predecessors from the time he took office. In the months between the introduction of the health care reform package in September 1993 and its defeat in September 1994, Clinton's average monthly approval rating from the Gallup Organization never rose above 55 percent. Worse, every month after the public met Harry and Louise, it fell below 50 percent. Since Clinton was less popular than his reform plan was originally, tying him to it could also erode support for it.

TABLE 7.1

Perceived Position of the Democratic Party, Democratic Presidents, Democratic Presidential Candidates, and People's Self-Placement on NES Health Insurance Scale, 1970–96

	Democratic Party	Democratic President	Democratic Presidential Candidate	Self-Placement
1970	3.17			3.87
1972	3.14		2.77	3.87
1976	2.90		2.98	3.95
1978	3.17	3.40		3.86
1984				3.98
1988	3.30		3.12	3.84
1992			3.40	
1994	2.71	2.26		4.00
1996		2.91	2.91	3.95

Source: American National Election Study, Cumulative File, 1948–2000.

This avalanche of negative rhetoric about the plan had the desired effect. One manifestation was that people began to perceive Bill Clinton as strongly favoring government involvement in health care, a striking change relative to the recent past. Table 7.1 tracks where Americans, on average, perceived the Democratic Party and their standard-bearer on national health insurance from the question's introduction in 1970 through 1996, along with where they placed themselves on the issue. The text of the question used by the NES is the following:

There is much concern about the rapid rise in medical and hospital costs. Some people feel there should be a government insurance plan which would cover all medical expenses for everyone. Others feel that all medical expenses should be paid by individuals, and through private insurance plans like Blue Cross or other company paid plans. Where would you place yourself on this scale, or haven't you thought much about this?

People are asked to place themselves and relevant political actors on a seven-point scale ranging from 1, a government insurance plan, to 7, a private insurance plan. Unfortunately, the NES failed to ask this question about either Clinton or the Democrats in 1992.

In the early 1970s, George McGovern's very liberal campaign clearly moved perceptions of Democrats to the left. In fact, public perceptions of the Democratic Party moved just over a quarter point toward the liberal pole of the scale between 1970, the election year before McGovern won the presidential nomination, and 1976. From the late 1970s through the 1980s, however, Americans saw the Democratic Party and its presidential candidates as only slightly left of center, just as they do for most other issues. The key word here is *slightly.* Not once during this period did the public view either a Democratic president, a Democratic presidential candidate, or the Democratic Party itself as much as a single point from the scale's midpoint.

This all began to change in the early 1990s. In 1994, Americans, on average, perceived Clinton at 2.26 on the scale, nearly a full point more progovernment than they perceived Dukakis in 1988, when he ran, in part, on a platform advocating universal health insurance. In fact, the public viewed Bill Clinton as a half point more liberal than they did George McGovern in 1972. Given that the average American's opinion on health insurance was exactly at the midpoint in 1994, perceptions of the president as extremely progovernment represented terrible news for his health insurance reform plan.

Public opinion about Clinton's position on health care is even more striking when viewed relative to perceptions of other presidents on other issues. Since 1970, the NES has asked respondents regularly where they perceive the president on a range of seven-point issue scales including defense spending, cooperation with the former Soviet Union, a woman's proper role in society, aid to blacks, the proper level of government services and spending, and, of course, health insurance. According to the NES Cumulative File, only Ronald Reagan on defense spending in 1982 and 1986 registered perceptions as far from the scale's midpoint as Bill Clinton did on health insurance in 1994.

Why did people see Clinton as so progovernment? Just like Reagan and defense spending, part of the explanation is grounded in reality. Clinton's plan did, in fact, provide the government with a more important role in the provision of health care than it presently had. However, private insurance companies would have continued to play a central role, much to the dismay of those on the left. The Clinton plan was certainly not a centralized health care system modeled on the Canadian or British system. Moreover, Americans are notoriously bad at correctly perceiving political reality. For example, only 40 percent of Americans knew that Republicans had the majority in both houses of Congress in 1995.

More important than reality is what people perceive reality to be. Attacks on the health plan were designed to cause people to perceive reality in a certain way. Whether it was by calling it too bureaucratic, too liberal, or too closely identified with an unpopular president, opponents were trying to paint the Clinton plan as outside the mainstream. And, of course, they succeeded.

HEALTH CARE REFORM AND POLITICAL TRUST

Rather than causing people to change their opinions through the sheer force of argument, political rhetoric is more often designed to make certain attitudes more salient when people are forming their opinions. This, in turn, affects the opinions that they ultimately arrive at. Since elites know that people carry around certain political predispositions in their heads, they use rhetoric to encourage them to think in terms of the predispositions most advantageous to their cause.

For example, consider the 1992 presidential election. Since he presided over the end of the Cold War and victory in the first Persian Gulf War, George H. W. Bush would have been greatly advantaged if the public evaluated the race in terms of defense and foreign policy. With the economy battling to emerge from recession, he would have been disadvantaged if the public evaluated the race in terms of economic growth. In the end, the economy became a more salient consideration to voters than was foreign policy, leading to Bush's defeat.

To the degree that attacks against the health plan were effective, then, it is because opponents placed the desired predispositions on the tops of people's heads when they responded to Clinton's health care reform plan. References to the problems of big government were designed to raise the importance of political trust, thus increasing its weight in evaluating health care reform. References to hyperliberalism and socialism were designed to make people think in ideological and partisan terms, causing people to weight them more heavily. And attacks on Clinton personally were designed to make personal assessments of the president more influential. To the extent that these things happened or failed to happen, a given strategy was more or less effective. I show below that the ability of opponents to make people think about health care reform in terms of how they felt about the federal government was the key to defeating the initiative.

EXPLAINING PERCEPTIONS OF BILL CLINTON
ON HEALTH INSURANCE

While it would be ideal for a survey organization to have asked people in September 1994 whether they supported or opposed the Clinton plan, how much they trusted the government, how conservative they were, how

Republican they were, and whether or not they approved of the president, no such survey exists. I have to rely on the 1994 NES, administered mostly in November, to assess the effect of each of the rhetorical strategies.

The NES did not ask people specifically whether they supported or opposed the Clinton plan. Instead, they asked people where they perceived Clinton on the seven-point health insurance scale described above. Specifically, respondents were asked to place Clinton between "a government insurance plan" at the one pole and "a private insurance plan" at the other. Since his plan failed because people came to see it as relying too much on government (Jacobs and Shapiro 2000), I need to explain why people came to identify Clinton so closely with a government run insurance plan. Hence, the dependent variable for this analysis is how far from the midpoint of the scale that people perceived Bill Clinton on health care. I calculate this by taking the absolute value of 4 minus people's placement of Clinton. There were a handful of people who placed Clinton to the right of center on this issue. Since they did not view Clinton as too progovernment, I code them as 0. This means that larger numbers correspond to more progovernment perceptions of Clinton.

Political trust should help explain these perceptions. I use the same political trust measure that I have used throughout the book. Similar to previous chapters, I must also account for other potential explanations, so as not to provide trust with too much credit. Since Fried and Harris (2001) suggested that many of the attacks on the plan were ideological, I include conservatism in the model as well. Moreover, since most of these attacks came from Republican partisans, I include the usual measure of partisanship. Conservatives and Republicans should both be more likely to view Clinton as more progovernment than liberals and Democrats, respectively.

Opponents also attacked Clinton personally. Hence, whether or not someone reports approving of the president should also be influential. Those who disapprove should be more inclined to respond to the charges against the plan and, hence, perceive Clinton as more progovernment than those who approve. In addition, I include a variable that asks people whether or not they believe they can afford health insurance. Those who do not feel that they can afford insurance may be more sympathetic to the Clinton plan and, as a result, see him as less progovernment.

I must also account for cognitive ability and social characteristics. Much research demonstrates that those who know more about politics tend to place political figures toward the poles of seven-point scales (e.g. Krosnick 1991). The reason is simple. Those who do not know much about politics tend to choose the midpoint rather than saying they do not know, whereas those who know more about politics realize that political figures generally have a position different from the midpoint. I also include the same battery of social characteristics used in the previous chapters to make the

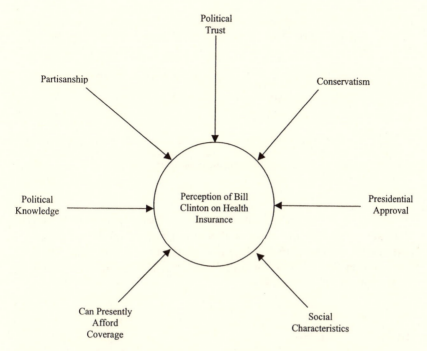

Figure 7.1. Perceptions of Bill Clinton on Health Insurance as a Function of Political Distrust, Other Symbolic Attitudes, Ability to Afford Health Insurance, and Social Characteristics.

estimates of the substantive variables more secure. Figure 7.1 summarizes the model graphically.

As I have done throughout, I map all the variables onto (0, 1) intervals to simplify the interpretation of the effects. So as not to confuse the reader, doing this means that a one-point change on the seven-point health insurance scale described above corresponds to a change of .166 (1/6) points after I have mapped it on a (0, 1) interval.

DATA

I use data gathered by the NES in 1988, 1994, and 1996. I am most interested in the 1994 data. These will bear most strongly on the reasons that the Clinton plan failed, given that the surveys were administered only two months after the plan's demise. To assess how 1994 was different, I use data from the most recent NES survey before 1994 that asked respon-

TABLE 7.2
Difference in Mean Perception of Democratic Standard-Bearer's Position on
Government-Sponsored Health Care by Political Trust, 1988, 1994, 1996

Year	At or above Trust Midpoint	Below Trust Midpoint	Difference (below – above)
1988	.408	.411	.003
1994	.552	.673	.121
1996	.442	.486	.044

Source: American National Election Studies, 1988, 1994, 1996.
Note: Figures are means.

dents to place prominent Democrats on the health insurance scale (the 1988 study) and the one soonest after (the 1996 study). If one variable is particularly influential in 1994, but not in the other two years, it explains why opinion about Clinton was so different in 1994 from opinions about Democrats in other years.

RESULTS

I have argued that opponents tapped into Americans' distrust of government when they attacked Clinton's health care plan and noted the sacrifices inherent in it. The results in table 7.2 provide some preliminary evidence for my argument. I again divide the samples into two groups, those scoring at or above the political trust midpoint and those scoring below it. In 1994, there is a large difference between trusters and distrusters in how progovernment they viewed Clinton to be on the issue. On average, those scoring below the midpoint perceived Clinton at .673 on the scale, whereas those scoring at or above the midpoint perceived him at .552. I find no such differences in either 1988 perceptions of Dukakis or in 1996 perceptions of Clinton. Political distrust may have increased perceptions of Clinton as progovernment in 1994 but had no effect in other years, suggesting that opponents' antigovernment charges against the plan, which were present in 1994, but absent in other years, worked.

This evidence would be more compelling if the differences between trusters and distrusters persisted after accounting for other factors. Table 7.3 presents the results from the model depicted in figure 7.1. To review, the dependent variable here is how far from the midpoint people perceive the Democratic standard-bearer, Michael Dukakis in 1988 and Bill Clinton in 1994 and 1996, on health insurance. The results in the first and

TABLE 7.3
Perceptions of Clinton's Position on Government-Sponsored Health Care as a
Function of Political Trust and Other Variables, 1988, 1994, 1996 (parameter
estimates)

Variable	1988	1994	1996
Intercept	0.075	0.295***	0.130*
	(0.047)	(0.049)	(0.069)
Political trust	−0.030	−0.191***	0.070
	(0.023)	(0.047)	(0.046)
Partisanship	0.104**	0.092**	0.080*
	(0.036)	(0.035)	(0.040)
Conservatism	0.180***	0.226***	0.237***
	(0.058)	(0.054)	(0.061)
Presidential approval		−0.015	−0.095***
		(0.023)	(0.028)
Age	−0.016	−0.003	−0.058
	(0.056)	(0.045)	(0.048)
Race	−0.020	−0.062*	0.049
	(0.035)	(0.034)	(0.035)
Gender	−0.013	0.047**	0.058**
	(0.023)	(0.020)	(0.021)
Education	−0.095*	0.122***	0.052
	(0.049)	(0.043)	(0.045)
Income	0.059	−0.020	0.037
	(0.050)	(0.044)	(0.042)
Political knowledge	0.429***	0.295***	0.232***
	(0.053)	(0.043)	(0.045)
Can afford health insurance		−0.001	
		(0.022)	
Adjusted R^2	.13	.14	.10
N	1,077	1,361	1,294

Source: American National Election Studies, 1988, 1994, 1996.
Note: Standard errors are given in parentheses.
*$p < .05$.   **$p < .01$.   ***$p < .001$. One-tailed tests.

third columns of table 7.3 demonstrate that political trust did not contribute to people's perceptions in 1988 or 1996.

In 1994, however, political trust has a very large effect. Specifically, the negative sign means that the less trustful people are, the more progovernment they perceive Clinton to be, other things being equal. The estimated effect of .191 means that a person who is most distrustful perceives Clinton as 19 percent further from the center than someone who is most trustful.

Trust's effect is noteworthy for two reasons. First, its magnitude is large. Recall that a one-point change on the seven-point scale corresponds to a .166-point change on the $(0, 1)$ scale, so an effect of .191 is quite substantial. Second, and more importantly, political trust only has an effect in 1994. This means that the antigovernment attacks did place political trust on the tops of people's heads when they were asked to think about Clinton and health insurance. When such rhetoric was absent from the information environment in 1988 and 1996, trust had no effect on perceptions.

In contrast, the other relevant variables generally exert about the same weight in each year under study. Take conservatism, for example. Its effect in 1988 was .180, in 1994 it was .226, and in 1996 it was .237. Since the 1994 effect is not much larger than in other years—indeed its effect was largest in 1996—the attacks stressing the plan's "extreme liberalism" or "socialistic" character failed to increase the weight that people placed on ideology. The personal attacks on Clinton were similarly ineffective. In fact, presidential approval is statistically insignificant in 1994 but significant in 1996, exactly the reverse pattern that one would expect if the personal attacks on Clinton had worked. In short, only the antigovernment messages had the desired effect.

In sum, by making political trust an important part of people's thinking at a time when Americans held the government in such low esteem, opponents of health care reform caused people to see Bill Clinton as a progovernment extremist. This, in turn, turned opinion against the initiative, ultimately leading to his most spectacular first-term defeat.

Trust and Perceived Sacrifice

Building on the theory and results presented in previous chapters, I argue trust exerts its influence among those who perceive that a government program will require sacrifice of them, but trust is less important among those who perceive that they will benefit. As a further test, I need to identify a characteristic that distinguishes those who perceived that the Clinton plan would require them to make a sacrifice from those who perceived they would benefit from it.

Fortunately, the NES asked people in 1994 whether or not they could afford health insurance. The Harry and Louise ads targeted people who

TABLE 7.4
Perceptions of Clinton's Position on Government-Sponsored Health Care with
an Interaction between Political Trust and Sacrifice, 1994

Variable	Parameter Estimate (SE)
Political trust	0.007
	(0.082)
Can afford health insurance	0.050
	(0.028)
Political trust × Can afford health insurance	−0.289**
	(0.098)

Source: American National Election Studies, 1994.
*p < .05.   **p < .01.   ***p < .001. One-tailed tests.

believed they could afford it under the present system. If they could be
convinced that that they would have to make sacrifices under the Clinton
plan, such as a reduction in services or choice or an increase in costs to
help pay for the presently uninsured, their support would likely decrease.
In contrast, those who say they cannot afford insurance are more likely to
perceive themselves beneficiaries. At a minimum, they should be unlikely
to perceive that they would need to make a sacrifice because they are not
particularly happy with the present situation. Political trust should influence perceptions among those who say they can afford insurance (those
making the sacrifice), but not among those who say they cannot (the potential beneficiaries).

To test this hypothesis, I add to my model an interaction between political trust and the respondent's statement on whether s/he can afford health
insurance. If the sacrifice hypothesis is correct, the effect of political trust
alone should be insignificant, indicating that it has no effect among those
who cannot afford health insurance under the present system. However,
the interaction between trust and whether a person can afford health insurance should be negatively signed and statistically significant, indicating
that trust's effect is large among those who say they can afford it.

The results in table 7.4, which are presented graphically in figure 7.2,
confirm my expectations.[1] The line reflecting those who say they can afford
health insurance is quite steep and negatively sloped, meaning that progovernment perceptions of Clinton decrease markedly as people become
more politically trustful. For example, a person who scores most distrustful on the political trust scale perceives Clinton as 28 percent closer
to the government-run health care pole than a person who scores most
trustful, which is more than a quarter of the scale's range. In contrast, the

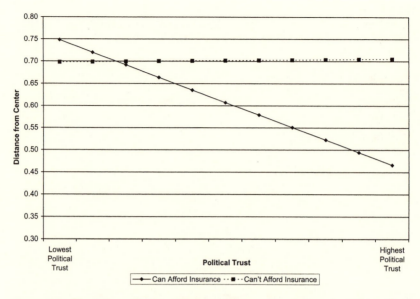

Figure 7.2. The Effect of Political Trust on Distance People Perceive Clinton from Center on Government-Sponsored Health Insurance, 1994.

line reflecting those who say they cannot afford health insurance is flat. Among these people, political trust tells us nothing about where they perceive Clinton.

I should also note that the effect of political trust among those making a sacrifice is enormous compared with the other variables. Trust's estimated effect in table 7.3 is .191, but this is an average effect for everyone in the sample, both those who perceive they will be making a sacrifice and those who perceive they will benefit. Since trust should only influence the opinions of the sacrificers, the average effect for the entire sample understates its effect for the sacrificers because the average includes the effect for beneficiaries as well, which is 0. When one focuses only on the sacrificers, trust's effect of .289 is far larger than any of the other variables in the model except for political knowledge, a remarkable finding.

The Implications of Health Care Reform's Defeat

Politics changed fundamentally after the effort to reform health care died. As Theda Skocpol (1996, 6) observed,

> Within weeks after the demise of health care reform the Democratic Party—
> legatee of the very New Deal whose achievements Clinton had hoped to imitate

TABLE 7.5
The Effect of Political Trust on Congressional Voting, 1992 versus 1994

	1992		1994	
	Below Trust Midpoint	At or Above Trust Midpoint	Below Trust Midpoint	At or Above Trust Midpoint
Voted for Democratic House candidate	58.37%	63.76%	41.11%	61.54%
Voted for Republican House candidate	41.63%	36.24%	58.89%	38.46%
Total	100	100	100	100

Source: American National Election Studies, 1992, 1994.

and extend—lay in shambles. Voters went to the polls on November 8, 1994, and registered widespread victories for Republicans running for state legislatures, for Republican gubernatorial candidates, for Republican Senate candidates, and—most remarkably—for Republican House candidates, who took control of that chamber after four full decades of continuous Democratic ascendancy. . . . The breadth and depth of the Republican victories seemed to render President Clinton an irrelevant lame duck for the remaining two years of his first term.

In addition to defeating health care reform, political trust was also a key element in the Republican sweep of the House. The results in table 7.5 make this clear. In 1992, whether or not a person trusted the government told us very little about how s/he voted in that year's House races. Those scoring below the trust midpoint provided 58 percent support to Democratic candidates while those scoring at or above the midpoint provided 64 percent support, a difference of only 6 percentage points. The distribution is markedly different in 1994. While better than 62 percent of those with a lot of government trust still voted for Democratic House candidates, only 41 percent of those with trust scores below the midpoint did. In other words, Republican support among distrusters was a whopping 21 percent higher than among trusters. Since the vast majority of respondents score below the trust midpoint, the advantage Republicans enjoyed because of the politicization of political trust was enormous.

Furthermore, the Republicans who rode the health care debacle to office were not old-style northeastern moderates. They were firebrand conservatives molded in the image of Rep. Newt Gingrich (R-Ga.) and his Contract with America. As a result, "[C]ongressional and public debates about government moved sharply to the right. Debates henceforth focused on *how* to reduce federal spending and balance the budget, whether to eliminate or merely sharply cut social programs. The focus of attention is no longer on how to create or even sustain national guarantees of security for the American citizenry" (Skocpol 1996, 7).

The campaign dialogue from the 2000 presidential election reflects the change. Democrat Al Gore was the deficit hawk, promising fiscal prudence over the expansion of government programs. Although the budget surpluses produced by the Clinton years provided great opportunities for activist government, Gore promised substantial tax cuts, albeit not as large as those proposed by George W. Bush. Though the health care problem increased unabated through the 1990s such that more than 40 million Americans had no medical insurance, Gore stopped well short of promising universal coverage, offering instead an incremental plan that would have initially covered only children. In fact, he painted his primary opponent, Senator Bill Bradley (D-N.J.), who advocated full coverage for all Americans, in much the same colors that the insurance industry painted Bill Clinton six years earlier.

For his part, Clinton never again proposed a government program of significant scope directed toward those near the bottom of the socioeconomic ladder. Instead, he seemed content to bolster his personal popularity by picking off some of the Republicans most politically popular ideas, such as supporting school uniforms, the V-chip to allow parents to block television shows with mature themes, and putting tens of thousands of new police on the streets.

Hoping to shore up his reelection prospects in 1996, Clinton also took his most decisive step, backing a welfare reform effort considered draconian by many on the political left. Although Clinton promised to "end welfare as we know it" in his first run for the White House, liberal Democrats surely did not think he would go as far as he did. The Welfare Reform Act of 1996 terminated AFDC as a federal program, with typically less generous state governments left in charge of deciding benefit levels. Among the provisions, able-bodied recipients of public assistance would be removed from the rolls after five years (individual states can mandate a shorter period if they choose) whether or not they had young children. Even single parents with children under six were required to have a 20-hour per week job within two years of receiving assistance, with the work requirement increasing to 30 hours per week in fiscal year 2000.[2] Clinton-style welfare reform can only be considered a serious assault on Lyndon Johnson's Great Society.

Likely thinking that public opinion had turned to the ideological right, Clinton himself turned to the right. A quick jog to the right would have been sufficient to bring policy in line with the low levels of trust that characterized this period. But as the economy grew, political trust increased through the rest of the 1990s. With conservatism constant and trust increasing, Clinton did not have to continue his move to the right. The leeway that higher levels of trust provide would have allowed him to pursue a more progressive public policy course during his second term. Since he and his advisors misinterpreted the change in public opinion as ideological, Clinton missed this golden opportunity.

CONCLUSION

I have shown in this chapter that a key reason for the failure of Bill Clinton's health care initiative was that people came to see him as too liberal on the issue. Of even greater consequence, people came to perceive him as too liberal because opponents of health care reform caused people to think about the Clinton plan in terms of how much they trusted the government. In 1994, but not in other years, those who were more distrustful perceived Clinton as more progovernment than those who were more trustful. While opponents also tried to engage people's ideology and their feelings about Clinton, they were only successful in engaging their distrust. With trust so low in 1994, however, this was sufficient to seal the fate of health care reform.

Providing further evidence for the theory presented throughout the book, trust was particularly influential among those who were relatively satisfied with the present medical insurance system. In 1994, political trust had a larger effect on this group's opinions than any other substantive variable. Also consistent with my theory, political trust had no effect among those who thought they might benefit from a new health care initiative. People only need to trust when they are making the sacrifices, not reaping the benefits.

These results are significant because Bill Clinton took a significant turn to the right after health care reform died in Congress. He had good reason to think that a right turn was a good idea, especially after his party lost control of both houses of Congress little more than a month after Sen. George Mitchell (D-Maine), the majority leader and major Clinton proponent on health care reform, declared the effort dead. There is no question that perceptions of Clinton's excesses on health care reform led to the sweeping Republican victory in 1994. As I have shown in this chapter, the main reason that people came to perceive Clinton as excessive on health care was because opponents of the reform effort activated the public's low levels of political trust.

CHAPTER EIGHT

Political Trust and the Future
of American Politics

IN THE MID-1960s, most Americans supported government programs designed to benefit those who were the object of racial discrimination and the less well off and believed the programs would work. According to a September 1964 poll taken by Gallup, twice as many Americans approved of the Civil Rights Act of 1964 as disapproved.[1] In August 1965, a solid plurality of Americans believed that the Johnson administration's War on Poverty would help wipe out poverty in the United States.[2] Americans trusted that the federal government would make judicious use of their tax dollars and be fair in its efforts to end discrimination between the races. Although support for redistributive spending and race-targeted policies was far from universal even in the Great Society years, it was sufficiently robust that Lyndon Johnson could pursue one of the most progressive public policy agendas in the nation's history.

Over the last 40 years, Americans have come to trust their government less, a change that has had far-reaching consequences. Most importantly, it has placed enormous constraints on progressives. In the aggregate, I have shown an impressive fit between how much Americans trust government and the liberalness of policy enacted by political elites. Politicians over the last 40 years have shown an uncanny ability to match how much government they give people with how much government people want, as manifested in their trust in government. Political trust provides a useful shorthand for elites because ordinary Americans have a much easier time articulating their feelings about government than their complicated and often contradictory ideological predispositions.

In addition, I have shown how this mechanism works on the individual level. Many liberal public policies require that the many make at least perceived sacrifices for the few. From the perspective of those making the sacrifices, moreover, such programs may carry perceived risk as well, such as when the sacrificers do not think highly of the beneficiaries of a government program. When the public does not trust that government will implement such policies efficiently or fairly, people will prefer that government not be involved. That is why political trust is only important in explaining the policy preferences of individuals who perceive that a policy requires a sacrifice or entails risk. This is important because programs that many perceive require sacrifice of them are the only ones for which public support has dried up considerably over the last 30 years.

Decreasing trust in government over the last two generations has undermined public support for federal programs like welfare, food stamps, and foreign aid, not to mention the entire range of race-targeted programs designed to make equality between the races a reality. Even though almost all Americans would like to rid the country of poverty and achieve greater racial equality, many do not trust the government enough to support the programs designed to realize these goals.

Even initiatives like health care reform, which are less obviously redistributive and certainly not as racialized, require trust in government to maintain support. At least this is true when opponents argue that reform will mean more government and will require sacrifice of those satisfied with the present system. Although a significant revival in political trust between 1994 and 2002 has put this issue back on the agenda for the 2004 presidential election, the failure of the Clinton reform effort suggests little or no change will occur in this or other similar policy areas unless the post-1994 increase in trust can be maintained. Given that both health care costs and the number of uninsured continue to grow, the fact that people will not support reform efforts that include government as a major player may become a problem of great consequence.

While most political commentators attribute the move to the right in American politics to a conservative turn in public opinion, this is not so. No matter the measure of ideology, I find no evidence of an ideological right turn. Moreover, if the public's ideological preferences had moved to the right, it would have caused increased support for limited government in almost all areas, something that has simply not occurred. While widespread public distrust favors the policy agenda of conservatives, it should not be confused with conservatism.

It should be troubling that at least part of the decline in political trust rests on misperceptions of political reality. While the federal government certainly wastes some percentage of tax dollars (the best estimates are below 5 percent), the percentage does not approach the average of nearly 50 percent that the public perceives. A relentlessly negative news media, which focuses far too heavily on the anomalous cases of waste, fraud, and abuse, bears much of the blame for this set of circumstance (see, for example, Patterson 1993; Capella and Jamieson 1997). Unfortunately, journalistic norms about what makes a good story ensure that this type of reporting will continue in the future.

More troubling is the degree to which Americans misperceive what government does, which also has a deleterious effect on political trust. Even though foreign aid and classic welfare programs combine to make up less than 10 percent of the federal budget, nearly half the public believes that one or the other is the single biggest item. Fewer than 15 percent of Americans correctly identify Social Security as the costliest federal program. These misperceptions have important consequences. I demonstrated in chapter 2 that, when asked to evaluate the federal government, people have on their mind "people on welfare," who receive relatively little from the government, but not "older people" or "the elderly," who receive quite a lot. Since most people would rather help older people than people on welfare, trust in government would increase markedly if the news media, in conjunction with political leaders, made a concerted effort to educate the public about what the government actually spends its money on. Support for redistributive, racial, and foreign aid programs would increase markedly as a result.

It is also interesting to note how inextricably political trust is tied to race. The results from chapter 2 and chapter 4 demonstrate that declining political trust in the late 1960s and early 1970s was, in part, the result of Americans' dissatisfaction with specific racial policies like busing and the government's more general efforts to integrate public schools and to provide aid to blacks. Thirty years later, trust and race are still joined, but in a different causal way. Now, in addition to low levels of trust undermining public support for race-targeted policies among whites, the results in chapter 5 demonstrate that antiblack stereotypes increase the negative effect that political trust has on whites' support for racialized redistributive programs, such as welfare and food stamps. If all whites thought well of African-Americans, political trust's effect on support for redistribution (and also the range of explicitly race targeted policies) would be minimal, which would increase support for these programs substantially in this environment with low political trust.

These results carry normative weight as well. In the case of poverty and race, for example, no institution or set of institutions other than the federal government has confronted these issues in a sustained and meaningful way. Perhaps in a perfect world, churches, volunteer organizations, and private enterprise could end poverty. But, in twenty-first-century America, none have the resources, or are willing to commit the resources, to even begin to play such a role. Similarly, some of the progress on school integration that was made between the 1960s and 1980s has been lost in the past decade. Although Americans express increasing concern about school integration, they are not particularly supportive of the federal government playing a role to ensure it. Since the recent return to segregation has been centered in the South and in the suburbs, it seems unlikely that any institution other than the federal government is positioned to confront this problem. Given that easily identifiable groups are disproportionately damaged by the present antiredistribution, anti–race policy political agenda— an agenda that has been fueled by declining political trust—the loss of political trust since the 1960s presents a threat to the representativeness of American political institutions.

POLITICAL TRUST AND POLITICAL ELITES

While this study has focused on mass behavior, declining political trust's effect on elite behavior is important, too, because it will further influence mass attitudes. When trust in government was high, progressives like John F. Kennedy, Lyndon Johnson, Hubert Humphrey, and Robert F. Kennedy were willing to lead public opinion on initiatives that benefited racial minorities and the poor. Their leadership was critically important. As Carmines and Stimson (1989) demonstrate, public support for civil rights increased most steeply *after* the Democratic Party signaled to its identifiers that they should support it. It is rare for the public to embrace a policy course that a solid core of elites does not first embrace.

As people's opinions of the federal government have soured, opinion leadership for progressive ideas has started to carry greater risk. Elites know that their support of government and its programs will draw the fire of opportunistic opponents. By advocating "big government" solutions, they will find themselves on the defensive, fighting an uphill battle to convince people that the institutions that they find untrustworthy are, in fact, trustworthy. Hence it is politically risky to tell Americans that government can play a constructive role in solving the country's social ills. Political elites too closely identified with government may pay for it with their jobs.

The rhetorical differences among Democrats of the last 40 years provide evidence that they realize these constraints. In his 1964 State of the Union Address, Johnson said, "This administration today, here and now, declares unconditional war on poverty in America." It is clear that the federal government will play a central role. In stark contrast, Jimmy Carter, in his 1978 State of the Union Address, said, "Government cannot eliminate poverty or provide a bountiful economy or reduce inflation or save our cities or cure illiteracy or provide energy." By arguing that government is incapable in a range of important tasks, Carter both reflects the extraordinary decline in public trust over the previous 15 years and reinforces it.

With hostility toward government and its social programs even higher in 1992 than it was in 1978, Bill Clinton ratcheted up the Democrats' rhetorical hostility during his first run for president when he promised to "end welfare as we know it," suggesting that he believed federal efforts to fight poverty had been a failure. Political elites on the left who once could be counted on to offer and support government efforts to aid those at the bottom of the socioeconomic ladder had made a decisive move toward extricating the federal government from the poverty-solutions business.

Such a rhetorical shift has profound consequences. Even people who might be inclined to support the federal government's efforts will have a hard time finding elites to legitimize their position. If elites fail to express confidence that government can solve social problems, then ordinary Americans will reflect this lack of confidence. The cycle is difficult, if not impossible, to reverse. As political elites perceive less public trust in government and less support for government programs, they talk less positively about them. In fact, they may find it politically advantageous to attack them. Other things being equal, public support will deteriorate further, as potential supporters find it increasingly hard to locate an elite voice to legitimize their belief that government can play an effective role. Indeed, even the most dynamic economy of the last 50 years followed by the galvanizing effect of the September 11 terrorist attacks only increased political trust to levels consistent with the Nixon years, not the Johnson years.

In that sense, declining political trust has both a direct and an indirect effect on support for progressive public policy. I have demonstrated that lower levels of trust directly undermine public support for specific programs. But the indirect effects might be equally important. Fearing reprisal from the voters, elites do not have the courage to advocate aggressive federal involvement in social policy. Since the public does not receive many strong messages in support of federal social programs, it will support them less as well. Absent some exogenous shock that has a sustained effect on the political system, both political trust and support for government-sponsored social programs are likely to remain low, at least relative to the Great Society years. Although the jury is still out on the post–September 11 environment, the consistent decreases in trust soon after a threat or military action has ended suggests that it will not provide such a sustained change.

WHAT THE RIGHT SHOULD LEARN

The findings presented in this book provide generally good news for those on the political right. With concerns about foreign threats so intense and feelings about the military so favorable in a post–September 11 world, it is clear that political elites can increase political trust simply by focusing on foreign affairs and domestic security. In 2001–2, survey researchers recorded a spike in political trust right after the terrorist attacks and again right after the passage of a congressional resolution authorizing war in Iraq. Political trust also increased markedly in the months after the first Gulf War got under way in early 1991 (Hetherington and Nelson 2003).

These higher levels of trust can be of political consequence as well. Conservative hawks can use this reservoir of good feeling toward government to press their aims abroad. In 2002, the NES asked respondents whether they favored or opposed going to war with Iraq. Among those with trust scores at or above the midpoint, 72 percent favored military intervention, compared with only 57 percent among those with trust scores below the midpoint. Moreover, it is not just the greater public anxiety caused by September 11 that explains this relationship. Back in 1990, just before the beginning of the first Gulf War, the NES asked Americans whether they thought that President George H. W. Bush's decision to send troops to the Persian Gulf was the right thing to do. Again, trust in government was important in understanding opinions. Of those scoring at or above the trust midpoint, 72 percent supported Bush's decision, while only 45 percent of those scoring below the trust midpoint did.[3] More trust increases support for military intervention.

The short-lived nature of the political trust rallies after September 11 and the second Gulf War suggests that the connection between trust and the welfare state will reemerge in the future, causing trust to drop again. Even so, a low-trust environment is still advantageous for those who want government to do less. While a conservative revolution would be better from the perspective of conservatives, a distrustful one is not bad. The Right has long fought against federal efforts at redistribution, has long argued for local control of racial matters, and has long opposed other efforts like the Clinton health care plan to extend the social safety net. Widespread political distrust aids these causes.

However, it is important that conservatives realize that political distrust does not advantage them in their efforts to trim all government programs. If they fail to connect government programs with the requirement that many people will have to make sacrifices for them, they will engage only conservatism. Since the majority of Americans are not conservative, such efforts will most often end in defeat.

The Republicans' mixed record after winning both houses of Congress in 1994 is instructive. In the months immediately after their victory, they did exceedingly well with the public, rendering President Clinton irrelevant in the eyes of some political commentators. They did this by implementing good-government reforms and railing against government excesses with a particular emphasis on redistribution. They lost their traction when they began to advocate things like eliminating the Department of Education, eliminating funding for the Corporation for Public Broadcasting, and slowing the growth of popular programs like Medicare. While former House Speaker Newt Gingrich (R-Ga.) and his followers surely saw their stock rise among conservative ideologues, the politically distrustful became concerned that the Republicans would cut programs that they or their parents would ultimately benefit from. Although most Americans do not want to spend tax money on welfare mothers, they do not mind paying for *Sesame Street*. As the outcome of the 1996 presidential election clearly demonstrated, the Republicans lost the battle when they moved to public policy areas on which distrust had no bearing.

George W. Bush's brand of "compassionate conservatism" provides a good mix for a politically distrustful electorate. Bush is certainly no friend of redistribution, having advocated and signed into law three sets of deep tax cuts that disproportionately favor upper-income Americans. These cuts greatly increased the size of the budget deficit, thereby reducing the amount of money government can spend on federal social programs. But he supports an increased government role in other areas where political trust has no effect on the public's policy preferences. For example, Bush proposes a larger federal role in education, especially in mandating that states impose achievement standards and testing regimes. In addition, rather than argue that Democrats are wrongheaded to advocate a prescription drug benefit for senior citizens, he proposed and actively worked to pass his own plan, albeit one less generous than Democratic initiatives and one that relies much more on the private insurance industry. In areas where the benefits of government programs will be distributed universally or nearly universally, Bush has generally supported at least the same amount of federal intervention. The one glaring exception is on the environment, an area where his administration received its most intense public criticism, especially in its early months.

A centerpiece of compassionate conservatism, Bush's faith-based initiative fits particularly well in a politically distrustful world. During the 2000 presidential campaign, Bush offered a plan to use federal money to help fund private, nonprofit, and church-based charitable services. Implicit in the plan is the notion that government has failed in its efforts to help those in need, whereas churches and community organizations have proven far more capable. Bush argues that, by using federal dollars, these types of organizations could increase their reach and effectiveness, doing more to solve social problems than government alone could.

The public has responded very favorably. Despite significant criticism from groups concerned about church and state separation, a solid majority of Americans continues to support faith-based antipoverty programs. For example, in July 2001, Opinion Dynamics asked a national sample the following question: "Based on what you know, do you support or oppose allowing government funds to be used by faith-based organizations, such as churches and synagogues, to deliver services to the needy?" Sixty-one percent of Americans registered support, and only 33 percent were opposed. Most Americans are so disenchanted with government that they are willing to move social services away from it, even if that might mean

violating constitutional restrictions on the relationship between government and religious organizations.

It is also important for conservatives to realize that their leadership prospects are, to some degree, limited by their own success. When people
perceive that government is doing its job well, political trust tends to rise.
But as I have shown throughout this book, increasing political trust increases the public's desire for liberal public policy, which is exactly the
opposite of what conservatives want to offer. This public demand for more
government is most often translated into an increase in the amount of
liberal public policy enacted by officeholders. Indeed, even Ronald Reagan
was forced to the left in his second term as political trust, and with it a
liberal policy mood, increased.

George W. Bush and the 107th and 108th Congresses have pressed a
very conservative policy course despite increasing levels of political trust.
This carries a certain amount of risk. These higher levels of trust have led
to more demand for government spending in many areas where Republicans are unlikely to want to spend. Between 2000 and 2002, the percentage of Americans who wanted to increase spending on federal welfare programs and on initiatives to aid blacks increased by 4 and 5 percentage
points, respectively. Even more dramatically, the percentage who wanted
cuts in these areas fell by 18 and 10 points, respectively. It is unclear
whether conservative Republicans can continue to dominate the national
government in the face of this opinion environment without a least a tack
to the left to satisfy the public. Furthermore, any efforts to privatize programs like Medicare and Social Security are clearly risky initiatives. Support for both programs as they are presently administered has remained
uniformly high over time. And even if political trust falls to never-before-
seen lows, it will have no bearing on support for these universal programs.
Should trust remain higher than it has through most of the last three
decades and should conservatives continue to pursue a diminished role
for the federal government, widespread voter anger and a backlash against
the Right could be the result.

What the Left Should Learn

If progressives desire a change in the post-Watergate policy direction, they
must start by finding a way to resuscitate the federal government's image.
Although Americans are not well informed about politics, they do know
enough to realize that the federal government is the root of federal programs. Hence, if they do not trust the federal government, they will want
to limit the number, size, and scope of its programs. The key for the Left,
then, is to take necessary steps to effect a sustained increase in political

trust. To do this, progressives must make efforts to redefine what government means in the public mind, have the courage to praise the things it does well, and fight the urge to criticize its unpopular elements for political gain. This is not to suggest a halt to criticism; such a strategy would neither be credible nor embody the progressive tradition. However, progressives should launch them judiciously because of the knowledge that such attacks will, at some level, undermine progressive policy goals in the future.

As I have noted, William Jacoby's (1994) work suggests that Americans do not associate government with many of the popular New Deal and Great Society programs. Instead they think about government in terms of unpopular redistributive programs like "welfare." This is because people wildly overestimate how much government spends on these programs. Those on the left must change this perception. The best way to do this is to redefine what "big government" means. The priming theory explicated in chapter 2 suggests that the criteria that people use to evaluate the government can change (see also Lock, Shapiro, and Jacobs 1999). The war on terrorism and the war in Iraq have recently imposed such a change. With a concerted effort, progressives can alter the criteria gradually over time onto the most favorable footing possible.[4]

If progressives provide an alternative vision of government as one that takes care of older Americans, protects the environment, builds highways, and the like, Americans will trust that version of government more than one that cannot police welfare cheats. By causing people to evaluate government on friendlier terms, political trust will increase, which, in turn, will increase support for social spending and race-targeted policies, too. In short, progressives need to change the information environment. They must provide some counterweight to, or perhaps even replace, Ronald Reagan's vision of government as something that spends most of its resources on welfare programs.

In addition, the increase in political trust caused by the greater emphasis on the military after September 11 should teach progressives that embracing patriotic symbols and a strong military is also helpful. Although social spending will have to compete with the military for scarce budgetary resources, connecting the government to the latter will almost certainly increase support for the former with the military now so popular. Indeed, the marked increase is support for various types of social spending recorded in the 2002 NES provides evidence. Progressive hawks have been few and far between since Senator Henry "Scoop" Jackson's (D-Wash.) death in 1983. Progressives would benefit from such a symbolic attachment.

Consistent with this approach, progressives must also raise the profile of government's successes. Government efforts to aid older Americans provide an excellent example. No one would argue that programs like Social Security and Medicare have been anything but stunningly successful in reducing poverty among the elderly. For example, a study performed by the Center on Budget and Policy Priorities found that 47.6 percent of older Americans in 1997 had incomes below the poverty line before factoring in their Social Security benefits. With Social Security benefits included, however, only 11.9 percent fell below the poverty line. In terms of numbers of people, the study estimated that Social Security lifted 11.4 million out of poverty.[5] Medicare has had similar benefits. Most consider these programs to be efficiently run, and they make up an enormous chunk of the budget. Proponents of an activist federal government should identify them as such. Moreover, such an effort would not be a cynical distortion. Progressives simply need to educate the public about what government really does. New Deal and Great Society programs actually did have some positive effects.

Recent Democrats have been too frightened to tell this story. Al Gore's presidential campaign provides a particularly fitting example. Recall that George W. Bush's most effective charge against the vice president was that Gore trusted the government while Bush trusted the people. It was a perfect chance for Gore to respond that he, too, trusted people more than government, but, of equal import, he believed that government accomplished a range of important tasks that almost all Americans support. In 1960, when Richard Nixon labeled John F. Kennedy a liberal, Kennedy defined what liberal meant by saying,

> If by "liberal" they mean, as they want people to believe, someone who is soft in his policies abroad, who is against local government, and who is unconcerned with the taxpayer's dollar, then the record of this party and its members demonstrate that we are not that kind of "liberal." . . . If by a "liberal" they mean someone who looks ahead and not behind, someone who welcomes new ideas without rigid reactions, someone who cares about the welfare of the people—their health, their housing, their schools, their jobs, their civil rights, and their civil liberties—someone who believes that we can break through the stalemate and suspicions that grip us in our policies abroad, if that is what they mean by a "liberal," then I'm proud to say that I'm a "liberal." (Dionne, November 1, 1988, A27)

Al Gore was no John Kennedy. Rather than defining what government meant to him, Gore attempted to counter Bush's charge by talking about how much more efficient he had made government through his Reinventing Government Commission. However, just as Republicans cannot argue that they care more than Democrats about the plight of the poor, Democrats cannot credibly argue that they are as opposed to government waste as Republicans are. Instead, the Left must associate government with popular, large-constituency programs in the public mind. The Right is much better at this kind of thing, successfully redefining global warming as climate change and Social Security privatization as personal retirement accounts. Regarding what government is, the Left needs to play the same game.

Shmuel Lock, Robert Shapiro, and Lawrence Jacobs (1999) provide some empirical evidence that positive affect toward government might increase if the criteria for evaluation changed. They asked a random sample of Americans, first, how much confidence they had in the federal government in general, and followed this question with a battery of questions about people's confidence in the government's ability to run several specific programs, such as the military, Social Security, the environment, Medicare, and aid to poor families. In addition, they asked a different random sample the same set of questions, but they started by asking people's assessments of the government's ability to run the specific programs and, after that, asked the question about confidence in the government in general.[6]

When people received the question on general confidence in government first, the distribution of responses basically mirrored the question on confidence in running programs for poor families. In other words, when people are not primed, they think about programs designed to benefit the poor when they evaluate the government in general. However, when respondents were first asked about specific programs like the military, Social Security, and the like, people rated the government in general more positively than when the general question was asked first.[7] This tendency was strongest among Democrats, which suggests the Left could shore up its core constituency by connecting government in general with popular government programs (see Lock, Shapiro, and Jacobs 1999 for more details).

Progressives must also be careful about the way they talk about Washington. Since most people tend not to trust government, gaining office and solidifying personal support by attacking it is a very attractive strategy. Indeed, even when Democrats controlled both houses of Congress, Democrats, including incumbents, were nearly as likely as Republicans to use antigovernment rhetoric in their Senate campaigns (Globetti and Hetherington 2000). Although such language clearly wins votes in a low-trust environment, progressives should fight the urge to use it unnecessarily because it comes with a cost. At a minimum, such antigovernment attacks solidify the conventional wisdom that government is untrustworthy, and they might even intensify already existing feelings of distrust. Jimmy Carter's experience should remind office-seekers that they will have little success making government work for them if they owe their election to running against it.

This is a particularly sticky situation for the Left during the period on which my analysis rests, with Republicans typically occupying the White House. Obviously, the out party must campaign against the government to convince voters that it should be the ruling party. Placing constant focus on government failures, however, will almost certainly cause people to trust government less. Hence, in their efforts to return to power, Democrats are necessarily forced to damage their future governing prospects. Their attacks will undermine political trust, which, in turn, will decrease the amount of liberal policy the public will want in the future. This certainly turned out to be the case for Jimmy Carter and Bill Clinton as they attempted to follow Republican presidents. When Clinton attempted to press a more liberal policy agenda in 1993–94 despite the low levels of political trust that he helped create, the voters repudiated his party in the next election. Perhaps worse, if the Republicans maintain control despite the attacks, they will face less public pressure to do things that conservatives would rather not do anyway. Indeed, such an environment may encourage the rollback of government services. Either way, Democrats face unique obstacles in an environment of low political trust.

Therefore, it is important for Democrats to tailor their attacks to target specific officeholders when possible. The late 1990s taught us that the public's perception of the president's trustworthiness and the government's trustworthiness do not necessarily move in tandem. As personal attacks on Bill Clinton's character intensified during his second term, the public came to see him as personally less trustworthy. At the same time, however, the nation's strong performance, particularly on economic matters, caused trust in government to increase. To the extent that the Democratic presidential hopefuls in 2004 can target President Bush's personal credibility and his personal policy decisions, those on the left will be better off. While such attacks will almost surely damage trust in government to some degree, the damage will be less than if people come to think that both the Republican president and the government as a whole cannot be trusted.[8]

Other avenues might increase political trust as well. Supporting good-government initiatives like campaign finance reform make good sense. At least part of the public's antipathy toward government is born of concern that it is run for the benefit of special interests or, worse, the personal interests of officeholders rather than ordinary people (Hibbing and Theiss-Morse 2002). Measures that can change this perception should increase political trust. Although many argue that the elimination of soft money under the McCain-Feingold campaign finance reform act will damage the Democrats electorally, the long-term benefits caused by increasing political trust should eventually offset the short-run costs. Virginia Chanley, Thomas Rudolph, and Wendy Rahn (2000) demonstrate that increasing trust will cause a more liberal policy mood. As Robert Erikson, Michael MacKuen, and James Stimson (2002) demonstrate, a more liberal policy mood will cause more progressives to be elected. And as I have shown in chapter 3, the combination of high political trust, a liberal policy mood, and progressives in the House and Senate explains almost all the variance in the amount of liberal public policy implemented over time. Trust is the catalyst. Increasing it will have the largest effect on increasing all the others.

The need for progressives to increase public trust in government is particularly strong given the demographic changes occurring in the United States because they present a unique opportunity. According to the 2000 census, the nation's fastest-growing racial and ethnic groups are Latinos and Asian-Americans. In addition to growing through a steady stream of immigration, both have higher birthrates than either whites or African-Americans. In fact, in 2003, Latinos passed African-Americans as the largest minority group in the United States. Since both Latinos and Asians now identify disproportionately with the Democratic Party, Democrats have an opportunity to dominate the next generation of American politics (Judis and Teixeira 2002).

The recent political history of California provides evidence of the opportunity at hand. From the early 1980s to the mid-1990s, Republicans did very well with Asian voters and were making significant inroads with Latinos, especially on social issues like abortion and school prayer. As a result, Republicans regularly dominated statewide elections, winning four straight gubernatorial races between 1982 and 1994. However, the anti-immigrant campaign waged by Republican governor Pete Wilson during the early 1990s, particularly his championing of Proposition 187, which eliminated a range of government services for legal and illegal immigrants, undermined Republicans' support from these minority groups. With Latinos and Asian-Americans making up an increasingly large part of California's population, no Republican has won a major statewide office since the Proposition 187 fight, with the exception of Arnold Schwarzenegger's quirky 2003 recall victory. Richard Nixon's and Ronald Reagan's home state has become a safe Democratic haven in presidential elections as well.

Unless conservatives can make significant inroads with racial minorities, the Democrats' electoral fortunes should improve as the non-Anglo population grows. The increasing non-Cuban Latino population in Florida will make it harder for Republicans to win there in the future. If California and New York continue to vote for Democrats, three of the four largest states may move largely beyond Republican control. In addition, the immigration of both Latinos and Asians into many Deep South states is worth watching. States like Louisiana, Georgia, and Texas might not be the Republican locks on the presidential level that they seem today.

But will more progressive public policy necessarily follow from Democratic electoral victories? If a large percentage of Americans continue to distrust the federal government, Democrats will not be able to accomplish much once in office. Recall that Bill Clinton came to Washington with solid Democratic pluralities in the electorate and in both houses of Congress, but his most lasting policy legacy will be welfare reform rather than comprehensive health care reform. A distrustful public defeated the latter but embraced the former, something that will surely repeat itself if people's feelings about the federal government do not improve. Without a strongly progressive spirit, which is impossible to maintain without significant public trust in government, the Democratic Party will look increasingly like the Rockefeller wing of the Republican Party in the 1960s. In fact, the Rockefeller Republicans might start to look relatively more progressive.

POLITICAL TRUST AND REPRESENTATION

The notion that people stand by the government even when it does not act in accordance with their self-interest or their policy preferences is particularly important to political minorities and those with limited resources. As E. E. Schattschneider (1960) has famously noted, the pressure group system sings with a decidedly upper-class accent, so the government will be particularly responsive to those with greater means. But in a democracy, the government should ideally represent all interests, not just well-heeled ones. For Schattschneider, strong political parties were important to provide voice to those who were not adequately represented by the pressure group system because parties were better able than any other political institution to socialize, or widen, the scope of conflict. If conflicts between people or interests remain private, the more powerful will always win the battles. For example, if a fistfight between Mike Tyson and me remained private, I would certainly lose. But if I could expand the scope of conflict to bring Lennox Lewis to fight on my behalf, I might fare better. Only when the scope of conflict is widened to include more people or interests can the less powerful succeed. The federal government is the ultimate arena for conflict socialization. If people do not trust it, few conflicts will be broadened to this level, which will be most damaging to the political interests of the weak.

An excellent illustration of Schattschneider in practice, and the importance of political trust along with it, is the civil rights movement. Following Reconstruction, the balance of power between whites and blacks in the states of the former Confederacy was one-sided. In terms of both raw numbers and political clout, whites could dominate blacks in any private conflict. Civil rights leaders achieved success by widening the scope of conflict to include northern activists, media elites, the Democratic Party, and, ultimately, the federal government. Only when the conflict was socialized, taking political decisions out of the hands of racist southern state governments and placing them into the hands of the federal government, did conditions for blacks change markedly.

Viewed in this light, widespread distrust of the federal government is problematic. At the root of Schattschneider's reasoning is that minority interests can use the federal government to help redress concerns. The results presented in this book suggest that a lack of public trust in government makes the federal government a less viable option. If the federal government is not a viable option, what institution will perform its role? Regarding race, for example, the federal government has done more to ensure fair outcomes for racial minorities than any other institution. Had the power of the federal government not been brought to bear on civil rights issues, it is unclear what other social force might have intervened to end segregation and obstacles to voting.

This is a truly troubling set of facts. What would have happened to the civil rights movement had political trust in the 1950s and 1960s been mired at levels like those of the late 1970s or the early 1990s? The federal courts might have still produced decisions like *Brown v. Board of Education* to end school segregation, but without Congress passing and the president signing the Civil Rights Act of 1964, no mechanism would have been in place to enforce the Court's decision. In fact, in 1963, fully nine years after the *Brown* decision, Alabama public schools were still completely segregated (Frankenberg, Lee, and Orfield 2003). Whites are much more likely to support race-targeted policies when they trust the government more, and their support affects what policymakers do. All this suggests that had the civil rights movement taken place when political trust was low, it would have been significantly less successful.

In a society comprised of majorities and minorities, it is impossible to represent minority interests fairly unless majorities are willing to make sacrifices for minorities when their interests do not overlap. Trust in governing authorities makes it easier for majorities to support such sacrifices. Even if the sacrifice is not real, only perceived, as is the case for most whites and affirmative action (Bowen and Bok 1998), trust in government helps build support for initiatives that assist minority interests. In fact, how much people trust the government is important not just when controversial policies such as affirmative action are at issue. It is important even when whites are deciding whether the federal government should ensure school integration and equal treatment in hiring for blacks.

The findings presented throughout this book reflect how determinative political distrust is in the current political climate. Though skepticism toward politics and politicians has always been a part of American political culture, it seems to have overwhelmed that culture today. With the news media fixated on government ineptitude and malevolence, the candidates themselves attacking Washington, and icons of popular culture lampooning political actors on a daily basis, citizens have come to evaluate political objects through this lens. Such attitudes undermine the government's ability to deal with poverty, protect minority rights, and extend the social safety net to areas that might require sacrifices of some Americans, such as health care.

Lyndon Johnson produced the Great Society in the mid-1960s, and Bill Clinton, a man in so many ways similar to Johnson, began to dismantle it in the mid-1990s. The most compelling explanation for this change in policy course is that Americans trusted the government when Johnson was president, but they no longer did when Clinton was in office. That change in public opinion has made created a much different country.

Notes

1. Stimson makes these data available on his website at http://www.unc.edu/~jstimson/heats.htm. His entries are the mean score of all available polls taken on each day of the campaign.

2. I thank Daron Shaw, a Bush campaign operative and a University of Texas political scientist, for his candor in talking about the campaign. This line of attack meshed nicely with the Bush campaign's attack on Gore's seeming inability to tell the truth. In that sense, it helped frame the race both in terms of Gore's personal untrustworthiness and the government's general untrustworthiness. The ad's timing could hardly have been better either. Soon after its debut, the accuracy of several Gore anecdotes came into question, including his claim that Florida classrooms were so overcrowded that students had to stand and that the same prescription medication for his mother-in-law cost several times as much as for his dog. Neither story was exactly true.

3. These data were taken from the 2000 National Election Study.

4. Dukakis turned a 16-point lead coming out of the Democratic convention into a near landslide defeat within three months.

5. One might suggest Richard Nixon as a successful former vice president, but he had been out of Washington for eight years before he won in 1968. Furthermore, he won, in part, because he ran an anti-Washington campaign.

6. It is also interesting to note that Bill Clinton's party lost control of both the House and Senate for the first time since the 1950s just two months after the defeat of health care reform. Among the casualties was none other than Harris Wofford.

7. As evidence, consider how long it took left-leaning politicians to criticize Sen. Trent Lott's (R-Miss.) racially insensitive comments at Sen. Strom Thurmond's (R-S.C.) one-hundredth-birthday party. Lott made his comments on a Thursday, and it took until the following Wednesday for the *New York Times* to run a story about it, largely because no one had had the courage to criticize Lott. When the *Times* finally did run a story about it, it appeared on page 28.

8. The poll was conducted from July 20 through September 25, 1995, by the *Washington Post*, Harvard University, and the Henry J. Kaiser Family Foundation.

9. Some might argue that Clinton's turn to the right actually caused the increase in political trust to occur. This is probably true to some degree, at least in the short run. Since trust was low in the early to middle 1990s, my theory suggests that people would have wanted less government. Clinton's conservative turn, then, might have increased trust, which, in turn, increased the public's appetite for more liberal public policy. It is not the case, however, that more conservative public policy always leads to more political trust, a point I take up in greater detail in chapter 3.

CHAPTER TWO

1. Indeed, the imperatives about participation for the politically trustful and distrustful are ambiguous. If one trusts, he or she might feel more loyalty to the political system and hence participate. Alternatively, that person might express his or her satisfaction with the political system by abstaining. Similarly, the distrustful person might feel the greatest need to participate to change the present state of affairs, or he or she might feel so bad about the system that abstention is the only solution. In fact, people with different psychological makeups likely react to these four situations in different ways. Hence we should find no relationship between political trust and political participation.

2. The last two times ABC News asked this question, the mean response was 47 cents in April 2002 and 46 cents in April 2000.

3. If one eliminates the local government option, almost all who would have chosen it choose state government instead. The percentage choosing the federal government remains constant (see Blendon et al. 1997).

4. Other dimensions might include their leadership qualities, their competence, and their compassion.

5. For a discussion of the problems associated with direct democracy, see Broder 2000.

6. Johnson was also fond of referring to the Supreme Court as "his Supreme Court" and the armed forces as "his military."

7. As reported in Paul Krugman's June 13, 2003, op-ed "Some Crazy Guy," *New York Times*, A33.

8. Although beyond the scope of this book, it is perhaps not surprising in this environment that the distribution of income has become increasingly uneven over the last 40 years as people lost trust in the federal government. Evening the economic playing field would require progressive tax policy, which might also be unpalatable to those lacking political trust.

9. One exception is that African-Americans were significantly less trustful of government than whites during the Nixon years. Since then, however, whites and African-Americans' mean trust score has been within five percentage points. Whites express more trust than blacks when a Republican is president, and blacks express more trust than whites when a Democrat is president.

10. There is evidence that 1964 might have been the high-water mark for trust since at least 1958. Although this exact battery of questions was first asked in 1964, several of the questions debuted in 1958. Of those that were asked in both years, all distributions were more trustful in 1964.

11. The difference in means is statistically significant for 1964 and 1966, and approaches significance in 1968 and 1970.

12. Although retrospective economic evaluations were very strong in both 1984 and 1996 as well, the mean for the five-point measure was statistically higher in 1998 than in either 1984 or 1996 ($p < .001$).

13. This poll was taken by National Public Radio, the Kaiser Family Foundation, and the John F. Kennedy School from May 26 to June 25, 2000.

14. Fifteen percent in a Harvard University–Kaiser Family Foundation poll taken just before the 1994 midterm election correctly identified Social Security as the largest federal program, but this is still a very low number.

15. The poll was taken between April 1 and April 4, 1995, by CBS News–*New York Times*.

16. This poll was taken by Schulman, Ronca, and Bucavalas of 3,246 Americans between April 4 and May 20, 2002. The research was funded by Pew Charitable Trusts.

17. If there were a feeling thermometer that allowed me to tap attitudes toward foreign governments, it would surely be predictive of people's feelings about the federal government as well.

18. The other three items in the NES's trust in government index are rarely asked by other survey organizations. However, changes in them tend to covary closely with changes in the standard trust item tracked in this section. For example, the percentage of trusting responses to each of the four items increased by between 10 and 12 percentage points between the 2000 and the 2002 NES. If all the questions were asked through all these surveys, the results would almost certainly mirror those presented here.

19. As evidence, there is a negative correlation between the number of days after the election a respondent took the NES survey and political trust. While the association is weak, it is suggestive that people were dissatisfied with the process and connected it to their feelings about government. This is particularly compelling given the fact that there is a statistically significant difference in means for political trust between people interviewed before the Florida Supreme Court ruled that the recount could go forward and after this decision, with opinion turning more negative.

20. Had ABC News prefaced the question by referencing redistributive programs in addition to health care, Social Security, and education, it is likely that a percentage even closer to 29 percent would have expressed trust in government.

21. Unfortunately, in February 2003 Gallup did not ask the question on the most important problem.

22. Robin Toner, "Trust in the Military Heightens among Baby Boomers' Children," *New York Times*, May 27, 2003, A1.

23. The first quartile in the distribution is .06 and the third quartile is .09.

24. In addition, a replication of the regression model presented in table 2.2 using 2002 data from the NES reveals that the effect of feelings about the military on feelings about the federal government was nearly three times larger than in 1996 and 2000. It is also noteworthy that the "people on welfare" thermometer was not a significant predictor of feelings about the federal government in 2002. With feelings about the military playing an enhanced role and people's feelings about welfare recipients playing a diminished role, it is little wonder than the mean score on the federal government feeling thermometer increased by more than five degrees between 2000 and 2002.

25. These data were taken from a Gallup Organization news release dated July 14, 2003, titled "A Turning Point for Consumer Perceptions," authored by Dennis Jacobe.

CHAPTER THREE

1. From the Funk and Wagnals *1965 Yearbook*, 17.

2. When one considers where the Republicans did well, it seems unlikely that 2002 foreshadows a fundamental shift of any sort. House elections were remarkably uncompetitive, with fewer than 10 percent of seats decided by less than 10 percentage points. In the Senate, most of the narrow Republican victories, which contributed to their reassuming the majority, took place in states that Bush won handily two years before. Indeed, it hardly seems surprising that a Republican Senate candidate might have won in North Carolina, Texas, New Hampshire, Colorado, Georgia, or South Carolina.

3. This variation in people's desire for more government tracks closely with changes in political trust over the same period. In fact, the correlation between the percentage of Americans who want more services and spending and mean political trust lagged by one election study is .76 ($p < .01$), suggesting that, as trust goes up, people's desire for more government in general follows, and vice versa.

4. Finding identical question wording is impossible, but, when asked by Harris on May 23, 2001, "Based on what you have read or heard, do you favor or oppose the tax cut plan before Congress?" 49 percent said they favored it. In May 1981, 64 percent told NBC News–Associated Press that they favored "cutting federal income tax rates by 10 percent a year for each of the next three years." Bush's second major tax cut passed in May 2003 was even less popular. A Harris poll conducted on May 21 found that only 45 percent favored "George W. Bush's tax cut plan."

5. The poll was taken between April 10 and 13, 2003, by Quinnipiac University Polling Institute.

6. The NES started to ask the conservatism question in 1972.

7. In fact, using survey data from 1972–2002, I find that the correlations between political trust lagged by one election study and the percentage of Americans who want to cut spending on welfare, food stamps, and assistance to blacks are −.90, −.74, and −.73 respectively. That is, in the aggregate, more political trust leads to less desire to cut these programs. These questions have been asked irregularly, so the number of cases is quite small for each. Even so, these correlations are all statistically significant at 95 percent confidence.

8. The *Washington Post* replicated this study using a national sample in the late 1990s and got basically the same distribution of opinion.

9. Carmines and Stimson use the terms "easy" and "hard" issues to make basically the same distinction.

10. Pew Foundation 2000.

11. Richard Fenno (1978) finds that individual members of Congress attempt to build constituent trust for just this reason. For example, "Congressman G's presentation of self builds the trust necessary to 'sell' his explanations at home and, hence, to cast votes more liberal than his district in Washington" (Fenno 1978, 154).

12. The measure of trust used here and in most of the aggregate-level figures throughout the book is the mean score of the standard trust (Trust) item. In several off-year elections, the NES failed to ask two or more of the four items that

make up the index. If I impute the means for the unasked questions based on the questions that were asked, I can compute an imputed index. This imputed index is highly correlated over time with the single trust measure ($r = .98$). Substituting one for the other makes no substantive difference to any of the findings presented throughout the book.

13. I wish to thank Bob Erikson for graciously providing these data, updating them for me, and guiding me in using them properly.

14. Since I only have trust data back to 1964, I lose the six bienniums between 1952 and 1964, which accounts for the smaller number of cases.

15. As Erikson, MacKuen, and Stimson (2002) also show, change in policy also reduces mathematically to Laws. The difference between the first pair of regressions and the third is the absence of the lagged dependent variable in the latter pair.

16. The sign on the correlation differs by which party controls the White House. Given that trust mirrors the party of the president to some degree, the sign is positive when Republicans are in control and negative when Democrats are in control.

CHAPTER FOUR

1. To make certain that these estimates do not suffer from specification bias, I estimate fully specified models for trust and the racial policies.

2. An insignificant effect might also indicate that the true lag differs from the lag between the two interviews.

3. The NES also asked questions about segregation, school integration, and public accommodations, but only in 1972 and 1976. Since four years is a very long lag, I only present the results for the aid to blacks and support for busing items.

CHAPTER FIVE

1. Since the NES did not ask the welfare question in 1984, this entry is necessarily an estimate. In the four studies that the NES asked about both food stamps and welfare programs (1992, 1994, 1996, 2000), people were, on average, 9.6 percentage points more likely to say they wanted to cut spending on the program. Hence, to estimate the percentage that wanted to cut welfare spending, I added 9.6 percentage points to the 33 percent who reported that they wanted to cut spending on food stamps in 1984. For figure 5.1, I also carry out this imputation for 1986, 1988, and 1990. If I compute the correlation between lagged political trust and the percentage favoring welfare spending cuts without these imputed values, the correlation is an even stronger $-.92$.

2. Robert Pear, "Anecdotes and the Impact They've Had on Policy," *New York Times*, December 27, 1983, B6.

3. Pear, "Anecdotes."

4. "Low Grades" 1998.

5. The survey was conducted between December 27 and December 29, 1994, by the Harvard University School of Public Health's Department of Health Policy and Management and the Kaiser Family Foundation.

6. People who live in districts with good schools will benefit indirectly from more federal spending in that it might increase their property values. In that sense, defining the beneficiary group is really quite difficult. If I do find significant results even with this slippage, they are all the more impressive.

7. I should also note that previous research has sometimes treated ideology and partisanship as endogenous to spending preferences (Rhodebeck 1993; see also Franklin 1984). The effect of the latter variables on the former, however, is substantially larger than the reverse. Since the degree of simultaneity is marginal, the estimated effects of a recursive model should be relatively accurate. To the degree that there is a discrepancy, the recursive model will likely give greater weight to ideology and partisanship at the expense of other variables. Should trust prove to be a significant predictor of spending preferences under these circumstances, the result is all the more impressive.

8. Some might suggest that trust and spending preferences cause each other rather than trust causing spending preferences. If this were the case, it would require a much more complicated statistical model. Theoretically, however, it is more plausible that political trust, an attitude primed constantly by the media, causes a person to form his or her spending preferences than vice versa. Empirically, I have shown elsewhere (Hetherington 1997; Hetherington and Globetti 2002) that spending preferences have no effect on trust once other relevant variables are taken into account. Furthermore, Chanley, Rudolph, and Rahn (2000) show that trust is a cause of policy mood, but not vice versa. Hence I estimate models that treat political trust as an explanatory, not a dependent, variable.

9. I should note that trust does have a significant effect on this item. Given that the beneficiary group is not clear, it is plausible to think that many might view spending in this area as requiring a sacrifice from which they might not benefit.

10. It is worth noting that opponents of environmental spending have begun to pitch the issue as a trade-off between jobs and the environment. If this choice begins to structure opinions, political trust might conceivably become important among those with jobs that are affected by the environmental movement, such as coal mining and logging.

11. The results are substantively equivalent if I use ordered logit or probit instead.

12. In 1994, there was a small spike in conservatism and in hostility toward spending on the environment. The former is likely the cause of the latter.

13. It is worth noting that people feel significantly better about "poor people" than they do "welfare recipients" (Gilens 1999).

14. The graphs for spending on welfare and food stamps follow the same general pattern, although the results are not quite as striking.

CHAPTER SIX

1. It is, however, clear that some people are lying. For example, whites are much more likely to provide racially tolerant responses to black than white interviewers (Kinder and Sanders 1996). In addition, people who say they do not have an opinion about racial policies most often are opposed to them (Berinsky 1999).

2. NES Cumulative File, 1948–2000.

3. NES Cumulative File, 1948–2000.

4. It is not that Americans abhor all preferences. There is little opposition to providing preferences to legacies, athletes, or students from different parts of the country. Racial preferences are unique in that regard.

5. See various NES studies taken between 1986 and 2000.

6. See 2002 NES, variable number 025125.

7. This essay is included in a more complete report called *Condition of Education, 1997*, National Center for Education Statistics, 97–991.

8. See "Gallup Poll Topics: Education," poll conducted August 1999, available at Gallup.com website.

9. According to the NES Cumulative File, the percentage of white nonsoutherners who supported a federal role in school integration dropped from 45.9 percent in 1970 to 20.7 percent in 1976. Of course, this also suggests an ambiguity in the direction of causality between political trust and support for a federal role in school integration during this middle period. There is little doubt that nonsoutherners' concern about federal integration initiatives undermined their political trust, although it is likely that the two attitudes were simultaneously related during this period.

10. If I confine the analysis to include only white respondents because they are more inclined to perceive that they are making a sacrifice, the correlation jumps to .85.

11. This correlation would surely be even stronger if a trust reading were available for 1962. It is worth noting that the data for several years in the NES Cumulative File are wrong for the question on fair treatment in jobs. The problems are particularly profound for 1986 and 1988. In addition, the correlation between lagged political trust and the percentage of whites that want the government to provide more aid to blacks is a statistically significant .52.

12. While much research suggests that the costs to whites are largely psychological and not material, this does not minimize the costs in the minds of most white Americans. This is evidenced by the success of political advertisements like Jesse Helms's "White Hands" ad and George H. W. Bush's ability to rouse public support for himself by his repeated vetoes of affirmative action legislation, which he termed a "quota bill."

13. The results are only stronger when I use ordered probit to estimate the models (see Hetherington and Globetti 2002).

14. Political trust has no effect on whites' support for racial equality in principle, which should not be surprising given that such support requires no tangible or perceived sacrifice.

15. None of the other items provides such an obvious test. For example, with affirmative action in hiring, it is hard to know who would feel most threatened. Working-class people might perceive the stakes are highest for them, but middle- and upper-middle-income people may perceive a strong threat as well. Hence I confine this analysis to education quotas.

16. These results replicate using the 1990 data as well (see Hetherington and Globetti 2002).

17. I use the 1992 NES data because all six of the racial policy items were asked in this survey and, with George H. W. Bush recently defeated by Bill Clinton, the trust measure is least likely sullied by partisan predispositions.

CHAPTER SEVEN

1. To create this figure, I multiplied each of the variables' parameter estimates by their sample mean.
2. Single parents who could not find care for their children under six were exempt. And states could also exempt single parents with children under one if they chose to do so.

CHAPTER EIGHT

1. The poll was taken in September 1964 by the Gallup Organization and was published in a document called *Hopes and Fears*.
2. This poll was taken by Opinion Research Corporation between August 2 and September 3, 1965. Forty-eight percent believed that the War on Poverty would "help wipe out poverty" in the United States. Only 37 percent thought that it wouldn't help much.
3. Both differences in proportions are statistically significant ($p < .001$). Moreover, in logistic regression models with support for the war in Iraq as the dependent variable and political trust, party identification, and liberal conservative self-placement on the right-hand side, political trust continues to have a statistically significant effect in both years.
4. While some might argue that changing the criteria that people are evaluating government on might break the link between political trust and support for social welfare programs, this is not the case. If I replicate the spending preferences models as closely as is possible using 2002 data, political trust is still a significant predictor of these preferences.
5. Press release from the Center on Budget and Policy Priorities entitled "Social Security Reduces Proportion of Elderly Who Are Poor from Nearly One in Two to Less Than One in Eight," April 8, 1999.
6. Unfortunately, they did not use the standard question on trust in government. However, it seems likely that the results reported would be similar if they had used the trust question rather than the confidence question.
7. I expect that the difference would have been even larger had programs for poor people either not been included on the list or, at a minimum, not been asked last in the list.
8. Obviously, Republicans, who generally support less government involvement, need to worry much less about the nature of their attacks. In fact, Fried and Harris (2001) note that Republicans in the late 1980s and early 1990s began to run their campaigns explicitly against Congress as an institution in an effort to discredit the institution, in addition to specific members of Congress. Their victory in 1994 suggests the potency of such institutional attacks when they come from the right.

References

Abramson, Paul R. 1983. *Political Attitudes in America: Formation and Change.* San Francisco: W. H. Freeman.

Anderson, Christopher J., and Andrew LoTempio. 2002. "Winning, Losing, and Political Trust in America." *British Journal of Political Science* 32 (2):335–51.

Ansolabehere, Stephen, and Shanto Iyengar. 1995. *Going Negative: How Attack Ads Shrink and Polarize the Electorate.* New York: Free Press.

Arrow, Kenneth Joseph. 1963. *Social Choice and Individual Values.* New Haven: Yale University Press.

Barnard, Chester I. 1958. *The Functions of the Executive.* Cambridge: Harvard University Press.

Berinsky, Adam. 1999. "Two Faces of Public Opinion." *American Journal of Political Science* 43:1209–30.

Bishop, George F., Robert W. Oldendick, Alfred J. Tuchfarber, and Stephen E. Bennett. 1980. "Pseudo-opinions on Public Affairs." *Public Opinion Quarterly* 44:198–209.

Blendon, Robert J., John M. Benson, Richard Morin, Drew E. Altman, Mollyann Brodie, Mario Brossard, and Matt James. 1997. "Changing Attitudes in America." In *Why People Don't Trust Government*, ed. Joseph S. Nye, Philip D. Zelikow, and David C. King. Cambridge: Harvard University Press.

Bobo, Lawrence. 1983. "Whites' Opposition to Busing: Symbolic Racism or Realistic Group Conflict." *Journal of Personality and Social Psychology* 45:1196–1210.

———. 1988. "Group Conflict, Prejudice, and the Paradox of Contemporary Racism." In *Eliminating Racism: Profiles in Controversy*, ed. Phyllis A. Katz and Dalmas A. Taylor. New York: Plenum Press.

Bobo, Lawrence, and James R. Kluegel. 1993. "Opposition to Race-Targeting: Self-Interest, Stratification Ideology, or Racial Attitudes?" *American Sociological Review* 58:443–64.

Bok, Derek. 1997. "Measuring the Performance of Government." In *Why People Don't Trust Government*, ed. Joseph S. Nye, Philip. D. Zelikow, and David C. King. Cambridge: Harvard University Press.

Bowen, William G., and Derek Curtis Bok. 1998. *The Shape of the River: Long-Term Consequences of Considering Race in College and University Admissions.* Princeton, N.J.: Princeton University Press.

Broder, David S. 2000. *Democracy Derailed: Initiative Campaigns and the Power of Money.* New York: Harcourt.

Brody, Richard A. 1991. *Assessing the President: The Media, Elite Opinion, and Public Support.* Stanford, Calif.: Stanford University Press.

Burnham, Walter Dean. 1970. *Critical Elections and the Mainsprings of American Politics.* New York: Norton.

Campbell, Angus, Philip Converse, Warren Miller, and Donald Stokes. 1960. *The American Voter.* New York: Wiley.

Cappella, Joseph N., and Kathleen Hall Jamieson. 1997. *Spiral of Cynicism: The Press and the Public Good*. New York: Oxford University Press.

Carmines, Edward G., and James A. Stimson. 1989. *Issue Evolution: Race and the Transformation of American Politics*. Princeton, N.J.: Princeton University Press.

Chanley, Virginia A., Thomas J. Rudolph, and Wendy M. Rahn. 2000. "The Origins and Consequences of Public Trust in Government: A Time Series Analysis." *Public Opinion Quarterly* 64:239–56.

Citrin, Jack. 1974. "Comment: The Political Relevance of Trust in Government." *American Political Science Review* 68:973–88.

Citrin, Jack, and Donald Philip Green. 1986. "Presidential Leadership and the Resurgence of Trust in Government." *British Journal of Political Science* 16:431–53.

Coleman, James S. 1990. *Foundations of Social Theory*. Cambridge: Harvard University Press.

Converse, Philip E. 1964. "The Nature of Belief Systems in Mass Publics." In *Ideology and Discontent*, ed. David Apter. New York: Free Press.

Converse, Philip E., and Gregory B. Markus. 1979. "Plus ca change. . . : The New CPS Election Study Panel." *American Political Science Review* 73:32–49.

Dahl, Robert Alan. 1956. *A Preface to Democratic Theory*. Chicago: University of Chicago Press.

Delli Carpini, Michael X., and Scott Keeter. 1996. *What Americans Know about Politics and Why It Matters*. New Haven: Yale University Press.

Dionne, E. J. 1988. "Describing Liberalism." *New York Times*, November 1, A27.

Easton, David. 1965. *A Systems Analysis of Political Life*. New York: Wiley.

———. 1975. "A Re-assessment of the Concept of Political Support." *British Journal of Political Science* 5:435–57.

Elliot, Euel, Barry J. Seldon, and James Regens. 1997. "Political and Economic Determinants of Individuals' Support for Environmental Spending." *Journal of Environmental Management* 51:15–27.

Erikson, Robert S., Michael B. MacKuen, and James A. Stimson. 2002. *The Macro Polity*. New York: Cambridge University Press.

Erikson, Robert S., Gerald C. Wright, and John P. McIver. 1993. *Statehouse Democracy: Public Opinion and Policy in the American States*. New York: Cambridge University Press.

Evans, A. S. 1992. "Black Middle Classes: The Outlook of a New Generation." *International Journal of Politics, Culture, and Society* 6:207–23.

Feldman, Stanley. 1983. "The Measurement and Meaning of Political Trust." *Political Methodology* 9:341–54.

Fenno, Richard F. 1978. *Home Style: House Members in Their Districts*. Boston: Little, Brown.

Finkel, Steven E., and John G. Geer. 1998. "A Spot Check: Casting Doubt on the Demobilizing Effect of Attack Advertising." *American Journal of Political Science* 42:573–95.

Fiorina, Morris P. 1981. *Retrospective Voting in American National Elections*. New Haven: Yale University Press.

Firebaugh, Glenn, and Kenneth E. Davis. 1988. "Trends in Anti-black Prejudice, 1972–1984: Region and Cohort Effects." *American Journal of Sociology* 94:251–72.

Frankenberg, Erica, Chungmei Lee, and Gary Orfield. 2003. "A Multiracial Society with Segregated Schools: Are We Losing the Dream?" Cambridge: Harvard University Civil Rights Project.

Franklin, Charles H. 1984. "Issue Preferences, Socialization, and the Evolution of Party Identification." *American Journal of Political Science* 28:459–78.

Free, Lloyd A., and Hadley Cantril. 1967. *The Political Beliefs of Americans*. New Brunswick, N.J.: Rutgers University Press.

Freedman, Paul, and Ken Goldstein. 1999. "Measuring Media Exposure and the Effects of Negative Campaign Ads." *American Journal of Political Science* 43:1189–1208.

Fried, Amy, and Douglas B. Harris. 2001. "On Red Capes and Charging Bulls: How and Why Conservative Politicians and Interest Groups Promoted Public Anger." In *What Is It about Government That Americans Dislike?* ed. John R. Hibbing and Elizabeth Theiss-Morse. New York: Cambridge University Press.

Fukuyama, Francis. 1995. *Trust: The Social Virtues and the Creation of Prosperity*. New York: Free Press.

Gamson, William A. 1968. *Power and Discontent*. Homewood, Ill.: Dorsey Press.

Geer, John G. 2003. "Attacking Democracy." Typescript.

Gilens, Martin. 1995. "Racial Attitudes and Opposition to Welfare." *Journal of Politics* 57:994–1014.

———. 1999. *Why Americans Hate Welfare: Race, Media, and the Politics of Anti-poverty Policy*. Chicago: University of Chicago Press.

Globetti, Suzanne, and Marc J. Hetherington. 2000. "Anti-government Campaign Rhetoric and Political Trust." Presented at the Annual Meeting of the American Political Science Association, Washington, D.C.

Grissmer, David, Ann Flanagan, and Stephanie Williamson. 1998. "Why Did the Black-White Score Gap Narrow in the 1970s and 1980s?" In *The Black-White Test Score Gap*, ed. Christopher Jenks and Meredith Philips. Washington, D.C: Brookings Institute.

Hardin, Russell. 2002. *Trust and Trustworthiness*. New York: Russell Sage Foundation.

Hart, Roderick P. 1994. *Seducing America: How Television Charms the Modern Voter*. New York: Oxford University Press.

Herrnstein, Richard J., and Charles A. Murray. 1994. *The Bell Curve: Intelligence and Class Structure in American Life*. New York: Free Press.

Hetherington, Marc J. 1997. "Negative News, Negative Consequences: One Reason Americans Hate Politics." Ph.D. diss., University of Texas at Austin.

———. 1998. "The Political Relevance of Political Trust." *American Political Science Review* 92:791–808.

———. 1999. "The Effect of Political Trust on the Presidential Vote, 1968–96." *American Political Science Review* 93:311–26.

———. 2001. "Declining Trust and a Shrinking Policy Agenda: Why Media Scholars Should Care." In *Communication in U.S. Elections: New Agendas*, ed. Roderick P. Hart and Daron R. Shaw. Lantham, Md.: Rowman and Littlefield.

Hetherington, Marc J., and Suzanne Globetti. 2002. "Political Trust and Racial Policy Preferences." *American Journal of Political Science* 46:253–75.

———. 2003. "The Presidency and Political Trust." In *The Presidency and the Political System*, ed. Michael Nelson. 7th ed. Washington, D.C.: CQ Press.

Hetherington, Marc J., and Michael Nelson. 2003. "Anatomy of a Rally Effect: George W. Bush and the War on Terrorism." *PS: Political Science and Politics* 36:37–42.

Hibbing, John R., and John R. Alford. 2004. "Accepting Authoritative Decisions: Humans as Wary Cooperators." *American Journal of Political Science* 48:62–76.

Hibbing, John R., and Elizabeth Theiss-Morse. 1995. *Congress as Public Enemy: Public Attitudes toward American Political Institutions*. New York: Cambridge University Press.

———. 2002. *Stealth Democracy: Americans' Beliefs about How Government Should Work*. New York: Cambridge University Press.

Howell, S. E., and S. B. Laska. 1992. "The Changing Force of the Environmental Coalition: A Research Note." *Environment and Behavior* 24:134–44.

Inniss, Leslie B., and Jeralynn Sittig. 1996. "Race, Class, and Support for the Welfare State." *Sociological Inquiry* 66:175–96.

Iyengar, Shanto, and Donald R. Kinder. 1987. *News That Matters: Television and American Opinion*. Chicago: University of Chicago Press.

Jacobs, Lawrence R., and Robert Y. Shapiro. 2000. *Politicians Don't Pander: Political Manipulation and the Loss of Democratic Responsiveness*. Chicago: University of Chicago Press.

Jacoby, William G. 1994. "Public Attitudes toward Government Spending." *American Journal of Political Science* 38:336–61.

Jamieson, Kathleen Hall. 1992. *Dirty Politics: Deception, Distraction, and Democracy*. New York: Oxford University Press.

Jennings, M. Kent, and Richard G. Niemi. 1968. "The Transmission of Political Values from Parent to Child." *American Political Science Review* 62:169–84.

Johnson, Haynes Bonner, and David S. Broder. 1996. *The System: The American Way of Politics at the Breaking Point*. Boston: Little Brown.

Judis, John B., and Ruy A. Teixeira. 2002. *The Emerging Democratic Majority*. New York: Scribner.

Kahneman, Daniel, and Amos Tversky. 1974. "Judgment under Uncertainty: Heuristics and Biases." *Science* 185:1124–31.

Karp, Jeffrey A. 1995. "Explaining Public Support for Legislative Term Limits." *Public Opinion Quarterly* 59:373–91.

Kernell, Samuel. 1977. "Presidential Popularity and Negative Voting: An Alternative Explanation of the Midterm Congressional Decline of the President's Party." *American Political Science Review* 71:44–66.

Key, V. O. 1949. *Southern Politics in State and Nation*. New York: Knopf.

Kinder, Donald R. 1983. "Diversity and the Complexity in American Public Opinion." In *Political Science: The State of the Discipline*, ed. Ada W. Finifter. Washington, D.C.: American Political Science Association.

Kinder, Donald R., and D. Roderick Kiewiet. 1979. "Economic Discontent and Political Behavior: The Role of Personal Grievances and Collective Economic

Judgments in Congressional Voting." *American Journal of Political Science* 23:495–527.

———. 1981. "Sociotropic Politics: The American Case." *British Journal of Political Science* 11:129–61.

Kinder, Donald R., and Lynn M. Sanders. 1996. *Divided by Color: Racial Politics and Democratic Ideals.* Chicago: University of Chicago Press.

Kinder, Donald R., and David O. Sears. 1981. "Prejudice and Politics: Symbolic Racism versus Racial Threats to the Good Life." *Journal of Personality and Social Psychology* 43:414–31.

King, David C. 1997. "The Polarization of American Parties and Mistrust of Government." In *Why Americans Don't Trust Government*, ed. Joseph S. Nye Jr., Philip D. Zelikow, and David C. King. Cambridge: Harvard University Press.

King, Gary. 1989. *Unifying Political Methodology: The Likelihood Theory of Statistical Inference.* New York: Cambridge University Press.

Kluegel, James R. 1990. "Trends in Whites' Explanations of the Black-White Gap in Socioeconomic Status, 1977–1989." *American Sociological Review* 55:512–25.

Krosnick, Jon A. 1988. "The Role of Attitude Importance in Social Evaluation: A Study of Policy Preferences, Presidential Candidate Evaluations, and Voting Behavior." *Journal of Personality and Social Psychology* 55:196–210.

———. 1991. "The Stability of Preferences: Comparisons of Symbolic and Nonsymbolic Attitudes." *American Journal of Political Science* 35:547–76.

Kuklinski, James H., Paul M. Sniderman, Kathleen Knight, Thomas Piazza, Philip E. Tetlock, Gordon R. Lawrence, and Barbara Mellers. 1997. "Racial Prejudice and Attitudes toward Affirmative Action." *American Journal of Political Science* 41:402–19.

Langer, Gary. 2002. "Trust in Government to Do What?" *Public Perspective* 13:7–10.

Lipset, Seymour Martin, and William Schneider. 1987. *The Confidence Gap: Business, Labor, and Government in the Public Mind.* 2d ed. New York: Free Press.

Lock, Shmuel T., Robert Y. Shapiro, and Lawrence R. Jacobs. 1999. "The Impact of Political Debate on Government Trust: Reminding the Public What the Federal Government Does." *Political Behavior* 21:239–64.

Lodge, Milton, and Bernard Tursky. 1979. "Comparisons between Category and Magnitude Scaling of Political Opinion Employing SRC/CPS Items." *American Political Science Review* 73:50–66.

"Low Grades for the Feds as Problem Solvers." 1998. *Public Perspective* 9 (February–March): 35.

Luhmann, Niklas. 1979. *Trust and Power: Two Works by Niklas Luhmann.* Chichester: John Wiley.

Luskin, Robert C. 1987. "Measuring Political Sophistication." *American Journal of Political Science* 31:856–99.

Mansbridge, Jane. 1997. "Social and Cultural Causes of Dissatisfaction with US Government." In *Why People Don't Trust Government*, ed. Joseph S. Nye, Paul D. Zelikow, and David C. King. Cambridge: Harvard University Press.

Mara, Gerald M. 2001. "Thucydides and Plato on Democracy and Trust." *Journal of Politics* 63:820–45.

Mayer, William G. 1992. *The Changing American Mind: How and Why American Public Opinion Changed between 1960 and 1988.* Ann Arbor: University of Michigan Press.

Mayhew, David R. 1991. *Divided We Govern: Party Control, Lawmaking, and Investigations, 1946–1990.* New Haven: Yale University Press.

McCombs, Maxwell E., and Donald R. Shaw. "The Agenda Setting Function of the Mass Media." *Public Opinion Quarterly* 36:176–87.

Mill, John Stuart. 1982. *On Liberty.* Harmondsworth: Penguin.

Miller, Arthur H. 1974a. "Political Issues and Trust in Government: 1964–1970." *American Political Science Review* 68:951–72.

———. 1974b. "Rejoinder to 'Comment' by Jack Citrin: Political Discontent or Ritualism?" *American Political Science Review* 68:989–1001.

Miller, Arthur H., and Stephen Borrelli. 1991. "Confidence in Government during the 1980s." *American Politics Quarterly* 19:147–73.

Miller, Arthur H., Edie N. Goldenberg, and Lutz Erbring. 1979. "Type-Set Politics: Impact of Newspapers on Public Confidence." *American Political Science Review* 73:67–84.

Miller, Arthur H., and Ola Listhaug. 1990. "Political Parties and Confidence in Government: A Comparison of Norway, Sweden, and the United States." *British Journal of Political Science* 20:357–86.

Mishler, William, and Richard Rose. 2001. "What Are the Origins of Political Trust? Testing Institutional and Cultural Theories in Post-Communist Societies." *Comparative Political Studies* 34:30–62.

Mueller, John E. 1973. *War, Presidents, and Public Opinion.* New York: Wiley.

Nelson, Michael. 2001. "The President as Potentate." *American Prospect* 12, no. 19.

Neuman, W. Russell, Marion R. Just, and Ann N. Crigler. 1992. *Common Knowledge: News and the Construction of Political Meaning.* Chicago: University of Chicago Press.

Neustadt, Richard E. 1990. *Presidential Power and the Modern Presidents: The Politics of Leadership from Roosevelt to Reagan.* New York: Free Press.

Oliver, J. Eric, and Tali Mendelberg. 2000. "Reconsidering the Environmental Determinants of White Racial Attitudes." *American Journal of Political Science* 44:574–89.

Orren, Gary. 1997. "Fall from Grace: The Public's Loss of Faith in Government." In *Why People Don't Trust Government*, ed. Joseph S. Nye, Philip D. Zelikow, and David C. King. Cambridge: Harvard University Press.

Page, Benjamin I., and Calvin C. Jones. 1979. "Reciprocal Effects of Policy Preferences, Party Loyalties and the Vote." *American Political Science Review* 73:1071–89.

Page, Benjamin I., and Robert Y. Shapiro. 1983. "Effects of Public Opinion on Policy." *American Political Science Review* 77:175–90.

———. 1992. *The Rational Public: Fifty Years of Trends in Americans' Policy Preferences.* Chicago: University of Chicago Press.

Pan, Zhongdang, and Gerald M. Kosicki. 1996. "Assessing News Media Influences on the Formation of Whites' Racial Policy Preferences." *Communication Research* 23:147–78.

Parker, Suzanne L. 1995. "Toward an Understanding of 'Rally' Effects: Public Opinion in the Persian Gulf War." *Public Opinion Quarterly* 59:526–46.

Patterson, Thomas E. 1993. *Out of Order.* New York: Knopf.

Pew Research Center. 1997. *Deconstructing Distrust: How Americans View Government.* Washington, D.C.: Pew Research Center for the People and the Press.

Popkin, Samuel L. 1994. *The Reasoning Voter.* 2d ed. Chicago: University of Chicago Press.

Putnam, Robert D. 1993. *Making Democracy Work: Civic Traditions in Modern Italy.* Princeton, N.J.: Princeton University Press.

———. 2000. *Bowling Alone: The Collapse and Revival of American Community.* New York: Simon and Schuster.

Reeves, Richard. 2001. *President Nixon: Alone in the White House.* New York: Simon and Schuster.

Rhodebeck, Laurie A. 1993. "The Politics of Greed? Political Preferences among the Elderly." *Journal of Politics* 55:342–64.

Rivers, Douglas, and Nancy L. Rose. 1985. "Passing the President's Program: Public Opinion and Presidential Influence in Congress." *American Journal of Political Science* 29:183–96.

Rosenstone, Steven J., and John Mark Hansen. 1993. *Mobilization, Participation, and Democracy in America.* New York: Macmillan.

Schattschneider, Elmer Eric. 1960. *The Semisovereign People.* New York: Holt Rinehart and Winston.

Scholz, John T., and Mark Lubell. 1998. "Adaptive Political Attitudes: Duty, Trust, and Fear as Monitors of Tax Policy." *American Journal of Political Science* 42:903–20.

Schuman, Howard. 1997. *Racial Attitudes in America: Trends and Interpretations.* Cambridge: Harvard University Press.

Schuman, Howard, Charlotte Steeh, Lawrence D. Bobo, and Maria Krysan. 1997. *Racial Attitudes in America: Trends and Interpretations.* 2d ed. Cambridge: Harvard University Press.

Sears, David O., Richard R. Lau, Tom R. Tyler, and Harris M. Allen Jr. 1980. "Self-Interest vs. Symbolic Politics in Policy Attitudes and Presidential Voting." *American Political Science Review* 74:670–84.

Sears, David O., Tom R. Tyler, Jack Citrin, and Donald R. Kinder. 1978. "Political System Support and Public Response to the Energy Crisis." *American Journal of Political Science* 22:56–82.

Simon, Herbert Alexander. 1947. *Administrative Behavior.* New York: Macmillan.

Skitka, Linda J., and Philip E. Tetlock. 1992. "Allocating Scarce Resources: A Contingency Model of Distributive Justice." *Journal of Experimental and Social Psychology* 15:179–88.

Skocpol, Theda. 1996. *Boomerang: Clinton's Health Security Effort and the Turn against Government in U.S. Politics.* New York: Norton.

Sniderman, Paul M., Richard A. Brody, and Philip Tetlock. 1991. *Reasoning and Choice: Explorations in Political Psychology.* New York: Cambridge University Press.

Sniderman, Paul M., and Edward G. Carmines. 1997. *Reaching beyond Race.* Cambridge: Harvard University Press.

Sniderman, Paul M., and Thomas L. Piazza. 1993. *The Scar of Race*. Cambridge: Harvard University Press.

Stimson, James A. 1999. *Public Opinion in America: Moods, Cycles, and Swings*. 2d ed. Boulder, Colo.: Westview Press.

Stokes, Donald E. 1962. "Popular Evaluations of Government: An Empirical Assessment." In *Ethics and Bigness: Scientific, Academic, Religious, Political, and Military*, ed. Harlan Cleveland and Harold D. Lasswell. New York: Harper and Brothers.

Sugrue, Thomas J. 1996. *The Origins of the Urban Crisis: Race and Inequality in Post-war Detroit*. Princeton, N.J.: Princeton University Press.

Tuch, Steven A., and Michael Hughes. 1996. "Whites' Racial Policy Attitudes." *Social Science Quarterly* 77:724–45.

Tyler, Tom R., and Peter Degoey. 1995. "Trust in Organizational Authorities: The Influence of Motive Attributions on Willingness to Accept Decisions." In *Trust in Organizations: Frontiers of Theory and Research*, ed. Roderick M. Kramer and Tom R. Tyler. Thousand Oaks, Calif.: Sage.

Voss, Stephen. 1996. "Beyond Racial Threat: Failure of an Old Hypothesis in the New South." *Journal of Politics* 58:1156–70.

Warren, Mark E. 1999. *Democracy and Trust*. New York: Cambridge University Press.

Wattenberg, Martin P. 1984. *The Decline of American Political Parties, 1952–1980*. Cambridge: Harvard University Press.

Wattenberg, Martin P., and Craig Leonard Brians. 1999. "Negative Campaign Advertising: Demobilizer or Mobilizer?" *American Political Science Review* 93:891–99.

Weatherford, M. Stephen. 1984. "Economic 'Stagflation' and Public Support for the Political System." *British Journal of Political Science* 14:187–205.

Weaver, R. Kent, Robert Y. Shapiro, and Lawrence R. Jacobs. 1995. "Trends: Welfare." *Public Opinion Quarterly* 59:606–27.

Williams, John T. 1985. "Systemic Influences on Political Trust: The Importance of Perceived Institutional Performance." *Political Methodology* 11:125–42.

Wilson, William Julius. 1987. *The Truly Disadvantaged: The Inner City, the Underclass, and Public Policy*. Chicago: University of Chicago Press.

Wlezien, Christopher. 1995. "The Public as Thermostat: Dynamics of Preferences for Spending." *American Journal of Political Science* 39:981–1000.

Zaller, John. 1992. *The Nature and Origins of Mass Opinion*. New York: Cambridge University Press.

Index

Page numbers in italics refer to tables or figures in the text.

ABC News polls, 32–33, 80, 156n.2
advertisements, political, 2, 26, 65, 121–24, 132–33, 161n.12
affirmative action programs, 101–2, 106–7, 109–12, 114–15, 117–19
Afghanistan, 31–32
African-Americans: affirmative action programs and, 101–2, 106–7, 109–12, 114, 117–19; assistance programs for, 45, 47, 82, 85–86, 91, 95–96, 109, 145; demographics and, 150; negative stereotypes of, 43, 64, 82–84, 93–96, 101, 108, 116–18, 140; trust levels of, 17; wage gaps and, 101–2
Aid to Families with Dependent Children (AFDC), 27, 36, 45, 69, 136
antipoverty programs, 66, 76, 87, *89–90*; Great Society and, 5, 20, 26, 35, 67–68, 72, 136, 147; negative racial stereotypes and, 43; nongovernment sources of, 140, 144–45; perceived risk/sacrifice and, 3–5, 49; regional differences and, 40; War on Poverty and, 20, 36, 138, 141. *See also* welfare programs
Armey, Dick, 41
Arthur Andersen & Co., 32
Asian-Americans, 150
Associated Press polls, 158n.4

Barnard, Chester, 53
Begala, Paul, 4
"big" government, 3, 19, 38–39, 42, 123–24, 141, 146
biological racism, 101
Bok, Derek, 10, 102
Borelli, Stephen, 23
Boston, Mass., 21
Bowen, William G., 102
Bradley, Bill, 136
Brown v. Board of Education, 69, 100, 152
budget, federal, 23, 43, 136; spending perceptions vs. reality and, 26–27, 29–30, 139–40, 146; waste in, 2, 10, 30, 52, 139
Bush, George H. W., 3, 23, 122, 124, 127, 143, 161n.12
Bush, George W.: approval ratings of, 30–31; campaign strategies of, 1–3, 147; "compassionate conservatism" of, 144–45; corporate scandals and, 32; faith-based initiatives and, 144; on government, 41, 144; personal trustworthiness of, 149; tax cuts under, 43, 136, 144
busing, 21, 68–69, 103, 105, 108, 140

California, 20–21, 150
campaign finance reform, 149
Carmines, Edward, 141
Carter, Jimmy, 3, 22–23, 47, 53; antigovernment stance of, 1, 22, 75, 141, 148–49; personal trustworthiness of, 11; policy liberalism under, 38; scandals under, 22
Carville, James, 4
CBS News polls, 27, 32
Center on Budget and Policy Priorities studies, 147
Chanley, Virginia, 149
child care programs, 85, 87, *90*
Citrin, Jack, 23
Civil Rights Act (1964), 20, 36, 68–69, 100, 103, 138, 152
civil rights movement, 20, 69, 151–52
Clean Air Act (1970), 75
Clinton, Bill, 3, 5, 41; antigovernment stance of, 1, 75, 141; approval ratings of, 29, 63–64, 124, 132; health care reform under, 4, 7, 19, 60, 120–37, 139, 151, 155n.6; optimism of, 23; personal trustworthiness of, 11, 13–14, 124, 149; policy liberalism under, 7, 36, 38, 58–61, 136–37, 149; scandals under, 23–24; welfare programs under, 45, 75, 136, 141, 150–51
Clinton, Hillary, 4, 122
college admissions quotas. *See* affirmative action programs

Congress, 25, 29, 34, 50, 162n.8
congressional elections: (1992), 41;
  (1994), 7, 24, 38, 40–41, 45, 59, 120–
  21, 135, 137, 143–44, 155n.6, 162n.8;
  (1998), 41; (2002), 40–41
conservatives/conservatism, 8–9, 38–61;
  "compassionate," 144–45; constant levels of, 3, 6, 77, 93, 98, 137, 139; feelings
  thermometer ratings of, 46; foreign aid
  programs and, 97–98; government spending support by, 82, 87, 91, 93; health
  care reform and, 124, 128, 132; ideological self-identification as, 42, 45–46, 60;
  lessons for, 142–45; limited government
  and, 42, 60–61, 75; race-targeted poli-
  cies/programs and, 108, 113–14
Consumer Product Safety Act (1972), 75
Contract with America, 24, 135
Converse, Philip, 40, 50
Corporation for Public Broadcasting, 143
crime prevention programs. See law-and-
  order spending
Cronkite, Walter, 22
Current Population Survey, 101
Czechoslovakia, 22

Daisy ad (1964), 122
defense spending, 23, 26, 41, 49, 87,
  126, 146
Degoey, Peter, 53
DeLay, Tom, 13, 41
Democrats/Democratic Party, 25; demographic changes and, 150; health care reform and, 125–26, 130; mid-term elections (1994, 1998) and, 41, 135,
  155n.6; National Convention (1968) of,
  22; policy liberalism and, 55–57, 126;
  presidential elections (1992, 2000,
  2004) and, 19, 41, 43, 149; race issues
  and, 101, 108, 141; vote choice and, 66
Denver, Colo., 21
Detroit, Mich., 20–21
distributive policies/programs: environmental protection, 3, 42, 49, 81, 85–87,
  144, 146–48; for highways, 3, 6, 25–26,
  47, 146; law and order spending, 41, 47,
  85–87; Medicare, 3, 26, 36, 143, 145–
  47; perceived risk/sacrifice and, 3–4, 6–
  7, 11–12, 48–49, 53, 66–68, 74, 76, 82–
  83, 85, 87, 90–98, 114–18, 124, 132–
  34, 138–39; public school funding, 36,
  42, 47, 82–83, 85, 87, 90; Social Secu-

rity, 3, 20, 26–27, 42, 47, 75, 81, 85–88,
  139–40, 145–48
Dole, Bob, 3, 41, 120–21
domestic security, 34, 142
Dukakis, Michael, 3, 126, 130
Duke, David, 108

earnings gaps, 101–2
Easton, David, 14–15
economic performance, 16, 18, 22–24, 30–
  31, 33–34, 58–59, 61, 65, 77, 82, 98,
  105, 127, 149
education. See public school funding
Education Department, U. S., 103, 143
education levels: ideology and, 40; racial
  policy preferences and, 108; spending
  support and, 82; trust measures and, 17;
  voter turnout and, 105
Eisenhower, Dwight, 63–64
elderly people, 17, 29, 82, 140, 146–47
Enron Corporation, 32
environmental protection programs, 3, 42,
  49, 81, 85–87, 144, 146–48
equal treatment policies, 106–7, 111–13; in
  hiring, 11–12, 101–3, 105, 107, 109,
  161n.15; in housing, 20, 69, 99–100;
  school integration as, 21, 68–69, 100–
  101, 103–5, 107, 109–10, 118–19, 140
Erikson, Robert, 37, 40, 53–55, 57, 149
European welfare states, 19–20
evolutionary psychology, 49–50

Fair Accommodations Act (1968), 69
Fair Housing Act (1968), 20, 36, 69
faith-based initiatives, 144–45
Fenno, Richard, 158n.11
financial aid (college) programs, 85, 87, 90
Fiorina, Morris, 9
Florida, 150
food stamp programs, 36, 45, 76, 139; ideological self-identification and, 42; negative racial stereotypes and, 5, 43, 47, 82–
  83, 95, 140; overestimates of spending
  on, 27; perceived risk/sacrifice and, 6,
  81, 85–86, 91–92
foreign aid programs, 27, 29, 45, 47, 81,
  85–86, 96–98, 139–40
Frankenberg, Erica, 103
Fried, Amy, 123–24, 128, 162n.8

Gallup polls, 30–31, 33–34, 104, 124, 138
Georgia, 150

Gilens, Martin, 77, 82–83, 93
Gingrich, Newt, 24, 135, 143
global warming, 147–48
Goldwater, Barry, 19, 79
Gore, Al, 1–3, 5, 10, 41, 136, 147
Great Society, 5, 20, 26, 35, 67–68, 72, 136, 147
Green, Donald, 23
Gregg, Judd, 120
Gulf of Tonkin incidents (1964), 13

Hansen, Mark, 105
Harris, Douglas, 123–24, 128, 162n.8
Harris polls, 158n.4
Harry and Louise ads (1994), 121–24, 132–33
Harvard University polls, 5, 80, 157n.14
Head Start program, 36
health care reform, 7, 60, 120–37, 139, 151, 155n.6; affordability and, 128, 132–34; Harry and Louise ads and, 121–24, 132–33; perceived risk/sacrifice and, 124, 132–34; as presidential campaign topic, 4, 19, 43
Health Care Task Force, 4
Health Insurance Association of America, 121
Helms, Jesse, 161n.12
Hibbing, John, 25, 50
higher-education quotas. See affirmative action programs
high-income people, 5, 82, 108, 151
highway programs, 3, 6, 25–26, 47, 146
hiring. See jobs, equal access to
housing, fair treatment in, 20, 69, 99–100
Housing and Urban Development Department, U. S., 36, 69
Humphrey, Hubert, 3, 141
Hussein, Saddam, 33

ideology, 7, 38, 40–46, 48, 60–61, 81, 100, 124, 160n.7. See also conservatives/conservatism; liberals/liberalism
income distribution, 17, 80, 101–2, 156n.8
inflation. See economic performance
information flow, two-sided, 19
information-processing theories, 25, 50–53
initiative, government by, 12, 16
Iran-Contra Affair (1985–90), 13, 23
Iran Hostage Crisis (1979–80), 22–23

Iraq War (2003–), 33–34, 142–43, 146

Jackson, Henry "Scoop," 146
Jacobs, Lawrence, 123, 148
Jacoby, William, 26, 146
Jarratt, Mary C., 79
jobs, equal access to, 11–12, 101–3, 105, 107, 109, 161n.15
Johnson, Haynes, 10
Johnson, Lyndon B.: AFDC and, 36, 69, 136; approval ratings of, 63–64; Civil Rights Act and, 36, 68–69, 138; Daisy ad and, 122; Fair Housing Act and, 20, 36, 69; Great Society and, 5, 20, 26, 35, 67–68, 72, 136, 147; personalization of politics and, 13; policy liberalism under, 19, 36, 38, 59, 61, 138; political trust under, 47, 59, 142; progovernment stance of, 141; Voting Rights Act and, 36, 68–69; War on Poverty and, 20, 36, 138, 141

Kaiser Family Foundation polls, 5, 25, 80, 157n.14
Karp, Jeffrey, 12
Kennedy, John F., 3, 5, 18–20, 22–23, 63, 141, 147
Kennedy, Robert, 22, 141
King, David, 23
King, Martin Luther, Jr., 22
Kosicki, Gerald, 82

Lance, Bert, 22
Langer, Gary, 33
Latinos, 150
law-and-order spending, 41, 47, 85–87
Lee, Chungmei, 103
Left, the. See liberals/liberalism
Leno, Jay, 52
Letterman, David, 52
liberals/liberalism, 5, 9, 60–61, 82, 108, 124, 126, 145–51
Lieberman, Joseph, 1
local governments, 10–11
Lock, Shmuel, 148
Los Angeles, Calif., 20–21
Los Angeles Times polls, 27
Lott, Trent, 155n.7
Louisiana, 150

MacKuen, Michael, 37, 53–55, 57, 149
Madison, James, 12

"Malaise Speech" (Carter), 22
mass media. *See* news media
McCain-Feingold campaign finance
    reform, 149
McGovern, George, 3, 75, 126
McIver, John, 40
McVeigh, Timothy, 14, 62
measurement methodologies. *See* research
    methodologies
Medicare, 3, 26, 36, 143, 145–47
military, the, 34–35. *See also* defense
    spending
Mill, John Stuart, 11
Miller, Arthur, 23
Mitchell, George, 137
mob rule, 12
Mondale, Walter, 3

National Association for the Advancement
    of Colored People (NAACP), 20–21, 105
National Election Study (NES): economic
    performance in, 24; feelings thermome-
    ter questions in, 27–29, 34, 46; food
    stamps in, 76; government services/
    spending support in, 42–45, 47, 81, 84–
    86, 91, 146; health care issues in, 125,
    128–30, 132; ideological self-identifica-
    tion in, 42, 45–46, 51, 60, 124; Iraq/
    Persian Gulf war support in, 143; panel
    studies by, 69; racial policy preferences
    in, 69–73, 102–3, 109; state/local gov-
    ernments in, 10–11; trust measures in,
    14–16, 18, 30, 78, 81, 158n.12; welfare
    programs in, 77–78
National Opinion Research Center surveys,
    100–101
NBC News polls, 158n.4
negative advertising. *See* advertisements,
    political
Nelson, Michael, 75
New Deal, 20, 26, 72, 147
New Frontier, 5, 20
news media, 10, 16, 25–26, 30–34, 52,
    122–23, 139–40, 160n.8
New York, 150
New York Times polls, 27, 32
Nixon, Richard, 14, 22, 38, 47, 75–76,
    142, 147, 155n.5. *See also* Watergate
    Affair (1972–74)

Oklahoma City bombing (1995), 14, 62
older people. *See* elderly people

Opinion Dynamics surveys, 144
Orfield, Gary, 103

Page, Benjamin, 39–40
Pan, Zhongdang, 82
partisanship, 48, 66, 81, 108, 113–14,
    160n.7
party identification, 9, 50–51, 78, 100
patriotic symbols, use of, 23, 61
Persian Gulf War (1991), 142–43
personal trustworthiness, 11, 13–14, 149,
    155n.2
Pew Charitable Trusts polls, 27
Pew Foundation studies, 52, 63
Piazza, Thomas, 106
policy liberalism, 6, 18–19, 37–39, 53–61,
    66, 78, 137, 145, 149
policy mood, 6, 39–43, 54–57, 66, 149,
    160n.8
policy satisfaction, 16
Potomac Association surveys, 76
poverty. *See* antipoverty programs
prescription drug benefits, 144
presidential elections: ideology and, 40–41;
    (1980), 41; (1992), 4, 41, 127; (1996),
    144; (2000), 1–3, 26, 30, 41, 136, 147;
    (2004), 19, 43, 139, 149; third-party
    presidential candidates in, 15
presidents: approval ratings of, 15, 25, 30–
    31, 63–65, 124, 132; personal character-
    istics of, 16, 61; personal trustworthiness
    of, 11, 13–14, 149, 155n.2. *See also indi-
    vidual presidents*
pressure groups, 4, 149, 151
PrimeTime Live (television program), 99
priming theory, 5, 25, 30–33, 35, 146,
    160n.8
principle-implementation gap, 100–106,
    114–15, 119
Proposition 187 (Calif.), 150
public school funding, 36, 42, 47, 82–83,
    85, 87, *90*
public transportation, desegregation of,
    101
Putnam, Robert, 9, 53, 105

Quinnipiac University polls, 43
quotas. *See* affirmative action programs

race riots, 20, 68
race-targeted policies/programs, 68–73,
    99–119, 138; education levels and,

108; negative stereotypes and, 82–84, 93–96, 108, 116–18, 140; perceived risk/sacrifice and, 3–5, 11–12, 114–18; racial equality and, 7, 100–106, 114, 119; regional differences and, 20–21, 103, 105

racial attitudes, 48, 82, 101–2, 107–8, 114, 119

racial equality, principle of, 7, 100–106, 114–15, 119

Rahn, Wendy, 149

rational choice theory, 49

"Rats" ad (2000), 2

Reagan, Ronald, 3; antigovernment stance of, 1, 76, 78–80, 146; approval ratings of, 64; defense spending and, 126; optimism of, 23; policy liberalism under, 38, 58–59; policy mood under, 40–41; tax cuts under, 43; welfare programs and, 26, 78–80, 146

recessions. See economic performance

redistributive policies/programs, 35, 39, 42–49, 61, 76–78, 80; antipoverty, 3–5, 20, 26, 40, 43, 49, 66, 76, 87, 89–90, 138; babysitter analogy and, 66–70; food stamp, 5–6, 27, 36, 42–43, 45, 47, 76, 81–83, 85–86, 91–92, 95, 139–40; foreign aid, 27, 29, 45, 47, 81, 85–86, 96–98, 139–40; overestimates of spending on, 26–27, 29–30, 139–40, 146; perceived risk/sacrifice and, 3–4, 6–7, 11–12, 48–49, 49, 53, 66–68, 74, 76, 82–83, 85, 87, 90–98, 114–18, 132–34, 138–39; policy liberalism and, 53; welfare, 5–6, 42–43, 45, 47–48, 76–83, 85–86, 91–93, 95, 107, 109–14, 136, 139–40, 145. See also race-targeted policies/programs

referendums. See initiative, government by

Reinventing Government Commission, 10, 147

Republicans/Republican Party, 5; demographic changes and, 150; health care reform and, 128; limited government and, 42, 60–61, 75; mid-term elections (1994, 2002) and, 7, 24, 38, 41, 45, 59, 120–21, 135, 137, 143–44, 162n.8; race-targeted policies/programs and, 108; Rockefeller wing of, 151; vote choice and, 66

research methodologies: cross-lagged models, 69–70; lagged measures, 78;

Laws measure, 53; measurement, 5, 8, 14–18, 35; panel studies, 69; policy liberalism and, 37; priming theory, 5, 25, 30–33, 146; regression analysis, 27, 66; survey participants characteristics and, 50–51, 128

retirement accounts, personal, 148

Right, the. See conservatives/conservatism

risk, perceived. See redistributive policies/programs

Rockefeller, Nelson, 151

Roosevelt, Franklin D., 20, 147

Rosenstone, Steven, 105

Rudolph, Thomas, 149

sacrifice, perceived. See redistributive policies/programs

Sawyer, Diane, 99

scandals, 16, 23–24, 65. See also specific incidents (e.g., Watergate Affair)

Schattschneider, E. E., 151–52

school integration, 72, 100–101, 103–5, 107, 109–10; Brown v. Board of Education and, 69, 100, 152; busing and, 21, 68–69, 103, 105, 108, 140; negative racial stereotypes and, 118; regional differences and, 103, 105, 119; resegregation and, 103–4, 119, 140

Schwarzenegger, Arnold, 150

science and technology programs, 85

self-interest: of politicians, 10, 25, 50, 149; of private citizens, 48–49, 81–82, 100, 106, 108

senior citizens. See elderly people

September 11 terrorist attack (2001), 8, 30–35, 41, 142–43, 146

Shapiro, Robert, 39–40, 123, 148

Shaw, Daron, 155n.2

Simon, Herbert, 53

Skocpol, Theda, 134–35

Sniderman, Paul, 106

social capital, 105

Social Security, 3, 20, 47, 75, 81, 85–88; ideological self-identification and, 42; overestimates of spending on, 26–27, 139–40, 145–48; privatization of, 145, 148

social trust, 9, 52–53

Soviet Union, 22, 85, 97

special interests, 4, 149, 151

stagflation. See economic performance

Starr, Kenneth, 24

state governments, 10–11, 40, 136
Stimson, James, 2, 37, 39, 41, 53–55, 57, 141, 149
Supreme Court, 25, 29

taxes: cuts in, 23, 43, 136, 144; income distribution and, 156n.8; payment of, 12
Taylor, Linda, 78–79
term limits, 16
terrorism. *See* September 11 terrorist attack (2001)
Tet Offensive (1968), 22
Texas, 150
Theiss-Morse, Elizabeth, 25, 50
third-party presidential candidates, 15
Tonkin Gulf Incidents (1964), 13
two-sided information flow, 19
Tyler, Tom, 53

ultimatum bargaining game, 49–50
unemployment. *See* economic performance
University of Cincinnati surveys, 50
University of Michigan surveys, 51

Vietnam War, 3, 13, 18–19, 21–22, 35, 77, 105
voter participation/turnout, 9, 64–65, 105
Voting Rights Act (1965), 20, 36, 68–69, 75

wage gaps, 101–2
Wallace, George, 22, 108
War on Poverty, 20, 36, 138, 141
wars, 16, 65. See also *specific incidents* (e.g., Vietnam War)
Washington Post polls, 5, 32–33, 158n.8
waste in government, 2, 10, 30, 52, 139
Watergate Affair (1972–74), 1, 3, 13, 18–19, 22, 24, 77, 105
Wattenberg, Martin, 78
wealthy people. *See* high-income people
Weatherford, Stephen, 24
welfare programs, 45, 76–81, 107, 109–14, 139–40, 145; AFDC and, 27, 36, 45, 69, 136; ideological self-identification and, 42; measurement error and, 16; negative racial stereotypes and, 5, 43, 47, 82–83, 95, 140; partisanship and, 114; people on welfare and, 29, 140, 157n.24; perceived risk/sacrifice and, 6, 48, 81, 85–86, 91–93; raised expectations and, 19–20
"welfare queens," 10, 26, 78
Welfare Reform Act (1996), 36, 136
White Hands ad (1990), 161n.12
Willie Horton ad (1988), 122
Wilson, Pete, 150
Wofford, Harris, 4, 155n.6
Wright, Gerald, 40

Zaller, John, 19